# THE EPISTLES OF JAMES, PETER AND JUDE

translated with an introduction
and notes by

## BO REICKE

This is Volume 37 of The Anchor Bible, a new translation in thirty-eight volumes, each with an introduction, notes, and comment. THE EPISTLES OF JAMES, PETER, AND JUDE is translated and edited by Bo Ivar Reicke, Professor of New Testament at the University of Basel, Switzerland.

The Anchor Bible marks the beginning of a new era of cooperation among scholars in biblical research: each volume is the work of an outstanding Protestant, Catholic or Jewish authority on the Bible, and the entire project is under the general editorship of William Foxwell Albright, Professor Emeritus of Semitic Languages at Johns Hopkins University, and David Noel Freedman, Professor of Hebrew and Old Testament Literature at Pittsburgh Theological Seminary.

The aim of The Anchor Bible is to make the Old and New Testaments accessible to the modern reader: its methods are to arrive at the meaning of the Bible through exact translation and extended exposition, and to reconstruct, as much as possible, the ancient settings of the biblical story.

*(Continued on back flap)*

The University Museum
University of Pennsylvania

# THE EPISTLES OF
# JAMES, PETER, AND JUDE

THE ANCHOR BIBLE is a fresh approach to the world's greatest classic. Its object is to make the Bible accessible to the modern reader; its method is to arrive at the meaning of biblical literature through exact translation and extended exposition, and to reconstruct the ancient setting of the biblical story, as well as the circumstances of its transcription and the characteristics of its transcribers.

THE ANCHOR BIBLE is a project of international and interfaith scope: Protestant, Catholic, and Jewish scholars from many countries contribute individual volumes. The project is not sponsored by any ecclesiastical organization and is not intended to reflect any particular theological doctrine. Prepared under our joint supervision, THE ANCHOR BIBLE is an effort to make available all the significant historical and linguistic knowledge that bears on the interpretation of the biblical record.

THE ANCHOR BIBLE is aimed at the general reader with no special formal training in biblical studies; yet it is written with the most exacting standards of scholarship, reflecting the highest technical accomplishment.

This project marks the beginning of a new era of co-operation among scholars in biblical research, thus forming a common body of knowledge to be shared by all.

*William Foxwell Albright*
*David Noel Freedman*
GENERAL EDITORS

# THE ANCHOR BIBLE

# The Epistles of
# James, Peter, and Jude

INTRODUCTION, TRANSLATION, AND NOTES

BY

## BO REICKE

Doubleday & Company, Inc.

Garden City, New York

1964

19677

# PREFACE

Commentaries on the books of the Bible may be written from various points of view. The special aim of this commentary on the epistles of James, Peter, and Jude is to place them in a setting that is historically realistic. Since the political and social problems of their time were of extraordinary importance to both the writers and the readers of these epistles, we pay special attention to them here.

As this commentary is not meant to be overly technical, we have not quoted at length the Greek and Latin texts which demonstrate the importance of political and social problems in the environment of the early church. Those who desire more detailed information on these matters are referred to the third main section of a book that we have published under the title of *Diakonie, Festfreude und Zelos* (Uppsala, 1951).

Some readers may say that the message these letters were written to convey is more important than their historical setting. This is true enough. But a knowledge of the specific concrete situation in which their message was first encountered is the best aid to receiving and understanding it in the specific concrete situation of today.

The author is much obliged to Professor A. V. Wallenkampf who made a helpful translation of the Swedish manuscript. Quite special thanks are due to Professor D. N. Freedman, one of the general editors of the Anchor Bible. He improved the exposition in countless points, and indicated where and how it might be clarified. It was an unselfish and prudent collaboration that cost him a considerable amount of time and energy.

Notwithstanding the great pains that these colleagues and the author have taken with the English wording, a modern reader will not always find the language fluent. This has become inevitable because the author wanted to keep his translation and exposition as much as possible in touch with the biblical texts, to give the reader a correct idea of their message.

*Bo Reicke*

# CONTENTS

## THE SECOND EPISTLE OF PETER

## THE EPISTLE OF JUDE

# PRINCIPAL ABBREVIATIONS

| | |
|---|---|
| Arist. *Pol.* | Aristotle, *Politics* |
| Barn. | The Epistle of Barnabus |
| CDC | Damascus Fragments (Qumran) |
| I Clem. | The First Epistle of Clement to the Corinthians |
| II Clem. | The Second Epistle of Clement to the Corinthians |
| I Enoch | First Enoch (Ethiopic Book of Enoch) |
| Eus. *Hist. eccl.* | Eusebius, *Church History* |
| IV Ezra | Fourth Ezra (Apocalypse of Ezra) |
| Herm. *Vis.* | Hermas, the Shepherd, His Visions |
| Ign. *Magn.* | Ignatius, Epistle to the Magnesians |
| Ign. *Rom.* | Ignatius, Epistle to the Romans |
| Jos. *Ant.* | Josephus, *Antiquities* |
| LXX | The Septuagint |
| Mart. *Epigr.* | Martial, *Epigrams* |
| Mishn. Shabb. | Mishnah, Shabbath |
| Philostr. *Vit. Apoll.* | Philostratus, *Life of Apollonius* |
| Plin. Min. *Ep.* | Pliny the Younger, *Letters* |
| 1QH | Qumran Hymns of Thanksgiving |
| 1QpHab | Qumran Commentary on Habakkuk |
| 1QM | Qumran War Scroll |
| 1QS | Qumran Manual of Discipline |
| Sir. | Wisdom of Sirach (Ecclesiasticus) |
| Suet. *Vit. Dom.* | Suetonius, *Life of Domitian* |
| Suet. *Vit. Ner.* | Suetonius, *Life of Nero* |
| Tac. *Ann.* | Tacitus, *Annals* |
| Talm. Jer. Ber. | Talmud of Jerusalem, Berachoth |
| Targ. Ps. | Targum to the Psalms |
| Xen. *Cyr.* | Xenophon, *Education of Cyrus* |

# GENERAL INTRODUCTION

Before examining the four epistles individually, there are some things that can be said about them as a group. In this General Introduction we shall look first at the relevant factors in the historical setting of the epistles, then at their literary form, at the contemporary religious climate, and finally at the content of the message they were intended to convey.

## HISTORICAL SETTING

As will be demonstrated in the special introductions to the four epistles, First Peter was probably written in the sixties, and James, Second Peter, and Jude in the nineties of the first century. In the categories of church history, these epistles belong partly to the last decade of the apostolic age, and partly to the last decade of the first post-apostolic epoch.

The apostolic age runs from A.D. 30 to 66, that is, it covers a little more than the second third of the first century. It was the period in which Peter, the first apostle, and James, the brother of Jesus, were the leading authorities in the church at Jerusalem. It is also the period in which Paul worked as a missionary to the Gentiles. The beginning of the apostolic age coincides with the crucifixion of Jesus, the date of which is generally supposed to be A.D. 30 (though other dates are possible). The end of this period is marked by the following three circumstances: 1) According to tradition, James was killed in 62 and Peter and Paul about 64; these events were results of the political difficulties the church experienced in the later years of the emperor Nero (54–68). 2) As a consequence of the same political troubles, the apostolic congregation moved from Jerusalem eastward about A.D. 65, and so lost its central importance for the church. 3) The primary cause of these political difficulties was zelotic Jewish nationalism which, in 66, led the Jews of Palestine to an open revolt against Rome and which, four years later, brought about the fall of Jerusalem and the end of Judaism as a political factor. Inevitably this changed the attitude of the church to the people of the old covenant.

The first post-apostolic epoch may be said to cover the years A.D. 66–96. In these years personal disciples of the apostles were still alive, and played important roles in the church. A definite beginning for this era is found in the outbreak of the Jewish-Roman war. It does not have such a definite end, but a caesura may be seen in the death of Domitian (81–96), because in the later years of this emperor the church suffered serious persecutions, which ended when the despot was murdered. During the whole of this period the relations of the church to homeless Judaism and to the Roman authorities remained serious problems, but the difficulties were more acute under Domitian.

Since the four epistles here treated are probably connected with the political troubles under Nero and Domitian, a brief historical survey with special attention to the relations between the church and the empire under these rulers will make it easier to understand the commentary that follows.

## 1. *The End of the Apostolic Age*

Nero was emperor of Rome from A.D. 54 to 68. A weak character, he behaved like an Oriental despot and contributed to the development of the emperor cult. He supported Greek art and literature with great enthusiasm, and was popular with the Greeks because he was reported to be willing to give Greece political liberty. There were influential courtiers who defended Jewish interests in the competition between Greeks and Jews characteristic of Alexandria and other eastern cities. But, in general, Nero was known to champion Greek civilization and despotic views of imperial sovereignty.

The threat posed by these two predilections of the emperor contributed to the rapid rise of Jewish zelotism, which in turn led to the war in A.D. 66–70. Josephus, who has described the history of this war, attributes the beginnings of the Zealot party to Pharisaic opposition to Rome occasioned by the great taxation that is mentioned in connection with the nativity of Jesus (Luke ii 1–5). It was after the middle of the first century, however, and especially in the days of Nero, that the zealots became really powerful and dangerous. Judging from the reports of Josephus, their number and their fanaticism increased enormously during this period until catastrophe was inevitable. By terroristic methods the zealots endeavored to defend the sovereignty of the Jewish poeple and their law against all Greek and Roman presumption. In their eyes it was offensive that Palestine should be governed by Roman procurators, as had been the case since A.D. 44 (the earlier procurators, among them Pontius Pilate, had only been responsible for Judea and Samaria). The zelotic opposition to the Roman government was in reality directed against the emperor, whose personal representatives the procurators were. Some zelotic leaders claimed to have messianic importance, which made the revolutionary attitude of these people appear still more serious. That the nationalistic zeal of the Jews was not confined to Palestine, but also influenced the Jews of the dispersion, is proved by the descriptions of Philo, of Luke in Acts, and of Josephus, as well as by the so-called Acts of the Alexandrian Martyrs. Nero, whose despotism was notorious, could not tolerate such flagrant insubordination on the part of Jewish activists. Even before the outbreak of the Jewish war the emperor and his advisers in Rome on several occasions had to deal with the political and social unrest stirred up by zelotic Jewish nationalism, for it had long irritated the Greeks of Alexandria and other cities.

The consequences of all this for the Christians in Palestine and in other parts of the empire were serious. Since the middle of the first century, when Jewish nationalism and zelotism first began to be a powerful factor and to raise difficulties for Greeks and Romans, the question of loyalty toward state and society had become quite acute for the church. In fact many Christians found themselves in a dilemma: whether or not to turn away from Jewish tradition to the Greek and Roman world.

Originally there was a genuine Christian desire to preserve contact with Judaism. From the time it came into being after the resurrection of Jesus, the apostolic congregation of Jerusalem took a positive attitude to the Jews, expecting to convert Judaism from within by representing the church as the true Israel (Acts i–v).

Twenty years later, a new factor was added, which influenced Christian relations with Judaism in a dramatic way. About A.D 51 the Judean church was severely persecuted by the Jews (I Thess ii 14). This was probably connected with the zelotic revival of those days, of which Josephus gives impressive reports. To many Christians of Palestine it must then have appeared necessary to accommodate to Jewish points of view and to avoid provocative contacts with Hellenism, in order to save the church from being further persecuted and even annihilated by the zelotic terrorists.

This is exactly what the attitude of Peter and James and other Christian Jews in the fifties would indicate. According to Gal ii 11–14 (about A.D. 55), Paul observed to his great disappointment that Peter dared not have anything to do with believers who were not circumcised, even though a few years earlier he had been willing to acknowledge such foreigners as fellow Christians (Gal ii 1–10). Paul ascribed this change of attitude to the influence of people around the Lord's brother James who had succeeded Peter as the leader of the Jerusalem congregation (he remained in this position until his death in A.D. 62). Paul's assumption is confirmed by Luke's narrative in Acts xxi of Paul's visit to Jerusalem about A.D. 58. According to James (Acts xxi 20), there were at that time thousands of Christian Jews in Palestine who made a bold stand for Jewish points of view, James calling them literally zealots of the law. Luke also quotes James as having suggested that Paul should pay regard to that powerful Christian zelotism when appearing publicly in the temple. Paul tried to do so, but it did not save him from being attacked by zelotic Jews (Acts xxi 27–31). The fact that James felt obliged to make concessions to such Jewish-Christian interests is also confirmed by Hegesippus, a well-informed traveler and collector of Christian traditions who lived about A.D. 160. Even though his story has a legendary form, the portrait which Hegesippus gives of James has biographical value, especially as it may not simply be traced back to New Testament narratives. According to Hegesippus, James maintained an intimate association with Judaism. As the leader of the Christians he prayed in the temple for the salvation of Israel, wore linen clothes like a priest, and had the ascetic behavior of a Nazarite. This made him popular with many Jews, to the extent that they called him the Righteous One, and his subsequent execution was deplored by many sincere Jews. James was certainly a peaceful man, and not a zealot. But his acceptance of some Jewish points of view, emphasized in a rather zelotic way by many of his supporters, made him appear to be a Jewish nationalist. There are also indications that James and his descendants were honored as representatives of the house of David. In any case there was the danger that the enthusiastic Judaists around James might be confused with Jewish nationalists in the eyes of the political authorities, who still regarded the Christians as being only a Jewish sect.

Now there is the paradox that James was killed by nationalistic Jews in spite of his prudent approach to Judaism. According to Josephus (*Ant.* XX. ix. 1:197–203), the high priest Ananus II used his temporary authority in the interregnum between the procurators Festus and Albinus, A.D. 62, to condemn James and some other men to be stoned, pretending they had transgressed the law. Josephus contends that, as an outspoken Sadducee, this high priest found James dangerous because of his messianic preaching. According to Hegesippus (Eus. *Hist. eccl.* ii. 23:1–19) it was Jewish scribes and Pharisees who brought about the stoning of James. There is no essential contradiction between the two reports, for while the high priest acted as president of the Sanhedrin, the scribes who represented the Pharisees were the most important members of this organization; and there had been the same collaboration of a Sadducean high priest with Pharisaic scribes in the trials of Jesus, the first apostles, Stephen, and Paul. Both these reports make it appear that James was the innocent victim of anti-messianic reactionaries who claimed to represent true Judaism. Maybe this simply implied that James was the object of Sadducean and Pharisaic envy. But it may also be that in his last years he provoked Jewish nationalistic feelings by criticizing that zeal for the law which he had previously encouraged Paul to respect in A.D. 58 (see above on Acts xxi 20). The pronouncedly anti-zelotic tone of the epistle of James seems to point in this direction, provided that James the Righteous was at least the authority behind its composition (compare the special Introduction to this letter). At any rate the relatively Judaizing attitude that the historical writers unanimously ascribe to James did not save him from being persecuted in A.D. 62 (as Paul had been four years earlier), and stoned by his own countrymen.

Sometime after this blow to Jewish Christianity, the Jerusalem congregation moved eastward, and so lost its general importance for the church. According to Eusebius, the new home of the Jerusalem Christians was Pella in Transjordan, although neither this writer nor other sources give details. In any case the migration obviously was away from the disorder and terror which the Jewish zealots caused in Palestine, and which soon afterward led to the outbreak of the Jewish-Roman war.

After that it did not seem advisable for Christians to sustain Jewish traditions. Even if the Jewish legalistic attitude, which James had supported in the fifties, preserved the congregations of Palestine from succumbing to the pressure of the zealots for several years, the eventual separation of Palestinian Judaism and Christianity became inevitable.

Long before this there had been criticism of Jewish attitudes in the early church. The necessity for Christians to give up one-sided Jewish traditions, like zeal for Jerusalem and external observances of the law, was evident to Stephen, Paul, and others who fostered the conversion of the Greco-Roman world. There is abundant evidence for that in the epistles of Paul, in which stress is placed on the need for a total break with the law as understood in Judaism, loyalty to the Roman state and society, and rejection of any civil aggressiveness. First Peter, which is very similar to the Pauline writings in spite of its attribution to Peter, also represents this positive, anti-zelotic view of state and society. In both cases it is not a question of any political opportunism but of an honest concern for the success of the gospel and the salvation of mankind.

However, it is another of the ironies of history that just as James was stoned in A.D. 62 by the command of leading Jews, in spite of his earlier efforts to preserve good relations with Judaism, so Peter and Paul were killed about A.D. 64 during a persecution commanded by the Roman emperor Nero, in spite of the exhortations to respect the Roman authorities and Gentile society found in their epistles. This martyrdom of Peter and Paul took place after the great conflagration of Rome in June 64, during the first persecution of the church initiated by the Roman authorities.

Tacitus, who has given the best report of the episode (*Ann.* xv. 44), tells us that Nero accused the Christians in Rome of having set the city on fire, because he wanted to remove the popular suspicion that he had arranged the destruction with the assistance of his chamberlains. Although Tacitus does not believe the Christians were responsible for the calamity, he thinks it was quite reasonable to punish them, because they represented a dangerous superstition, hated mankind, and were pernicious criminals.

Yet there must have been some more specific reason for Nero to indict the Christians. This had not happened before, since Christianity was earlier regarded as a form of Judaism and shared the religious privileges of the latter. Now the Romans began to discover the differences between Jews and Christians, perhaps because some representatives of Judaism drew their attention to it. But how could Nero and his people fail to see that the disciples of Christ were innocent believers in a kingdom that was not of this world? The answer is that some Christians may have preached against Rome, as later John the Revelationist did in Asia Minor. It must be observed that Paul, in the epistle to the Romans, is seriously concerned because he finds inclinations to social unrest in the congregation (Rom xii 18–xiii 14, xvi 17–20). He rejects this as "zeal" (xiii 13), and recommends loyalty to the political authorities. And in the First Epistle of Clement, written in the name of the Roman congregation about A.D. 95, in order to admonish the Corinthian brethren to give up their revolutionary attitude and obey the authorities, the martyrdoms of Peter and Paul are expressly said to have been caused by "zeal" and "strife" (I Clem. 5:2–7). The meaning is that dissatisfaction and rebelliousness in the Roman congregation had once led to the persecution in which Peter and Paul were killed, and the Corinthians are warned to avoid stirring up similar difficulties. By speaking repeatedly of "zeal," the author suggests an analogy to Jewish zelotism, which meant opposition to Rome. It is likely, however, that in Rome the opposition was supported by strong Gentile elements and had not only political, but also social objectives, as the Roman congregation included the poor, slaves, and prisoners of war. It is to be observed that after the burning of Rome a general resistance to the emperor appeared, which led to political intrigue and conspiracy involving men like Piso and Vinicianus. This may have placed the Christians in Rome in a more exposed position. At any rate First Clement, which is a product of the Roman congregation, clearly indicates that a sort of Christian zelotism in Rome was a leading reason for Nero to attack the believers there. So the apostles Peter and Paul died as martyrs because of a social aggressiveness in the Roman congregation for which they were not responsible and which they had vigorously rejected, as their epistles show.

These circumstances have to be considered in connection with one of the four epistles here treated, namely First Peter, which seems to have been written from Rome shortly before Nero's persecution. It regards martyrdom as inevitable, but rejects rebellion of any kind, because a loyal and quiet civil life is expected to impress authorities and private individuals, and to convert them.

## 2. *The Post-Apostolic Period*

After the death of the leading apostles, James, Peter, and Paul, the first post-apostolic epoch of the church's history began with the troubles of the Jewish-Roman war. Jewish zelotism, which became more and more desperate in the sixties, led to an open revolution in Palestine in A.D. 66. After some hesitation Nero sent Vespasian with a strong army to occupy the country. Titus completed the campaign and destroyed Jerusalem in A.D. 70.

Vespasian was made emperor in the year before the fall of Jerusalem, and governed the empire with a steady hand, A.D. 69–79. His son Titus succeeded him and made himself popular in his short reign, A.D. 79–81.

Domitian, the younger brother of Titus, then occupied the throne A.D. 81–96. His despotic ways provoked the criticism of senators, aristocrats, and philosophers, whom he therefore determined to suppress. Later Roman historians present a malignant portrait of Domitian, for they belonged to the aristocratic party that gained new importance after his death. The personal deficiencies of the man certainly facilitated their caricatures. But in point of fact Domitian was an ambitious monarch, who worked with unusual energy, if not always with the happiest methods, to save the empire from outside disturbance and from internal corruption. Domitian also was popular with the soldiers and with the lower classes. It was only in the last years of his life that he persecuted indiscriminately those whom he thought to be conspiring against him. That he demanded extraordinary veneration in public affairs, to the point normally accorded the divine, only meant that the emperor cult had developed a little further than under his predecessors. There is nothing to prove that Domitian required sacrifices from all people of the empire, as was the case with later monarchs (including the glorious Trajan). He permitted the Jews to practice their faith, if they paid a special tax of about one dollar a year.

These were the Flavians, Vespasian and his sons Titus and Domitian, who ruled Rome during the critical first post-apostolic period in the history of the church. Although the Christians did not have much direct contact with them, it is important to consider the personal characteristics of the Flavian autocrats in order to understand the position which, in their days, the church took in relation to the state.

1. Under the government of Vespasian and Titus the Christians seem generally to have been on good terms with the authorities, and to have been tolerated by them. For the Neronic persecution and the catastrophe of zelotic Judaism showed with the force of events that the policy of loyal submission to the Roman state and society advocated in the epistles of Paul and in First Peter had been justified. And it was only later that Domitian changed the picture. To subsequent generations of secular and ecclesiastical writers he seemed to be a second Nero, a foolish tyrant who also persecuted the church. But in fact he was not greeted with fear and hatred from the beginning, or at least not in all circles. The historical evidence is more complicated than it appears to us if we study only the negative caricatures of Domitian delivered by later historians. It should also be noticed that the positive view of the heathen state and society, which, for missionary purposes, had been represented by the epistles of Paul and by First Peter, was still defended by those later writings of the New Testament known as the Pastoral epistles and the General epistles, and that some of these were probably written under Domitian.

We are here concerned with James, Second Peter, and Jude, which belong to the so-called General epistles. As will be shown in the commentaries that follow, these books seem to reflect the situation under Domitian, a date of composition at that time being the most plausible one. They have, in common with the Pauline and Pastoral epistles, a remarkably positive attitude to state and society, and condemn revolutionary tendencies and social hostility. Essentially the same view is represented by First Clement. And this is a most important circumstance, for it is an established fact that First Clement, which has numerous connections with the General epistles, and was once esteemed equal with them as Holy Writ, was composed in the very capital of the empire about A.D. 95, when Domitian's excesses had been flagrant for some years. This shows that Christian authors were still, even under Domitian, anxious to preserve that loyal attitude to heathen society recommended by Jesus (when discussing tribute to Caesar), by Paul and others. What we have here is a genuine Christian tradition of opposition to social agitation, developed in the epistles of Paul, continued by the Pastoral epistles, and reiterated by Second Peter (iii 14–16). The personality and policy of Domitian certainly showed real deficiencies, so that it may appear strange that under him social open-mindedness should be defended by James, Second Peter, and Jude. But the fact that First Clement was composed during the last years of this emperor proves that despite all the difficulties and problems accumulating for them, it was still natural for leading Christians to regard a co-operative attitude to state and society as essential for the success of the gospel.

2. In contrast to the positive view taken by such leading Christians, a critical and even revolutionary attitude to society may have been represented by some elements in the church. Possibly it had already started under the first Flavians, but at any rate the opposition seems to have assumed major proportions during the last years of Domitian. This view explains why James, Second Peter, Jude, and First Clement are so eager to admonish their readers not to participate in materialistic aggressiveness, or "zeal," as they sometimes call it on the analogy of Jewish zelotism. But we must remember that Christian opposition to Rome also had an idealistic background, as exemplified in the book of Revelation where a severe but purely religious criticism of the emperor and the empire is expressed.

This opposition to the *status quo* may further be supposed to have had different causes and different aspects:

a) A fundamental reason was the impatience that many felt, because the consummation ("the end of the age") did not come as soon as it was expected. Paul had already been obliged to discuss this in his earliest writings, First and Second Thessalonians. Eschatological impatience led to social disorder. Dissatisfied believers materialized eschatology, hoping to have the final triumph and joy of the faithful realized in empirical forms on earth. In the post-apostolic period the problems were even more acute, because there were by now thousands of believers belonging to the poorer classes, and including numerous slaves, whose condition was far from happy. They wanted the church to improve their social status. In antiquity people generally expected religious and social organizations to save them from the hardships of life. And as the church was easily linked with the popular fraternities and societies of the time, its promise of another life was understood by many in a materialistic way. In their impatience the poor and the slaves demanded that victory and bliss should be realized here and now. This inevitably led to social unrest and opposition to state and society.

b) Jewish influence on the church complicated the situation. The importance of the Jewish question in books like John, Titus, Hebrews, and Revelation makes it clear that Judaism, even after the political catastrophe of the fall of Jerusalem, affected Christianity both positively and negatively. This was so mainly for two reasons. First, after A.D. 70 many Jews were offered a new home in the church. Second, Judaism was still a religion officially recognized by Rome, whereas Christianity was not, but might at any moment be persecuted under the severe legislation against corporations. In so far as Jewish antagonism to Rome continued to live an underground life in the Flavian period—and this is confirmed by the apocalypses of Baruch and Ezra, to say nothing of the new fanatic revolts of the Jews at the beginning of the second century—the social impatience felt by some elements of the church received inspiration from this source. Such antisocial influence from circumcised people is condemned by Titus i 10. There were also Christians who believed that a return to the Jewish community would save the church from being persecuted. Such opportunistic inclination to Judaism is repudiated by the epistle to the Hebrews, as well as by the epistle of Barnabas.

c) Another temptation for the Christians of those days was presented by certain philosophical schools which were most influential and popular in the Flavian period: the Stoics and the Cynics. Their professional representatives went around preaching freedom and criticizing society on piazzas and streets, in halls and temples, and in the houses of the rich. Stoicism had outstanding representatives among the Roman aristocrats themselves. The Stoics, and with them the Cynics, constantly referring to reason, preached a deterministic materialism, championed a republican government, and therefore in the days of the Flavians appeared as radical enemies of the established order. Vespasian and Domitian regarded their propaganda as criminal, the former expelling the philosophers from Italy in 71, the latter persecuting them in 89, and then expelling them in 93 or 95. Fourth Maccabees and other Jewish books show that Hellenistic Judaism already had taken over elements of Stoicism and related systems. This process was continued in Christian circles, especially since the Stoic-Cynic ideal of freedom and equality appealed to many. But in so far as philosophical rationalism led to intellectual presumption, and social radicalism implied envy, animosity, and belligerence, it was the duty of leading Christian personalties, such as the authors of the epistles dealt with in this study, to remind their readers of the fact that genuine wisdom is not impatient, but humble. It may also be observed that Domitian extended his persecution of the philosophers to idealists like the popular neo-Pythagorean preacher Apollonius of Tyana, who is reported to have opposed the emperor with bitter irony. He was not connected with the church, but in some ways resembled the Christian preachers. In this context it is also necessary to consider Gnosticism, an idealistic philosophy that entwined itself about Judaism and Christianity (Col ii 8, 16–23; I Tim vi 20). Its source was not Greek theory, but Oriental mysticism. In addition to the intellectual arrogance to which Gnosticism easily led, and which Paul had criticized in his correspondence with the Corinthians and others, there was the danger of isolation from man and society. This also the writers of the General epistles rejected. They wanted their readers to be good citizens, to avoid revolutionary movements, and so to facilitate the church's mission to the Gentiles.

These three factors: a) social animosity, b) Jewish influence, and c) contemporary philosophies, were also operative among the Roman aristocrats, representing the senatorial party, who developed a strong opposition to Domitian.

With regard to (a), the social hostility that was so easily stirred up by the fraternities and societies, among which the church was popularly placed, it must be observed that most corporations had rich patrons and benefactors who often used their influence with the members to serve their own political purposes. Such corporate propaganda, called *ambitus*, was prosecuted as illegal, but flourished nonetheless. As the conflict between the senatorial party and Domitian became increasingly severe, and was marked by the emperor's persecution of his aristocratic enemies, the poor Christian congregations were evidently compromised by their connections with senators, noblemen, and other rich people. The danger was that the believers might be persuaded to join the political opposition, and thus be led into unchristian arrogance on the one hand, and unnecessary persecution on the other.

As for (b), the connections with Judaism, one may consider the case of Clement and Domitilla. Flavius Clemens was Domitian's cousin and the father of his presumptive successors; he had also just served as consul with the emperor, and must be regarded as second only to the latter in the empire. In A.D. 95 he was put to death by Domitian because of "atheism," which means non-belief in the official gods, and because of a tendency toward Jewish customs. His wife, Flavia Domitilla, another relative of the emperor, was exiled for the same reason, according to the historians Suetonius and Dio. However, the well-known catacombs which carry Domitilla's name show that in fact she had embraced Christianity. Is it not probable that Flavius Clemens shared his wife's faith and that he also was a Christian? The fact that Clement and Domitilla were officially accused of atheism in connection with Judaism does not conflict with this view. The epistle to the Hebrews shows that some Christians were again willing to accept the Jewish label in the Flavian period, since Jews were allowed to affirm "atheism" in the sense of non-commitment to the official deities, if they paid the annual tax required by the emperor. In this case, however, the Jewish privileges did not save the noble couple. They were punished mainly because of their high rank; and since they were not of Jewish descent, it was difficult for them to claim to be Jews. The episode reveals that the church had made contacts with members of the very highest aristocracy, whose biblical faith was supposed to be more acceptable if presented as Judaism. Nevertheless, such dangerous converts increased the risk of persecution. The sudden attack on Clement and Domitilla was probably unjust; there is no reason to believe they were involved in criminal activity. But it is worth noticing that Domitian was murdered some months later by Domitilla's steward who was also a Christian, and committed the deed in collaboration with some chamberlains after negotiations with Nerva, the leader of the senatorial party. Thus there was a real possibility of Christian involvement in the political intrigues of the Flavian period. The New Testament authors we are discussing had good grounds for their warnings.

As for (c), the connections between Christians and the current philosophies, these were in part the result of contacts with noble Romans, for philosophy was strongly supported by the latter, many of them being philosophers themselves. The more the church was able to win rich and important people, the deeper its involvement in contemporary philosophical movements became. But there was the danger of intellectual interests other than Christian being involved here, as is remarked by the authors of the Pastoral and General epistles when they speak of "knowledge" and "wisdom" in critical terms.

The attitude toward state and society of the epistles here treated is optimistic and positive in spite of the tendencies we have just discussed. This is not because of any political conservatism, respect for the mighty, or desire to avoid trouble, but rather a simple conviction that social obedience and patience are necessary for a Christian and valuable for the success of the gospel, and that God himself will judge iniquities.

A different picture of the state was given by John the Revelationist, who may be supposed to have written the Apocalypse about A.D. 96. Following Jewish apocalyptic tradition, he foresaw that the Roman tyranny would develop in such a way that religious veneration of Rome and the emperor would include the demand for participation in sacrifices by all and pass into the category of demonism. In his last years Domitian fulfilled this prediction by persecuting those who did not acknowledge the public gods, as in the case of Clement and Domitilla. He probably allowed his officials to arrange such persecutions in Asia Minor also, as is reflected in the book of Revelation. Pliny confirms this by writing in A.D. 112 as governor of northwestern Asia that Christians living there had been persecuted about twenty years earlier. Trajan authorized Pliny to require sacrifices in veneration of the emperor, and later autocrats even obliged their officials to do so. The book of Revelation rightly condemns such an arrogant demand which faithful Christians could not fulfil.

The contrast between the General epistles and Revelation is very instructive. According to the former, Christians should respect state and society in the midst of all iniquity. This still appeared to be possible when the General epistles were composed. John, on the other hand, saw that Rome had gone too far in requiring absolute subservience. But the Revelationist by no means recommended political intrigues and social aggression; he shared the early Christian conviction affirmed by the General epistles that patient suffering is necessary for the diciples of Jesus and that the iniquities of this world are to be rectified by God and his Messiah, not by human violence.

## FORM AND CONTENT

### *Literary Form*

The four writings treated in the present volume are usually called "epistles," and this is a useful way to characterize them. A literal translation into current English of the Greek word *epistolē* would of course be "letter," but while the New Testament epistles are similar in many ways to the varied documents we would now call letters, they differ in that they more frequently have a public character and are never private communications. For this reason the word "epistle" with its more formal connotation is generally used.

Besides the five historical books of the New Testament, the twenty-one epistles are, if not the largest, at least the most numerous category of New Testament writings. For the rest, the church has accepted only one prophetic or apocalyptic book. The Old Testament also contains in addition to the historical and prophetic books a group of poetic-didactic books called "the writings" (Job, Psalms, etc.). About the only resemblance between the "writings" and the "epistles" is that both include productions of widely varying dates, some being among the earliest and some among the latest in the literary periods of the Old and New Testaments respectively. Otherwise, "the writings" comprise widely differing literary forms and were the last group to be recognized by Judaism as canonical, while the epistles represent a homogeneous literary category which, if we disregard oral traditions, was the oldest and most important within the early church.

Partial precedents in Jewish and Greek practice contributed to the development of the New Testament epistle form. Jewish congregations were accustomed to correspond with each other, with political authorities, and with the religious leaders in Jerusalem. Not much is left to us of that correspondence. In the Greek world letters and epistles were quite normal instruments of private and public communication, as thousands of papyri and other documents show. Standard phrases of Jewish and Greek letters are reflected in the openings and conclusions of the New Testament epistles.

Thus the Jewish initial address "X to Y" (e.g., Ezra vii 12) is generally used in the epistles of the New Testament (Rom i 1, 7a, etc.; also I Pet i 1; II Pet i 1; Jude 1). After this address, Oriental and Jewish letter writers inserted a wish for "peace" (e.g., Ezra iv 17). This custom was also taken over by writers of New Testament epistles. In a few cases the Greek salutation "X (wishes) Y grace" was preferred (Acts xv 23, xxiii 26, and James i 1). But to avoid the implications of the Greek conception of "grace," the phrase was extended into a wish for "grace and peace" (I Thess i 1). Paul generally fortified the religious sense of this double expression by further adding the words "from God the Father" (Rom i 7b, etc.). In the epistles of Peter and Jude there is another addition, the standard phrase being "grace be with you, and may peace abound" (I Pet i 2b; II Pet i 2, and, with slight changes, Jude 2). Here the wish for peace may even have had a cautionary significance, warning the congregation against embroilment in political quarrels (in I Pet v 14, the wish for peace is repeated at the conclusion of the epistle).

At the end of a letter, a Greek writer commonly inserted greetings from and to several individuals. This custom is also reflected in the New Testament (Rom xvi 21–23, etc., and I Pet v 12–14a, but not James, Second Peter, or Jude). Although concluding letters with a signature was not usual in antiquity, the author who dictated a letter to a stenographer sometimes added a greeting with his own hand. Paul on occasion did this (I Cor xvi 21, and elsewhere). In most of the New Testament epistles the actual subscription is a blessing or a praise which emphasizes their character as religious messages (Rom xvi 25–27; I Cor xvi 23 f., etc.; also I Pet v 14b; II Pet iii 18b; Jude 24 f.).

On the other hand the central parts of the New Testament epistles do not reflect the influence of Jewish and Greek letter traditions in the way that the salutation and conclusion do. The heart of the epistles is generally a doctrinal section followed by a series of admonitions. These may be regarded as following the forms of Jewish, Greek, and Christian preaching. Analogies are found in the parenetic speeches of Enoch (in the books of Enoch), the patriarchs (in the Testaments of the Twelve Patriarchs), and similar authorities represented in Jewish traditions, and to some extent also in the moral speeches and essays (*diatribaí*) of Greek philosophers. But, beyond that, Christian preaching made the main parts of the New Testament epistles an essentially new creation, developed to its highest point by Paul.

Most New Testament epistles are not literary substitutes for conversation, like private letters, but ways of speaking publicly to congregations that could not be addressed in person. This is clearly true of the earliest New Testament epistle, First Thessalonians (v 27). So the rhetorical setting, which was always of great importance in antiquity, must be kept in mind. If a church authority could not visit the believers he wanted to address, he preached to them in writing. Someone read his epistle aloud to the congregation and the people were able to listen to the voice of the writer, as though the latter were speaking personally. As inspired communications that still preserve the characteristics of preaching, the New Testament epistles are unique literary productions.

The rhetorical core is stronger in the later New Testament epistles, inasmuch as the forms of preaching continued to evolve. One example is the baptismal sermon which consisted of catechetical instructions and exhortations presented to candidates for baptism. Another special form of preaching, though only practiced as a literary genre, was the "testament." It was taken over from Judaism, where it is found in the last part of First Enoch and in the Testaments of the Twelve Patriarchs. It is in the form of a farewell speech given by a man of God just before his death. The form and imagery of the epistles treated here may often be explicated by a reference to such preaching traditions. In James and Jude we find hortatory preaching in general, in First Peter and First John reflections of baptismal sermons, in Second Peter the pattern of a "testament."

It is worth noticing that the authors of Hebrews and the General epistles, which are the latest epistles of the New Testament, have diluted and partly dropped the phrases traditionally belonging to a letter and concentrate on rhetorical exposition. (Exceptions are Second and Third John, which have the form of actual letters.) Thus the salutation does not mention any definite person or congregation as recipient. It either has a general character—which is the meaning of the expression "General" or "Catholic epistles"—or it has disappeared, as in Hebrews and First John. The characteristic greetings at the end of a letter still have a personal quality in First Peter. But this is hardly the case with Hebrews, and they have been completely omitted in James, Second Peter, First John, and Jude.

The amount of preaching in these writings did not prevent the church from calling them "epistles." Fundamentally they were written messages like the Pauline epistles, and some of them still have a few resemblances to actual letters. It was possible to present them as epistles in spite of the predominant rhetorical element because from the very beginning the apostolic epistles were intended to be read publicly to the congregations (see above on I Thess v 27). Epistolary and rhetorical factors accordingly were accepted as parallel constituents. In spite of the decline of the former and the predominance of the latter, the writings continued to be regarded as epistles.

### Religious Environment

The epistles of James, Peter, and Jude are parts of the Bible in that they have been officially adopted into the canon, but they also belong there because of the intimate relation of their religious ideas to the main biblical tradition. It is true that it took a long time for the church to recognize all of them as canonical. While First Peter, like First John, was accepted in the second century, the rest of the General epistles were not generally acknowledged until the fourth century. Nor should it be denied that our epistles have peculiarities which, despite the resemblances, make them different from the Pauline epistles, and more like Hebrews, First John, and First Clement. But if the four epistles are studied from a historical point of view without dogmatic prejudices, there is no doubt that their ideological framework is the biblical tradition.

It is also evident that the authors of the four epistles were conscious of representing biblical tradition, for they expressly refer to what God and Christ had done (the *Heilsgeschichte*) and to what the prophets and the apostles had said (the "apostolic tradition"), e.g., James i 18, v 10; I Pet i 10–12, ii 21–25, iii 18–22; II Pet i 16–18, iii 2; Jude 5, 14, 17.

To understand what this participation of the authors in biblical tradition means, we must ask to which historical expressions of biblical faith our epistles are specially related. Not all issues of Israelitic-Jewish religion and early Christian faith need be taken into account, but only those which had particular relevance to the ideological background of the writings in question.

The Old Testament was the normative source of religious knowledge for all Jewish believers—with the exception that the conservative Sadducees like the Samaritans acknowledged only the Pentateuch. Jesus and his apostles took over the Old Testament as Holy Writ from Judaism, although they understood it in their own way. They rejected superficial observance of the law and found it essential to fulfil the commandment of love contained therein. They read the story of God's dealings with Israel as a preparation for the kingdom they were ordained to preach and understood Moses and the prophets to have predicted the coming of Christ, the punishment of the wicked, and the salvation of the faithful. In this way the Old Testament was a permanent source of inspiration for Jesus and his disciples and was believed to have been written directly for the edification of the church. The four epistles we are concerned with here also show this general dependence on the Old Testament.

With regard to the new faith and piety taught by Jesus on the basis of the Old Testament, the closest Jewish analogy is found not in the temple cult, nor in the religious views represented by the priests or the rabbis, the Sadducees or the Pharisees, but rather in the apocalyptic-pietistic movement which in the second preChristian century found expression in the book of Daniel and other apocalyptic works and in the days of Jesus was represented by certain fervently messianic congregations, including the penitential movement of John the Baptist.

The discoveries of ancient Jewish manuscripts in the Judean desert near Qumran confirm this. It is not possible to relate here the story of these discoveries which, so far as scholars are concerned, began in 1948. But some facts connected with the Qumran material are of interest, as they help in understanding the religious environment shared by John the Baptist, Jesus himself, the apostles, and the first Christians. There is no evidence that John the Baptist and Jesus were followers of the Qumran movement. John may possibly have had some connections with Qumran, but his baptism and preaching were essentially new. Above all, there is nothing to prove that Jesus had personal contacts with the sect, which is not even mentioned in the New Testament; his words and works cannot be traced to Qumran. Our purpose is simply to consider some analogies that will help us to understand what John, Jesus, and the first Christians preached, and which show that Christianity arose in apocalyptic-pietistic circles like those of the Qumran community.

Qumran—located near the northwestern shore of the Dead Sea —was the center of a group of apocalyptic pietists, who studied the Old Testament as prophecy of their present situation and coming salvation. They represented the apocalyptic pietism that had been developed in the second century B.C. and which found literary expression in the book of Daniel. In their library, deposited in caves near Qumran before A.D. 68, they also had books similar to Daniel, especially First Enoch and some Testaments of the Twelve Patriarchs, which modern scholars, long before the Qumran discoveries, had found significant as providing analogies to the preaching of Jesus and the New Testament. Furthermore, the Qumran library contained several texts not hitherto known. The most important of these had been in the first cave to be discovered at Qumran: i.e., the War Scroll (1QM), the Manual of Discipline (1QS)—which is related to the Damascus Fragments of an old Cairo collection (CDC)—the Hymns of Thanksgiving (1QH), and several commentaries on Old Testament books, especially the Habakkuk Commentary (1QpHab).

Characteristic of the Qumran union were the following convictions. Existence was supposed to be dominated by two contradictory principles, light and darkness, truth and falsehood. The old covenant between God and Israel, broken by the people's false leaders, was now replaced by a new covenant, that is, the Qumran union itself. In this covenant the Old Testament, understood as prophecy, was being fulfilled. Entrance into the new covenant required obedience to the law, genuine repentance, purification of the heart, sacrifice of the whole person instead of temple offerings, and surrender of private possessions. The holiness of the members was confirmed through baptisms and common meals. Messianic expectations were also expressed. But above all the Qumran believers were convinced that they had already crossed the threshold of the eschatological age foretold by the Scriptures. God, according to his secret plans, would lead his elect to a glorious consummation.

In spite of many peculiarities, Qumran piety, next to the preaching of John the Baptist, is the form of Judaism which is closest to early Christianity, from external as well as from internal points of view. The earlier comparisons of the New Testament faith with the apocalyptic pietism of books like Daniel, First Enoch, and the Testaments of the Twelve Patriarchs are supported by the Qumran discoveries; and the Jewish environment of Jesus and the first Christians is illuminated by the new material at quite essential points.

This insight may also be applied in part to the General epistles. Although they were composed relatively late and for readers who belonged to the Greek world, there are expressions in them which remind us of the Qumran texts. These will be dealt with in detail in the commentary.

However, the essential background of the epistles we are concerned with is found within the New Testament tradition. Jesus, his preaching and activity, is in the center. The epistle of James includes sayings which, though not quoted as words of Jesus, are very similar to sayings of his preserved in the gospels, in particular the Q material (sayings common to Matthew and Luke). James probably was inspired by such traditions. On the whole the General epistles are based on the preaching and work of Jesus, though they scarcely provide contributions to his biography. Also, these four epistles, while differing from the Pauline epistles in details, represent the attitude of Paul in condemning political action on the part of Christians. Though written comparatively late, they definitely belong to the apostolic tradition, as they themselves claim.

On the other hand, the readers of the four epistles lived in a Hellenistic environment. Their language was Greek, and their way of thinking, their religious, metaphysical, and social ideas necessarily bore a Hellenistic stamp. They were influenced by the popular vocabulary of the philosophical movements such as Stoicism and Gnosticism which controlled much public and private thinking. The authors of the General epistles were obliged to adapt their expositions to the Hellenistic thinking of their readers. These circumstances have given many expressions and concepts used in the four epistles a pronouncedly Hellenistic appearance (e.g., James i 17: "the Father of the Luminaries with whom there is no change of position, nor any periodic concealment"; or II Pet i 4: "in order that you might become partakers of divine nature"). These Hellenistic figures, however, are only dashes of color used by the authors to make their expositions more attractive to their readers.

### Christian Message

There are several theological interconnections among the four epistles treated here. With regard to the epistles of Peter this is due to direct influence, for the First Epistle was known to the author of the Second, as the latter indicates (II Pet iii 1). Scholars have also endeavored to find some influence of Second Peter upon Jude or vice versa, since the central part of Second Peter runs parallel with Jude, but important differences make it unlikely that either epistle was the source of the other. It is better to suppose that they depended on a common tradition of preaching. James does not have such literary connections with the other General epistles, but there are common theological features. Though the General epistles are not a homogeneous group like the Pauline epistles, they may be regarded as belonging, together with Hebrews and First Clement, to a specific branch of early Christian literature, to be distinguished from the Pauline branch. At the same time we must recognize that First Peter is also very much like the Pauline writings.

These four epistles are not as concerned with the passion of Jesus Christ as are the epistles of Paul. If we except First Peter, their subject matter is more the Christian congregation, its present and future problems, than the life and death of Jesus. Certainly the works of God and Jesus Christ in the past are often referred to, and remain fundamental. But there is a shift in attention from Christ to the Christians, from the past to the present and future. This is due to the acute social problems and political pressures which confronted the faithful. Golgotha is still the basis of Christian life, but the actual starting point of the exposition is rather the believer's conversion and baptism. It is just because Christology was supposed to be known already through preaching and catechism that the authors were able to concentrate on the burning problems of political and social ethics.

The essential concern of the four epistles is to inculcate the right attitude of Christians toward their worldly environment. They should prove the genuineness of their faith by being obedient and patient followers of Christ, behave as good citizens, and not drift into worldly intrigues in order to improve their situation, nor into provocative criticism in order to demonstrate their dissatisfaction with non-believers. Social aggressiveness spoils Christian faith, love, and hope. It poisons the believer's mind, irritates the surrounding society instead of leading it to conversion, and implies distrust in God who, after having tested his faithful, is alone expected to judge all iniquity. In short, the four epistles preach the ideals of faith, peace and love, patience and obedience (James i 3, iii 17 f.; I Pet i 2, iv 8; II Pet i 2, 6 f.; Jude 2, 20 f.).

Eschatological problems were connected with social issues because instead of the victory that many expected to come immediately, there was continued discrimination and oppression. So the exhortations to faithfulness, patience, and long-suffering are completed by references to the certainty of the future consummation. James starts with the problem of the present temptations (i 2) and ends with assurances about the final salvation (v 7–11, 17–18). First Peter begins with the object of Christian hope (i 3–13), follows this with advice for coping with life in a troublesome environment, and ends with another reference to the future glory (v 10). Second Peter first draws attention to the endurance necessary for entrance into the eternal kingdom of Christ (i 3–11), and then affirms the certain coming of this glory by a reference to Christ's transfiguration (i 12–21). The criticism, which follows, of materialistic seducers who promise freedom is also intermingled with

eschatological references (ii 1–22). Finally, a thorough discussion
of the eschatological problem is offered, leading to the conclusion
that the approaching end makes peaceful endurance necessary (iii
1–18). Jude also rejects the same materialistic seducers mentioned
in the middle part of Second Peter, with similar references to eschatological data (15, 21, 24).

It is therefore evident that in these four epistles the exhortations
to a peaceful and patient Christian life in loyalty to state and society
are to be understood in an eschatological perspective. The emphasis
of the authors on co-operation with secular authority should not be
interpreted as appeasement but as an attitude of unconcern for
the values of this world in light of its imminent destruction and
the coming of the reign of God. The four epistles are intended
to convey more than merely abstract morality. In fact, the wisdom
they preach is supremely practical. Did not Jesus say, "For what
shall it profit a man, if he shall gain the whole world, and lose
his own soul?"

# THE EPISTLE OF JAMES

# Introduction

The epistle of James addresses forceful admonitions to Christians in countries outside of Palestine.

Its *author* calls himself, in i 1 "James, the servant of God and of the Lord Jesus Christ." No other information is given about the writer. If he is to be identified with a James mentioned elsewhere in the New Testament, the most likely candidate is James, the brother of Jesus. It is true there are two apostles named James, the sons of Zebedee and Alphaeus, but they do not seem to be indicated here. James the son of Zebedee was executed around A.D. 43 (Acts xii 2), before this epistle could possibly have been written. James the son of Alphaeus did not have the importance in the early church or the authority implicitly claimed by the author of the epistle. It is only James the brother of Jesus, later called the Righteous One, who can be seriously considered, since he played an influential role in the church at Jerusalem from A.D. 44 to his death in A.D. 62 (Acts xii 17, xv 13, xxi 18; Gal ii 9). However, we shall see that although much of the content and philosophy of the epistle is consonant with what is known of the teaching of James the Righteous, there are objections to identifying him as the actual writer.

Little is known about the life of James the Righteous, but he seems to have been a man of pious and peaceful disposition. The admonitions of the epistle to patience, steadfastness, humbleness, and perseverance through tribulations would have found favor with him. Many of the exhortations show similarities to the Sermon on the Mount and other words of Jesus found in the Q tradition (material common to Matthew and Luke). If we suppose that James preached after the fashion of his brother Jesus, these echoes of the gospels suggest that the epistle of James was at the very least inspired by and in accordance with the teachings of the Righteous One.

But even the old church did not acknowledge him to be the actual author (Eus. *Hist. eccl.* ii. 23, 24 ff.), and with good reason. Except for the name at the head there is no reference to him or his life in the entire epistle. It is highly improbable that James could write Greek, yet not only the language of the epistle but even the ideas have an unmistakable Greek stamp. The brother of Jesus was a Jew, and Gal ii 12 and Acts xxi 20–24 imply that he recommended observance of the Jewish law as late as A.D. 55 and 58. Paul, Luke, Josephus, and Hegesippus all portray James as one who endeavored to preserve contact with Judaism. Yet the epistle of James is expressly anti-zelotic. It does not recommend observance of the law in any specifically Jewish sense and certainly does not support Jewish nationalistic ambitions. That after A.D. 58 his views did undergo such a basic shift is not impossible; his death at the hands of nationalistic Jews in A.D. 62 may have been the result of just such a change. But under this hypothesis we would expect to find some of this personal history touched upon in the epistle. James would have owed his hearers an explanation of the about-face in his teachings. But nowhere in the epistle is there any indication of a strong concern for Jerusalem and Judaism. The message is directed toward converts who have joined Christian congregations in the dispersion, that is, the Roman empire. Not problems of the Jerusalem church but persecutions by heathens, relations with secular powers, and other problems of the churches in the Greco-Roman world are treated by the author.

Whether we adopt the view that James the Righteous remained an advocate of *rapprochement* with the Jews or that he later reacted against the zelotic terror, in either case it is unlikely that he would write the kind of letter we have in the epistle of James. We come to the conclusion that it is a production of a later author. He may very well have been a disciple of James the Righteous and in a position to write in his name in admonishing Christians to be patient and peaceful. The echoes of the Synoptic gospels and the use of the name James would associate with hallowed tradition what is essentially a practical sermon advising Gentile Christians on their conduct in the world and guarding them against zelotism.

The *readers* of the epistle are called in i 1, "the twelve tribes in the dispersion," so they are evidently thought of as living out-side Palestine in various areas of the Roman empire. A certain Jewish-Christian point of view is inherent in the text, but no opposi-tion to Gentile Christianity is discernible. Circumcision is no problem at all, and when the author refers to the law, it is without any suggestion that this should constitute a subject for discussion between Jewish and Gentile Christians. The problems are placed on a com-pletely different plane than in the Pauline epistles. Here the readers are addressed as the twelve tribes of Israel, not in opposition to Gentile believers but as the Christian church in general, regarded as the heir of Jacob and his twelve sons.

The *time* of composition probably does not coincide with the time of Paul's activity in view of the non-controversial manner in which the author speaks of the tribes of Israel, the law, etc. James's rejection of an empty Christianity which is in name only and of a faith which does not lead to works or deeds of love (i 22–27, ii 14–26) can hardly imply any polemic against Paul. The latter is not referred to at all in the context. Paul's opposition was to works and observances of the law as tickets for entering the house of righteousness, but he was just as thoroughly convinced as James that the faith of those inside must express itself in works of love, Gal v 6. In the epistle of James the problems are of another kind entirely. Either the epistle came into existence before Paul's ministry, or a considerable time after. It is practically im-possible, however, that the work is pre-Pauline. The persecutions mentioned in i 2 f., 12 f., ii 6, iv 6, v 10 f., refer to Christians outside of Palestine, but none are known prior to Paul's time. Many other details in the epistle make sense only at a later stage in the development of the church. Readers are warned against in-timate association with the rich of the world, i 2–7, iv 13–v 6, and against being influenced by mundane wisdom or philosophy, iii 13–17. They are admonished not to be impatient in waiting for the Lord's return, v 8, and to assume responsibility for the apostates from the faith, v 19 f. These are all conditions of a period later than Paul's ministry.

As indicated in the General Introduction, the church in the Ro-man empire was first generally persecuted toward the close of the reign of Domitian, A.D. 81–96. During the reign of this emperor too, certain internal political conditions prevailed, on the basis of

which it is possible to explain the situation described in the epistle
of James: The senators and the rich were involved in conspiracies
against Domitian; in this they were supported by the Stoics and
other philosophers, and probably also by certain prominent Jewish
proselytes; the poorer classes, on the other hand, sided with the
emperor. The recipients of the epistle of James appear to have been
stirred to social discontent and political aggressiveness, as is demonstrated by the repeated warnings against combativeness, malicious
speaking, a treacherous state of mind, etc. The author recommends
instead of this, humility, patience, i 2 ff., 12, 19 ff., etc., and loyalty,
i 25, ii 8, iii 17, iv 6, 10 f. In this connection the gospel is called
"the law of liberty" and "the royal law," by which expressions the
writer designates the universal law of love. Undoubtedly the appeal
is to avoid social aggressiveness. The author further sides openly
with the poor against the rich, i 10 f., iv 13–v 6, and condemns
particularly attempts by the recipients to secure supporters among
Romans of senatorial or noble rank, ii 1–7 (as pointed out in the
commentary below, these were the only ones allowed to wear
golden rings). He is also against mundane wisdom or philosophy
which leads to disputes and strife, i 5, iii 13–16. Finally, Jewish
motifs are interspersed throughout the epistle, e.g., when the author
calls his readers the twelve tribes, i 1, their church a synagogue,
ii 2, and in his admonitions repeatedly refers to the law which, however, is interpreted as being identified with the commandment of
love, i 25, ii 8–12, iv 11. The different factors by which the recipients
of the epistle of James appear to be influenced seem to fit especially
well with social and spiritual conditions in the Roman empire during
the reign of Domitian.

Therefore we conclude that the epistle of James came into existence around A.D. 90. Second Peter and Jude as well as Hebrews
and First Clement (one of the Apostolic Fathers) probably belong
to the same period. With reference to their contents, these writings
are comparable to the epistle of James.

The *purpose* of the epistle of James is to admonish the recipients
to Christian patience, e.g., i 21, v 7–11. They ought not to become aggravated over the trials that they must endure as Christians, i 2–
18, v 9–11, nor manifest envy and hatred toward their neighbors,
i 19–21, iii 1–iv 12 (the recipients are explicitly castigated in

iv 2 as murderers and zealots, struggling and fighting). Furthermore the readers are told to direct their attention no longer toward external means in order to vaunt themselves in this world: ii 1–13 (against preference for rich proselytes), ii 18–26 (against proselyting without requiring a change of mind), iii 13–18 (against wisdom or philosophy regarded as a means of self-arrogation), iv 13–17 (against commercial ethics). Above all one should not become impatient when the day of the Lord is delayed, but steadfastly wait for it, i 6, v 7–11, 17 f.

The *form* of the epistle of James is exceedingly simple. It consists of a series of admonitions on different themes which are dealt with one after another without any clearly discernible plan. There is a greeting in i 1, which gives the work the appearance of an epistle. But it is not really a personal letter at all. James is rather to be regarded as a circular, the contents of which are equivalent to a sermon. With regard to its diction, the epistle of James is to be compared with the productions of Hellenistic sermonic literature. The reader is especially reminded of a Jewish-Hellenistic collection of admonitory speeches called the Testaments of the Twelve Patriarchs.

The reason for the apparent lack of system in the epistle of James is not, as some hold, that the author has collected admonitions and sayings from various sources at random without reworking and classifying them. The order of the material is rather dependent on the conditions current in the communities which stir and trouble the author. If the reader fails to realize how concrete and disturbing the evils are, against which the author is fighting, then he will misjudge the text and label it trite moralizing. Only as the reader perceives the acutely contemporary character of the epistle throughout and the author's strong personal involvement, will he be able to sympathize with the presentation.

In spite of the relative lack of plan, division of the contents of the epistle of James into different main sections is possible. We would propose the following outline, dividing the book into five parts (corresponding for the most part to the five chapters of the book), each with two sections, with the exception of Part Four, which has three sections (including the first verses of chap. v).

1. Greeting, i 1

PART ONE

2. *Patience in the midst of afflictions*, i 2–18
   a. *Afflictions lead to steadfastness and perfection*, i 2–4
   b. *Wisdom obtainable through prayer to God*, i 5–8
   c. *Riches nothing over which to boast*, i 9–11
   d. *Perseverance in tribulations produces blessedness; God is not the cause of tribulations, but man's own lust*, i 12–18
3. *The importance of being a doer of the Word*, i 19–27

PART TWO

4. *The impropriety of currying favor with the rich*, ii 1–13
5. *The worthlessness of a faith not practiced*, ii 14–26

PART THREE

6. *The danger of a poisoned tongue*, iii 1–12
7. *True wisdom involves humble living*, iii 13–18

PART FOUR

8. *The combativeness of the recipients*, iv 1–12
9. *Business ethics*, iv 13–17
10. *Judgment on the unrighteous rich*, v 1–6

PART FIVE

11. *Patient waiting for the Lord's return*, v 7–11
12. *Manual of discipline*, v 12–20
    a. *No swearing, but praying, singing*, v 12–13
    b. *The healing of the sick*, v 14–18
    c. *The salvation of apostates*, v 19–20

The Christian importance of the epistle of James has been the subject of lively discussion. Martin Luther's dislike of this writing is well known. In his introduction to the New Testament of 1522 he calls it "a rather straw-like epistle" in comparison with John, I John, Romans, etc. There were two reasons for his skeptical attitude toward James: The great reformer thought that the epistle of James, through its emphasis on the perfection of faith through deeds, was in opposition to Paul's teaching on justification by faith, and he missed in this epistle statements concerning Christ's suffering and resurrection. In spite of this, Luther did not exclude James from the canon, because he found there was still much good Scripture in it. Later reformers, like Karlstadt and Oecolampadius, wished to ascribe only deutero-canonical rank to the epistle of James. During the following centuries doubts about the full canonicity of the epistle of James were less common. Today's critical research, however, has questioned its apostolic origin and its Christian nature. Among other attacks on it, efforts have been made to show that James was an originally Jewish writing with only superficial Christian additions here and there.

With reference to these criticisms, the following may be stated in defense of the epistle of James. As has been pointed out above, and as will be further developed in the commentary to follow, James's teaching does not really conflict with Paul's statements regarding justification by faith. Whether its author was an apostle or not is not of decisive importance with regard to the value of the epistle. As to its Christianity, it is true that the very name of Jesus Christ appears only in i 2 and ii 1, but this is not decisive either. Even if the two passages were deleted, it would still be impossible to make the epistle of James simply a piece of Jewish literature. In order to do so, it would be necessary to remove one passage after another so that in the end hardly anything would remain. The term "faith" appears for instance in i 3, 5, and plays a basic part in the rest of the epistle. Although this faith is regarded as incomplete without deeds of love, it is faith alone which constitutes the religious fellowship of the recipients, and not any special nationality as was the case with the Jews. The recipients are also, in accordance with New Testament usage, called "brethren" and "beloved" (i 2, 16, etc.). Even if directly christological expressions are lacking in this admonitory epistle, it nevertheless presents a Christian eschatology, cf. v 7 where the readers are advised to trust and hope in the Lord's coming. Other similar testimonies might be cited. That the author was dependent on Jewish traditions is an indisputable fact, but this is equally true of Peter's sermons at the beginning of Acts, and no one questions their Christian orientation.

The Christian character of the epistle of James cannot be denied without doing great violence to its integrity.

It is equally unjust to regard the author of the epistle of James as solely a moralist. On the contrary, here is a writer who speaks with personal warmth for what he regards as right, and with prophetic force against what he regards as unjust. His message is grounded in the conviction that real evils threaten the life of the young church, and drastic remedies are needed.

# Translation and Comment

## 1. GREETING
### (i 1)

I  1 James, servant of God and of the Lord Jesus Christ, with greetings to the twelve tribes in the dispersion.

### COMMENT

The James mentioned in vs. 1 was doubtless understood to be the Lord's brother, James the Righteous, who was the head of the Jerusalem congregation about A.D. 48–62 (cf. the Introduction above). Throughout the epistle the writer speaks with an authority suitable to the leading figure in the church at large, but hardly to any other James in the early church. As already pointed out, it is not likely that James the Righteous actually composed a Greek letter of this sort; in addition the contents of the epistle are more in harmony with a later situation of the church in the Roman empire. Yet the writer wishes it to be understood that the original inspiration came from that same James, though he does not directly identify him as the brother of the Lord. Quite modestly he presents him as "the servant . . . of the Lord Jesus Christ." The writer of the epistle of Jude likewise uses the well-known name of James, the kinsman of Jesus, and modestly calls himself the "servant of Jesus Christ, brother of James," Jude 1. The expression was apparently influenced by James i 1 and implies that the author of Jude was, like James, understood to be a brother of the Lord. Such attributions to leading authorities were not uncommon in early

Christianity. It was not regarded as a deception of any kind, in so far as the writer had the right to speak for and in the name of the church leader. This was probably the case here, for the epistle of James contains older material that may well have originated with the brother of Jesus, and in any case appears to have been expressed in his spirit. The actual writer may have been a disciple of James the Righteous, familiar with the preaching of the apostle, and justifiably speaking in his behalf.

## 2. PATIENCE IN THE MIDST OF AFFLICTIONS
## (i 2–18)

*Afflictions lead to steadfastness and perfection, i 2–4*

I  2 Regard it as a complete joy, my brothers, when you fall into various trials, 3 since you know that the testing of your faith produces endurance. 4 And let endurance take full effect so that you may be mature and perfect, lacking in nothing.

### COMMENT

The readers of the epistle have exhibited dissatisfactions and impatience because of the afflictions to which they have been exposed, vs. 2. Though the author speaks generally of different kinds of trials, the nature of these afflictions may be inferred from subsequent passages as persecution, sickness, and poverty. It is not simply a matter of individuals being exposed to personal difficulties, but of congregations undergoing trials of their faith. Whenever the believers as a group are involved in the ordeal of suffering, it ought not to be endured with grumbling, but accepted joyfully (cf. Matt v 11 f.). According to vs. 3 the trials are also wholesome, since they constitute a testing[1] of the faith which in turn leads to steadfast endurance. This steadfastness, however, ought to take full effect, vs. 4, that is, remain effective to the very end. The goal for Christians, and the author may have in view the final judgment, is to be perfect, thoroughly sound and flawless.

*Wisdom obtainable through prayer to God, i 5–8*

5 Now if any of you lacks wisdom, let him ask it from God who gives to all men generously and ungrudgingly, and it will be given to him. 6 Let him ask in faith, however, without doubting. For the doubter is like a wave of the sea driven by the wind and tossed hither and thither. 7 Let that man never imagine that he will receive anything from the Lord— 8 a double-minded man, unstable in all his ways.

### COMMENT

Wisdom is necessary in dealing with trials and afflictions; it may be obtained through prayer to God, vs. 5a. With this divine wisdom the readers will be able to endure suffering with patience and to escape ultimate danger and temptation. As we know from iii 13–18, they had sought a more practical wisdom from worldly sources. Through the "wisdom" described in that passage as leading to social unrest, they have been drawn into a struggle to improve their lot in life. The viewpoint corresponds to that of certain materialistic philosophers, belonging to the ranks of the Cynics and Stoics, who were sharply critical of prevailing conditions in the empire during the reign of Domitian (when the epistle of James seems to have been written). These advocates of wisdom may also be compared with intellectual critics of society today, who combine a materialistic philosophy with ruthlessly aggressive tactics. It is likely that James has such sources of "wisdom" in mind when he advises his readers to strive after the true wisdom that comes only through prayer. He is confident that such prayers will be answered positively, vs. 5b. He knows that God gives to everyone without reservation, or "outright,"[2] and ungrudgingly. The gracious manner of God's giving is emphasized in contrast with the way people act, even the Christians. As opposed to God who gives "outright," single-mindedly, the querulous man in vs. 8 is said to be "double-minded." And unlike the One who generously distributes his gifts, the readers are repeatedly described as being full of wrath and greed.

But if we ask God for wisdom, vs. 6a, we must do so in faith, not in doubt. The doubter is not anchored in God, vs. 6b, but is like an ocean wave driven to and fro by the wind. The thought here centers not so much on shifting sentiments, as on the instability of the whole personality under the influence of changing circumstances (cf. Eph iv 14). An unstable or vacillating person cannot expect to be heard by God, vs. 7. He does not give his heart undividedly to God, vs. 8, but is double-minded: that is, he is divided in his interests; his eye is not "single" but sees double (Matt vi 22), and he tries to serve both God and Mammon (Matt vi 24). He is unsettled in all his ways, uncertain in his decisions and his deeds.

## Riches nothing over which to boast, i 9–11

9 Let the humble brother glory in his exaltation, 10 and the rich brother in his humiliation, because as a flower of the grass he will pass away. 11 For when the sun rises with its burning heat, "the grass withers, and its flower falls off,"[a] and the beauty of its appearance fades away. In this way also, the rich man will perish in the midst of his enterprises.

[a] Isa xl 7

### COMMENT

In these verses, the author expresses his concern over the readers' preoccupation with the question of wealth. In view of this, James emphasizes the worthlessness and futility of earthly riches. Among the crowd of those struggling to gain possessions, the only one deserving of praise is the humble man, vs. 9, who has gained thereby a true sublimity. The rich man, on the other hand, vs. 10, may take pride only in being humbled. As a possessor of worldly wealth, he will fade away as a flower of the grass. In vs. 11, the image is

taken up in a paraphrase of Isa xl 7. (The same verse is quoted
in more detail by I Pet i 24, though not with reference to riches,
but to worldly propaganda.) When the sun rises, its burning heat
destroys the flower of the field—its beauty affords no protection,
but perishes with the flower. Likewise the rich man, in spite of his
impressive appearance, will fade away in the midst of his "ways,"
that is, his plans and undertakings. This will take place when the
sun of the new age, Christ, appears in his effulgent glory.

*Perseverance in tribulations produces blessedness; God is not
the cause of tribulations, but man's own lust, i 12–18*

12 Happy is the man who endures trial. For when he has
become approved he will receive the crown of life which the
Lord has promised to those who love him.

13 Let no one say when he is tempted: "I am tempted by
God." For God cannot be tempted by evil, and does not himself tempt anyone. 14 But every man is tempted, since he is
drawn away and enticed by his own desire. 15 Then when desire
conceives, it gives birth to sin, and when sin has ripened, it
produces death. 16 Do not go astray, my beloved brothers.

17 Every gift which is good,
     and every bequest which is perfect
is from above, since it comes down from the Father of the
Luminaries with whom there is no change of position, nor any
periodic concealment. 18 With good will he has begotten us
by the word of truth so that we may be a first fruit among his
creatures.

COMMENT

The first part of vs. 12 is reminiscent of the beatitudes of Jesus
in the Sermon on the Mount, especially Matt v 10 ff., where persecutions are said to lead to blessedness. The latter part of the same
verse echoes Rev ii 10 in its reference to the crown of life as the
reward of those who persevere in tribulation. The crown or wreath

of victory is also mentioned as a representation of eternal reward in I Cor ix 25; II Tim ii 5, iv 8; I Pet v 4; Rev iii 11. God is said to have promised this reward to those who love him, cf. Rom viii 28; I Cor ii 9; James ii 5. Thus there are striking analogies elsewhere in the New Testament to every phrase in vs. 12. It is clear that the thoughts expressed here are typically Christian. The author wishes to emphasize that the present trials will effect their reward, the gift of eternal life, since they furnish the believers an opportunity to prove their love to God.

The trials, vs. 13, are not to be regarded as temptations sent by God himself.[3] It is to be remembered that God is untouched by evil.[4] Therefore, the readers must not charge God with mercilessly trying and tempting men, as though he did not understand their frailty.

The truth is that man is tempted by his own lust which draws and entices him, vs. 14. According to James, lust is the root of evil. In this he, like Paul in Rom vii 7 f., 19–23, has probably adopted the rabbinic teaching concerning the evil instinct by which man has been mastered since the fall in the garden of Eden. This evil propensity explains the dominion of sin and death in the world, vs. 15, since it conceives and gives birth to sin, which in turn produces death. The line of reasoning is very close to what we have in Paul's writings except that the law is not mentioned. In both instances the background is Jewish speculation about Adam and the fall, although Greek psychology has contributed the idea that "lust" produces such disastrous results. For people today influenced by modern psychoanalysis, it is not at all difficult to understand James at this point, though fundamental differences exist. In this context the chief object is not to present ingenious explanations of existing conditions in life, but to show how man through his lust opens the way to temptations and trials.

It is a grievous self-deception, against which the author urgently warns his readers, vs. 16, to blame God for these trials. God is the only giver of good and perfect gifts, as vs. 17 stresses through the citation of a hexameter otherwise unknown.[5] Human beings make donations and distribute gifts, as in antiquity the rich often did in order to gain the favor of the masses. Such gifts, however, have no lasting value. The only true giver is God, and his gifts are perfect. These come from above, from the one who is the

"Father of the Luminaries," that is, of the celestial bodies. An interesting parallel to this expression occurs in the Qumran Manual of Discipline (1QS iii. 20), where God is called the "Prince of the Luminaries." James adds that with him unlike the heavenly bodies, there is no change of conjunction or any darkening according to periodicity.[6] On the contrary, God is constant in his love for man.

The Christians are also the children of God's love, vs. 18. God is said to have brought them into being through his beneficent good will.[7] On account of this concern, he has begotten "us" who are believers through the word of truth. The last expression emphasizes that the believers have been born to a new life, by accepting the message of the gospel in their hearts. The same thought appears in I Pet i 23; it may also be compared with the representation of baptism in Titus iii 5 as the bath of new birth. Born to new life in this way, the Christians have become a kind of "first fruit" among God's creatures. This signifies that they stand above other creatures in rank, but they must also present themselves as an offering to God. So the first fruits, according to Deut xxvi 1–11, etc., are to be sacrificed to the Lord, and the martyrs, according to Rev xiv 4, are to be set apart as a first-fruit offering to God and the Lamb.

# 3. THE IMPORTANCE OF BEING A DOER OF THE WORD
## (i 19-27)

I  19 Although you have knowledge, my beloved brothers, let everyone be swift to hear, slow to speak, slow to anger. 20 For a man's wrath does not achieve the righteousness of God. 21 Therefore, put away all filthiness and accumulation of evil, and with humility receive the implanted word that is able to save your souls.

22 Furthermore, become doers of the word, and not hearers only who deceive themselves. 23 For if anyone is a hearer of the word, and not a doer, he is like a man perceiving the shape of his natural features in a mirror. 24 When he has caught a glimpse of himself and then goes away, he immediately forgets what he looked like. 25 But the one who gazes into the perfect law of liberty, and remains there, and does not become a forgetful hearer, but an effective doer, shall be blessed in his doing.

26 If anyone thinks he is religious, and fails to bridle his tongue but deceives his own heart, then his religion is vain. 27 A religion which is pure and undefiled before God the Father is to care for orphans and widows in their distress, and to keep oneself unspotted by the world.

## COMMENT

The introductory clause in vs. 19a presents certain linguistic difficulties, if the reading given by the oldest manuscripts is retained. A verb meaning "to know" appears here.[8] The form of the verb used[9] may be understood either as the indicative, "you know," or the imperative, "know!" If the verb is imperative, the following admonitions could be regarded as the object. Such a possibility is in harmony with biblical usage (cf. "hearken" in ii 5). But this supposition runs into the difficulty that the first of these admonitions is followed by "however,"[10] which destroys the suggested dependence on the imperative "know." If on the other hand the verb is indicative the meaning is absolute since there is no direct object: "You have knowledge." The difficulty is that this verb is hardly ever used in an absolute sense; it customarily is qualified by an object. Aside from this there is no serious problem of interpretation, while other attempted solutions involve glaring linguistic anomalies. It is preferable therefore to render the verb as indicative. The knowledge or information, which the brothers are said to possess, may simply be understood as the result of their instruction in the Christian doctrine. Since the recipients of the epistle are described as recently converted to the Christian faith, e.g., in vss. 18, 21, 22, it would be natural for the author to refer to their newly gained knowledge of the gospel. The author recognizes that such knowledge exists, whether it is to be regarded as common Christian knowledge, or as a special wisdom, as "gnosis" reserved for the initiated. In either case he stresses that this knowledge must not be misused, but that all should train themselves to listen, rather than to talk. A defense of the text of the oldest manuscripts can thus be made, and a logical connection established between the parts of vs. 19. On the other hand, it must be acknowledged that the later Byzantine manuscripts present a simpler, more comprehensible text: "Consequently,[11] my beloved brethren, let each man," etc.

Everyone ought to be ready to listen when God's word is proclaimed, vs. 19b. In humble and obedient submission to the word, each individual ought to show his knowledge of the faith. On the other hand, no one should be eager for the role of speaker. Apparently, many of the recipients were enthusiastic preachers, with the result that there was a great deal of talking and witnessing on the part of the laymen of the church (cf. also iii 1). The author admonishes these talkative laymen rather to listen humbly when the word is proclaimed by its rightful ministers. The worst is, however, that these talkative individuals excite themselves to anger. Even in our day this excitement to anger is noticeable among demagogues who thunder against existing conditions and against their fellow men.

The epistle of James is directed against those who have appeared both as religious prophets of doom and as political agitators. It is evident from vs. 20 that these demagogues imagined that by their angry sermons of condemnation, they could hasten the manifestation of God's righteous judgment, but the author declares this to be impossible. The "righteousness" of God in their view is tantamount to improved economic conditions, as is also shown by related passages in chapters ii and iv.

There was constant agitation among the heathen against the Roman imperium, but it was equally true of Jewish apocalyptic circles. The stimulus for provocative and seditious speeches against the social order may have come from one or both of these sources. In either case the readers are admonished in vs. 21a to overcome this evil enterprise by avoiding all filthiness and wickedness. The practice of putting off the old humanity with its contamination was conceived quite concretely like the shedding of a garment and associated particularly with newly converted members as they entered the life of the church (cf. Eph iv 22; Col iii 8; I Pet ii 1). In all likelihood the author of James had in mind recently baptized members when he uses the phrase, "putting away," and follows it up with the illustration of the "implanted" word, vs. 21b. For in the thought of the early church "implanting" was a figure for baptism (cf. Rom vi 5), though in this passage the word is viewed as being implanted into the believers, not the other way around. Otherwise the planting of the word in the life of man may also be compared with Jesus' parable of the sower, which describes the different ways in which the word is received by various kinds of people (Matt xiii 3–9, 18–23, with parallel texts). According to James, the readers ought to receive the word with humility, because it is able to save their souls. They must not allow the proclamation of the word to become an occasion for showing rancor and wrath against society. Some have misused the gospel in this respect. Already in the early church revolutionary spirits were stirred to attacks on the existing order, on the basis of a materialistic interpretation of the hopes for the future. This sort of thing may happen in communistic circles, and did also happen in Germany during the Reformation and in Great Britain during the seventeenth century. In view of the dangerous possibility, James places major emphasis on the necessity of meekness or humility. For him it is not a matter of routine instruction, based upon theoretical or psychological considerations, but of vital importance in view of the tumultuous circumstances in which his readers find themselves, and to which he has reacted deeply and strongly.

There is a question concerning people who attend worship services in order to hear the preaching. Outwardly at least, they profess Christianity, but in reality they are Christians in word only. Satisfied with a formal confession of the Christian faith, they are not prepared to assume responsibility for its wider implications and certainly do not expect to carry these out in daily life. For this reason the readers are urged in vs. 22 to become "doers" of the word, and not merely listeners who deceive themselves. Among the Dead Sea scrolls there are texts that contain interesting analogies to this motif. In the Commentary on Habakkuk (1QpHab vii. 11, viii. 1, and xii. 4), the faithful are presented as "doers of the law." In the Manual of Discipline (1QS ii. 25b–iii. 12), the importance of being converted to a real practice of the covenant is emphasized. The self-deception rebuked by James probably involves the expectation of these would-be Christians that they would gain the salvation of their souls, which God's word brings (vs. 21), merely by listening to the proclamation of the word or by participating to a convenient extent in the instruction and services of the church.

An illustration is offered in the next two verses which is designed to show how meaningless such a mere confession of the evangelical faith really is. In a few words the author depicts a man who sees "the shape of his natural features" in a mirror (vs. 23) and then goes away (vs. 24) forgetting the face reflected in the mirror. As is clear from what follows, the mirror is used as a symbol of God's word, and its function is to enable the new man in Christ to appear. The word of God had already been described in vs. 18 as begetting believers to newness of life. According to early Christian thinking what is involved is not simply rehabilitation, but renovation or regeneration so that a new man steps forth (cf. John iii 5; Eph iv 24; Titus iii 5). Thus in the illustration of the mirror, the man who delves into the word is brought to newness of life. The author probably has in mind the moment when the believers, through baptism and confession of faith in Jesus Christ, were born again in a unique way through the power of the word; for his words are directed primarily to those who have recently been received into church fellowship (cf. vss. 18, 21, 22). If this individual forgets the newness of life he now possesses through the life-giving power of the word, so that he reverts to the previous pattern of his life, then it is evident that he attributes no particular importance to the word and the new birth. He is like the man who thoughtlessly sees his face in a mirror and then goes off forgetting the image that he saw and giving no further thought to his appearance. Viewed in this light, the illustration of the man looking at himself in the mirror becomes comprehensible, and the details contribute touches of color and meaning to the whole. The reference to the image in the mirror is related quite naturally to the new birth through the word (vs. 18), and the new person who has come into existence through it.

It is interesting to notice that this author, so often charged with making an inadequate adaptation of Jewish or Hellenistic moralism to the Christian faith, represents ethics as fulfilling the life of the new man which the Christian has become once and for all through the word of God. That in this connection the imperative is based on a perfect indicative (i.e., what a Christian must be is what, through the grace of God, he has already become), is also characteristic of the New Testament way of thinking (cf. Rom vi 3–6, viii 11 f.; I Cor vi 16; Eph iv 13). On the whole the author demonstrates considerable independence of Jewish and Greek moralism.

That person on the other hand, vs. 25, who looks deeply[12] into the perfect law or "the law of liberty" and abides in it so that he becomes a real "doer," will be blessed through his doing. As is evident from the context, and also from a comparison with ii 8, the "law" here refers to the gospel or the word of salvation to which the writer has referred repeatedly in the foregoing passage (vss. 18–24). The fact that the gospel is called "law" does not involve any attempt to reintroduce external observances, but is rather prompted by a desire to overcome Jewish nationalistic zeal for the law and present the gospel of love as the true law. The emphasis is not on the word "law," but on the qualifying attributes "perfect" and "of liberty." In contrast to other patterns of human behavior, the gospel is perfect, that is, it leads to perfection, and gives its adherents freedom. The freedom mentioned here is to be understood in connection with the remark in vs. 21 that God's word saves the souls of the believers. Thus the law of liberty is identical with the gospel of salvation, cf. ii 12. The expression itself, "law of liberty," is partly reminiscent of Stoic phraseology. It may have been inspired by the Stoic ideal of freedom, according to which men ought to strive for independence from every passion of the soul, such as anger, fear, etc. Freedom of this kind is of interest here since in vss. 19–21 the author admonishes his readers to shun wrath and all evil passions. This does not mean that he wishes to disseminate Stoic teaching, but only that he has adapted himself to a way of thinking characteristic of the environment of his readers. Philo of Alexandria speaks in a similar way about freedom in connection with God's word. James, however, by calling the gospel "the law of liberty," emphasizes its difference from the law understood as a means of Jewish self-assertion. Although the Maccabees had heroically defended the independence of the Jewish people and their law, and later efforts at independence were based upon strong national feeling coupled with intense messianic expectations, it is nevertheless fair to say that Jewish zeal for the law often led to revolutionary aggressiveness, not only on the part of the zealots, but also of the other religious groups. Jesus, Stephen, the Jerusalem Christians, and later Paul, were bitterly persecuted in the name of the law. So was James the Righteous himself, when he was put to death in A.D. 62. In the days of the Flavian emperors Jewish apocalypticists continued to produce grim prophecies against the Romans, and thus prepared the bloody revolt that broke out under Hadrian. All this shows that zeal for the law might provoke violent passions. In the present context James warns his readers against being enslaved to such passions (vs. 14), especially wrath (vss. 19 f.). Most probably he expresses a sharp difference with Jewish-national fervor when he calls the perfection of the law, which is found in the gospel of love, "the law of freedom." This law does not involve slavery to evil passions, or the illusory freedom of political independence, but the true liberty of eternal salvation. It is entirely to the point, therefore, when James adds that adherence to this law of liberty will lead to blessedness for the one who obeys it and really practices it.

The recipients of the epistle wish to be known as God-fearing people, vs. 26. Apparently they support religious institutions and interests. Their piety should not be understood in the modern sense of personal devoutness, which would be anachronistic, but rather in the light of the Roman attitude toward religion and atheism.

Godlessness and irreligion were denounced by the emperor and the imperial officials, as antisocial tendencies. The author does not defend the interests of the state, but he thinks that it is not right for people to pretend to be religious while attacking society with an evil tongue, as do many of the readers. If they claim to belong to the Christians and yet do not control their tongues, then their religion is vain. If they indulge in such malicious complaining against the authorities, as apparently they have, they deceive their hearts. The latter expression may be taken to mean that they try to silence their consciences and persuade themselves that their outspoken criticism is quite compatible with their Christian confession. In contrast to this it is pointed out in vs. 27 that the characteristic of a religion which is pure and blameless in the eyes of God is works of love in behalf of orphans and widows. To be "doers" of the law does not mean to observe external rules, an opinion to which a one-sided Paulinism has led many interpreters of this epistle, but rather to perform works of love within the church. This implies no contradiction to the teachings of Paul. It is only necessary to realize that the law here spoken of is the law of love. Such works of love will enable the readers to keep themselves unspotted by the world and its ugly intrigues in which, according to what follows, they have hitherto been involved (cf. also iv 4; II Pet ii 19–22).

## 4. THE IMPROPRIETY OF CURRYING FAVOR
## WITH THE RICH
### (ii 1–13)

**II** 1 My brothers, do not use the glorious faith in our Lord
Jesus Christ as a pretext for currying favor with people. 2 Thus
if a gentleman with a gold ring in a splendid garment enters
your synagogue, and a poor man in filthy clothing also comes
in, 3 and you pay attention to the one who wears the splendid
garment and say: "Please sit here in the best place," while you
say to the poor man: "You stand there, or sit at my feet":
4 have you not made distinctions among yourselves, and become
judges with wrong standards?

5 Listen, my beloved brothers. Did not God choose the poor
in the world [to be] rich in faith and heirs of the kingdom
which he has promised to those who love him? 6 But you have
dishonored the poor man. Is it not the rich who oppress you,
and who drag you before the courts? 7 Is it not they who revile
the good name invoked upon you?

8 If, on the contrary, you fulfil the royal law according to
the scripture: "You shall love your neighbor as yourself," you
do well. 9 But if you try to curry favor with people, you commit sin, being convicted by the law as transgressors. 10 For
whoever keeps the whole law but fails at one point, has become
guilty of all. 11 Thus the one who says: "Do not commit adultery," has also said: "Do not kill." If you do not commit adultery
but kill, you have become a transgressor of the law. 12 Speak
and act, as [those who are] going to be judged by the law
of liberty. 13 For the judgment will take place without mercy for
the one who has shown no mercy. But mercy will triumph
over judgment.

## COMMENT

The readers of the epistle have a weakness for the rich and powerful. According to vs. 1, they make their glorious[13] faith in the Lord Jesus Christ, a pretext for[14] efforts to curry favor with people.[15] This is evident, vs. 2 points out, when a rich man and a poor man simultaneously visit the assembly of the readers, or their "synagogue" as the author expresses himself in conformity with certain Jewish interests among them. In this connection the rich man is said to wear a gold finger ring, which indicates that he was of senatorial rank or a Roman nobleman. During the early years of the empire only such men had the right to wear a gold ring. When it is added that he wears a "splendid garment," this may indicate that he is seeking political office and adherents. For according to the New Testament and also extra-biblical documents a "splendid garment" signifies a white toga. Such robes were often worn by politicians who were candidates for elective office. At any rate it would be apparent to the readers that the rich man under discussion was a representative of the aristocracy and that his connection with the Christians was supposed to be beneficial to both groups. The magnates of the Roman empire were interested in acquiring the political support of different organizations by generosity toward their members. And they used the organizations to win clients in an even more direct way than certain politicians today who seek to win "supporters." Simultaneously the religious and the secular organizations of antiquity were eager to secure mighty and wealthy protectors. According to vs. 3, this is also true of the readers of the epistle. In their eagerness to please the rich man who enters their congregation they hurry to offer him an important seat, while the poor man must stand, or sit on the floor.

Such behavior produces dissension in the Christian congregation, vs. 4. For the unity of the church is dissolved if such differences in rank are accorded recognition. At the same time the Christians act as judges with faulty standards[16] by estimating people according to their material possessions.

According to vs. 5, there is a higher standard for judging people, which the Christians are to follow: before God the poor are the most valuable and have been chosen by him (cf. I Cor i 27 f.) to be rich in faith and to inherit the kingdom that he has promised to those who love him (cf. above, i 12). Faith and hope of an eternal inheritance are true riches. To dishonor the poor man, as the recipients do according to vs. 6a, is a grave violation of God's will.

Clearly the epistle of James sympathizes with the poor, as do Luke and Paul, confirming the characteristic "pauperism" of the early church (cf. i 9–11). The opposition to the rich seems stronger here than anywhere else in the New Testament. However, this is not due to any ill will in principle toward possessions and money, but is based on experiences of the author with the policy of the rich, which had encouraged a factional spirit among the Christians and proved harmful to the peace and unity of the community, as the following verses indicate.

The rich oppress the Christians, vs. 6b, and drag them before the courts. Most likely this is not meant to characterize the rich in general, because wealth does not always imply prosecution of Christians. The statement was made rather in view of specific difficulties encountered in the days of James. It is possible that some rich people had been irritated by Christians, and dragged them before courts. But there is no explicit evidence of this practice. And it is not clear how the present obsequious behavior of the Christians could produce so vicious a reaction, or on the other hand, how this danger could be avoided by abandoning the present course of action. We do know that during the reign of Domitian it was dangerous to have connections with senators and rich men, since they and their retainers were subject to prosecution by the Roman authorities (as illustrated by the emperor's attack on Flavius Clemens; see the General Introduction). This danger would be avoided by not permitting such rich men to control a Christian community.

The statement in vs. 7 that the rich revile the name of Christ may also be understood in an indirect manner. For the rich man spoken of in the preceding verses, who visits the Christian congregation, can hardly be thought of as reviling the Christians after having been treated so courteously by them. But as a representative of the aristocracy, which was in opposition to the imperial power especially in the days of Domitian, such a rich man might very well help to give Christianity a bad reputation among the authorities and the people.

It is interesting to notice that at the end of the verse the author avoids stating directly that the believers have been baptized into the name of Christ, but speaks indefinitely about the good name once invoked upon them. Possibly the caution here, as elsewhere in the epistle where basic Christian truths are only alluded to, depends on a wish to avert misuse of the epistle by non-Christians.

To counteract the eagerness to curry favor with influential people, vs. 8, the author quotes a well-known passage of the Old Testament,[17] Lev xix 18. It is the biblical commandment of love which James, like Jesus in Matt xxii 39 and Paul in Rom xiii 10, presents as the fulfilment of the law. No more than elsewhere in the epistle does he think of the Pharisaic law with all its rites and precepts of purification, but rather of that essence of God's law which is love to one's neighbor, as enjoined by the gospel. This commandment of love is called "the royal law," or rather "the imperial law," inasmuch as its promulgator is Christ, regarded as the true king, superior to the Roman emperor. Probably the expression has also been chosen in order to emphasize that the gospel of love, in contradistinction to objectionable tendencies among the readers, fulfils the law of society. Partiality toward the rich is a transgression of the law of love, vs. 9, since it contravenes the will of God by discriminating against the poor, whom he has chosen.

It is important to obey the whole law, as vs. 10 stresses, for if one fails at a single point, then the law is broken. This remark indicates that among the readers there was an effort to observe the revealed law after the Jewish pattern. The author points out that such zealots for the law do not keep the law, since they violate it at a basic point. According to vs. 11, they are certainly rigid with reference to the commandment against adultery (Exod xx 14), but do not really obey the commandment against murder (Exod xx 13). Of course the readers do not commit murder in the common meaning of the word, but the author understands the commandment against murder in the broadened and deepened sense which Jesus gave to it in the Sermon on the Mount (Matt v 21f.). He interprets their wrath and hard words against the people in the community as a violation of this commandment. In this way he demonstrates that the zealots for the law do not themselves really keep the law.

Whatever they say or do, the readers must remember that they will finally be judged by the law, vs. 12, that is, not by the Jewish law, but by its perfection in the law of real liberty or salvation, which is the law of love. Confronted with the law in this form the believers, as is evident from vs. 13, will have a judgment that is both sterner and milder than under the law of Moses. On the one hand, the judgment will be administered without mercy to those who have shown no mercy. According to Matt xxv 41 the Son of man will consign "the bucks," or those who have not shown mercy toward the least of his brothers, to eternal fire. On the other hand, it is clear that mercy surpasses or triumphs over[18] judgment: that is, for those who have practiced mercy there need be no fear of judgment. This was also pointed out by Jesus in the parable of the final judgment, for according to Matt xxv 34 the Son of man will invite "the sheep" or those who have truly shown mercy toward the least of his brothers to enter the promised kingdom.

# 5. THE WORTHLESSNESS OF A FAITH NOT PRACTICED
## (ii 14–26)

II  14 What good is it, my brothers, if someone says that he possesses faith but does not have works? Can his faith save him?

15 If a brother or a sister is naked and lacks daily food, 16 and one of you says to them: "Go in peace, be warmed and be fed," without giving them what the body needs, what good is it? 17 Thus faith also, if not accompanied by works, is dead in itself.

18 Now someone may say: "You have faith, and I have works. Show me your faith without works, and I will show you my faith through my works. 19 You believe that God is one. [In this] you do right. Even the evil spirits believe and tremble." 20 Please consider, foolish man, that faith is useless without deeds.

21 Was not Abraham, our father, justified by deeds when he offered his son Isaac on the altar? 22 You see that his faith worked together with his deeds. So his faith was made perfect by his works, 23 and the [word of] scripture was fulfilled which says: "Abraham believed God and it was reckoned to him as righteousness,"ᵃ and he was called "a friend of God."ᵇ 24 You see that it is through deeds that a man is justified, and not through faith alone.

25 The same was true of Rahab, the harlot. Was she not

ᵃ Gen xv 6
ᵇ Isa xli 8

justified because of her deeds when she received the messengers and sent them away by another road? 26 Just as the body without the spirit is dead, so also faith without deeds is dead.

### COMMENT

It must be noted that in vs. 14 the discussion is about a person who only asserts that he has faith. This person has no real faith, since his faith does not find expression in deeds. The author does not take issue with faith itself, but with a superficial conception of it which permits faith to be only a formal confession. He desires to point out that a Christianity of mere words does not lead to salvation.

In accordance with this, vss. 15–16 describe a situation in which a vital faith will manifest itself in appropriate deeds. A Christian is to give clothing and food to a freezing and hungry brother or sister. It is not enough to speak comfortingly about the problem in terms of spiritual warmth and spiritual food and leave the needy person to shift for himself with the well-meaning words, "Depart in peace." In the early church this blessing was pronounced by the deacons at the close of holy communion. It may be assumed that the author was acquainted with this or a similar custom and directs his admonitions especially to the deacons. In any case true worship is not only a matter of formulas and ceremonies, but also of active works of love (as was previously pointed out in i 27). Faith without deeds is dead, vs. 17; this conclusion is further emphasized in vss. 20, 24, and above all in vs. 26. Once again it is clear that the deeds approved are not technical observances, but acts of love. In this connection it is quite impossible to speak of any direct or indirect contradiction of Paul, who, according to Gal v 6 and other passages, emphasized that faith should be realized in deeds of love.

After this discussion of the duty of the believers—perhaps especially of the ministers of the church—to exercise true charity toward the destitute, the following verses deal with the general obligations of those who have been recently converted to the Christian faith. It appears from vs. 18 that an effort has been made to facilitate a Gentile's transition from paganism to Christianity by assuring him that faith alone is sufficient, and that accompanying deeds are not

necessary. Thus if anyone finds it difficult to accommodate himself
to the practice of true Christian piety, it will suffice for him to
make a confession of faith, while others assume the responsibility
for deeds. Such a distinction between confession and performance
was incorporated in principle in Pharisaism. The Pharisees recognized that it was impossible for all individual Jews to fulfil the demands of the law. So the members of the Pharisaic fellowships
accepted vicarious responsibility for satisfying these requirements
and performing good works on behalf of the masses. Even more
drastic modifications of the legal stipulations were made for the
sake of the half-proselytes or "God-fearers." For these, chief importance was attached to the confession of Jewish belief. The heathen thus found the way made easier to become adherents of
Judaism. The present passage in James may contain a criticism of
such arrangements. It seems to presuppose an agreement between
a Christian missionary and a Gentile regarding his acceptance of
the Christian religion on particularly favorable terms. The new-
comer need only profess a certain minimum faith. The representatives of the church assume responsibility for the requisite deeds,
and so contribute to the well-being of the newly converted person
himself, since he thereby becomes an object of their charity. With
reference to faith, vs. 19 indicates that a simple monotheistic af-
firmation is supposed to be sufficient for reception into church fellowship. The author ironically quotes the zealous proselyter to the
effect that even the evil spirits cherish a similar faith in God. In
this way Christianity would simply be identical with natural religion.
James characterizes such reasoning as an unworthy way of gaining
proselytes. When he has the speaker add that even the evil spirits
tremble before God, he probably alludes to the fact that some
Christian leaders, like Jewish proselyters, are eager to win large
groups of peripheral adherents who are thought of as "fearing God."
Such a Christianity of mere words is worth nothing according to
James. Its spokesmen are reminded in vs. 20 that faith without deeds
is useless. This statement (as also vss. 17, 24, and 26) is the
conclusion to what has preceded, and not an introduction to what
follows; thus the expression "foolish man" refers to the proselyter
just mentioned, and not to the readers in general.

In support of the thesis that good works are necessary, Abraham's
exemplary behavior is then referred to in vs. 21. The progenitor of

Israel was not justified by faith alone but rather through his deeds, in particular because he offered his beloved son Isaac on the altar. Although the illustration may appear strange to the modern reader, it is readily understandable in the context. First, the reference to Abraham is entirely in order, in view of the key place of the patriarch, as the father of the faithful, in the thought of first-century Judaism and Christianity. Second, Abraham's willingness to offer to God his dearest and most precious possession is an example to believers and a lesson concerning the spirit of sacrifice and quality of giving expected of them. Third, the allusion to the altar may reflect the practice in the early church of placing the love offerings on the table or altar. Whether or not the custom and the connection are to be assumed here, they best explain the symbolism of the passage (as is also the case in Heb xiii 10, 16). There is no criticism of Paul's teaching in this passage, in spite of the fact that in Rom iv 3 and Gal iii 6 Paul refers to Abraham's faith as an Old Testament confirmation of the doctrine of justification by faith alone. It is possible that James has in mind a current misrepresentation of the Pauline position on this question, but there is no indication of any disputation with Paul or his disciples. The author simply expresses his concern that the faith of the newly converted, misconstrued as a formula of salvation, be not isolated from the larger area of Christian life and practice. The example of Abraham shows, vs. 22, that faith must be accompanied by deeds so that they complement and enrich each other. Faith constitutes the foundation but reaches fruition in works of mercy. According to vs. 23, the important word of Scripture[19] in Gen xv 6 about Abraham's justification is to be understood in this way: Abraham's faith was perfected through his deeds. The conclusion is, vs. 24, that man is justified by deeds, and not by faith only. While the writer appears to contradict Paul's teaching on justification by faith, this is not actually the case. James is also concerned with the problem of justification, but he views justification in the light of the last judgment, while Paul has in mind conversion and baptism. Paul rejected works of the law, but he encouraged acts of Christian love even as James, though the latter speaks of these as obligations of the law of liberty. Paul was also convinced that the final judgment will be decided on the basis of a believer's deeds, I Cor iii 13 ff.; II Cor v 10 f. This is fully in accord with Jesus' description of the last judgment according to Matt xxv 31–46. Note especially the phrases "inasmuch as you have done it," and "inasmuch as you have not done it," vss. 40, 45.

In vs. 25 the story of Rahab is offered as another example of the importance of good works, though the illustration seems rather farfetched. It is surprising to find Rahab, who contributed to the fall of Jericho (Josh ii), and who is here explicitly called a harlot, praised as a model of justification by faith and works. This woman, however, was highly esteemed in the early Christian church. In addition to her distinction as an ancestress of Jesus (cf. Matt i 5), she is singled out as a good example in Heb xi 31 and in I Clem. 12:1, 8 (writings which appear to be related to James in background and origin; compare the remarks on the dating of James in the Introduction).

What the author wishes to emphasize is Rahab's helpfulness toward the emissaries of God's people. She received them hospitably and sent them safely away along another road. The Christian congregations ought to receive the representatives of the church in the same way and equip them for their further journeys. Rahab thus becomes a type of the Christian congregation, which, in accordance with the thinking of Jesus and the apostles, might well be symbolized by the figure of a woman (cf. Luke xv 8–10; II Cor xi 2). That this pagan and previously unchaste woman was saved from destruction was not due solely to her faith, as Heb xi 31 points out, but also to her performance of a good deed. Faith without deeds is like a body without spirit, vs. 26. A modern reader would rather be inclined to reverse the image and picture works as the corporeal element made alive by the working of faith, the spiritual factor. But the author views faith as the formal confession of Christianity, so he is correct in describing it as a body which needs to be animated by the spirit of Christian living and doing. Here again we see how far James is from controverting Paul on the subject of faith and works of the law: the latter is not under discussion in this passage.

## 6. THE DANGER OF A POISONED TONGUE
### (iii 1–12)

**III** 1 Do not many of you become teachers, my brothers, since you know that we [teachers] will receive a severer condemnation, 2 for in many respects all of us give offense.

If anyone does not give offense in [his] speech, he is a mature man, who is able to bridle his whole body as well. 3 For if we place bits in the mouths of horses so that they may obey us, then we control their whole body. 4 Consider the ships too which are so large and are driven by fierce winds: they are guided nonetheless by a tiny rudder, wherever the pilot's impulse directs. 5 In the same way the tongue also is a small organ, but it makes great boasts. Consider how small a fire ignites a mass of wood. 6 Indeed, the tongue is a fire. As [representing] the world of iniquity the tongue is placed among our organs; it contaminates the whole body, and inflames the wheel of being, as it is inflamed by Gehenna. 7 All kinds of beasts and birds, reptiles and sea animals, can be tamed, and have been tamed by mankind. 8 But no human being is able to tame the tongue. It is an uncontrollable evil, full of lethal poison.

9 With it we bless the Lord and Father, and with it we curse men who are made after the likeness of God. 10 So from the same mouth proceed blessing and cursing. This, my brothers, ought not to be so. 11 Does a fountain pour from the same spout what is sweet and what is bitter? 12 My brothers, is it possible for a fig tree to yield olives, or a vine figs? Neither can salt water produce sweet.

COMMENT

Many of the believers felt themselves called to be teachers or preachers, vs. 1. Laymen should not enter lightly upon this office, since serious risks are entailed in offering public testimony to the faith. Being a preacher involves a grave responsibility, and as his privilege is greater, so his condemnation will be the more severe. At the same time, the author concedes in vs. 2a that no preacher is faultless, and modestly includes himself in this category. If therefore the proclamation of the word ought to be reserved for those who hold the office of preachers, their position far from assuring their salvation places them in greater jeopardy.

What a man does with his tongue is fraught with momentous consequences, vs. 2b. A carefree, thoughtless exercise of the gift of speech can bring a man to destruction more quickly than anything else, since the tongue has so much influence (cf. "every idle word," Matt xii 36 f.). Control of speech is the only way to perfection, and means control of the whole body. Why does the author talk in this manner about the "body"? He is actually thinking of the congregation whose "tongue" is the teacher or preacher. His purpose is to warn against provocative or demagogic speaking. Thus the "body" is here, as often in the writings of Paul, a symbol of the church; this view is confirmed by the illustrations that follow.

The author reminds the reader in vs. 3 that it is possible to control the movements of a large horse by putting a bit in its mouth. This illustration would not be applicable to the case of an individual and his own body, since for the normal person there is no difficulty in controlling bodily movements. It only becomes relevant when the tongue is thought of as a means of governing the actions of a separate body of much larger size. In this way a church leader who regulates the preaching may control the whole group of believers. The same is true of the illustration of the ship in vs. 4. For the early Christians a vessel was a favorite symbol of the church (cf. I Pet iii 20 and several passages in the Apostolic Fathers). The meaning of this passage becomes clear if it is recognized that the ship represents the church, and the rudder, which actually resembles a tongue, corresponds to the proclamation of the message

within the congregation. The author has made a point of the fact
that the ship has been driven hither and thither by strong winds.
These winds represent various human interests, as in Eph iv 14.
The situation of the Christian congregations is fraught with danger
as the powerful tongues twist and turn the believers in opposite
directions where the winds blow. But by means of the true rudder
or through the proclamation of the word the pilot of the symbolic
vessel is able to bring it to its predestined goal. The pilot or captain
is evidently the leader of the congregation, though behind him
looms the figure of Christ. This conclusion is in agreement with the
literary and artistic traditions of the early church. Thus, in spite
of its small size, vs. 5a, the tongue is a powerful member of the
body which can boast of great deeds.

With regard to its ability to bring about disastrous effects the
tongue may also be compared with a fire, vs. 5b, which though
small to begin with can burn up an abundance of material.[20] In
the view of the author the material set on fire by the tongue is
nothing less than the whole world. According to vs. 6 the tongue
is set among the organs of the body as typifying the world of unrighteousness[21]; its devilish power contaminates the whole body.
It is further described as setting fire to "the wheel of being," which
signifies existence. The strange expression calls to mind the cyclic
theories of human existence commonly associated with Indian and
other Oriental philosophies. But the author was probably more dependent on Stoic ideas concerning different aeons of the world and
the destruction of the universe in fire, a theme also found in the
other General epistles (cf. especially II Pet iii 7, 10). Thus the
tongue is regarded as the instrument by which the great world fire
is kindled and spread. It has begun to burn the world prematurely,
and hastens the day of the final conflagration. And it is the Christians primarily who suffer from the fire kindled by the evil tongue,
being persecuted by the destroying powers, represented in particular
by the worldly authorities (cf. I Pet iv 12; Jude 23). The destructive
flames that reach out toward the unwary believers and have already
singed them, have their source in the underworld, for the fire of
the evil tongue (cf. Prov xvi 27) is in turn kindled by the flames of
hell.

The dangerous power of the evil tongue is also the subject of
the following verses. Man is able to tame all the animals of the

world and has already accomplished this in part, vs. 7. According
to Gen i 28, ii 19, ix 2, man is also commissioned to rule over
all the animals. But he is not master of everything in the world,
vs. 8: no man can prevail over the tongue. How does this pessimistic
conclusion fit the author's purpose of persuading his readers to
control their tongues? The answer must be that man alone and
unaided cannot control his tongue, but that with Christ's help it is
possible. As in the preceding illustration of the ship, in which Christ
must be thought of as the ultimate guide in spite of the fact that
he is not directly mentioned, so here the author does not name
him, but leaves it to the readers to draw the necessary inference
concerning their Lord and Savior. Therefore, it is the tongue of the
natural, unredeemed man which cannot be tamed. It is said to be
"an uncontrollable evil, [and] full of lethal poison," like a snake
that is too elusive to catch, but whose fangs are deadly.

Unhappily the tongue of many pretended Christians, vs. 9, has
assumed a double function. With the same tongue believers bless
God and curse men, who are created in the image of God. The
recipients of the epistle seem to find this natural. In their eagerness to appear as prophets of doom they believe that it is part of
the Christian message to pronounce curses upon degraded mankind.
In vs. 10 the author condemns this practice and asserts that blessings and curses ought not to issue from the same mouth. For, according to vs. 11 this means that two incompatible elements have
been combined, inasmuch as blessings belong to the world of God
and curses to the sphere of evil. It is against nature for both sweet
and bitter to proceed from the same source. In the case of the
Christian preacher and what issues from his mouth, it is also
against God. Sweet and bitter waters never flow out of the same
fountain, since they cannot rise from the same spring. In this illustration the bitter water, as in Exod xv 23 which is quoted in Heb
iii 8, etc., represents dissatisfied and angry reactions; in vs. 14 James
returns to the subject which has an important role in the context.
Preaching is also compared with water in John vii 37 f. The anomaly
of having these contradictory elements of speech united on the
tongues of the recipients is further illustrated in vs. 12 by a description of trees and their fruits, reminiscent of Matt vii 16 ff. (with
parallels). Figs are sweet, and a fig tree cannot yield bitter olives,
no more than sweet figs can grow on a vine with its sour fruit. In

the same way salt water cannot produce sweet. There is an absolute difference in kind between the true Christian message and the expressions of the poisonous tongue. Bitter dissatisfaction has nothing to do with the gospel, and it is impossible to oscillate between the one and the other.

## 7. TRUE WISDOM INVOLVES
## HUMBLE LIVING
### (iii 13–18)

III  13 Whoever is wise and perceptive among you, let him show through his excellent conduct his achievements in wise humility. 14 But if you cherish bitter jealousy and ambition in your hearts, do not boast and lie against the truth. 15 This "wisdom" does not come down from above, but it is earthly, sensual, demonic. 16 For where jealousy and ambition are found, there will be instability and every foul deed. 17 But the wisdom from above is first of all pure, then peaceful, reasonable, tractable, full of mercy and good fruits, impartial and not hypocritical. 18 And the fruit of righteousness, which is peace, is sown by the peaceful.

### COMMENT

Among the readers there were many who were proud of their wisdom and intelligence. In i 5 the author had hinted that this wisdom had been gained from the wrong sources and not from God. Now the writer, vs. 13, gives his readers to understand that such pretended wisdom is not in accordance with the principles of Christian faith. The one who[22] is really wise and intelligent must manifest his achievements or show what he is able to do[23] through good Christian behavior. And this must be done in humility of wisdom, that is, in wise humility, or possibly in humility as concerns wisdom.[24] The recipients of the epistle do not behave so. According to vs. 14 they strive after wisdom as a means of success in society only, displaying bitter aggressiveness[25] and ambition.[26] It is possible that in doing so they seek support from the Stoics, the Cynics, or some other school of philosophy which at this juncture was similarly critical of society and the authorities. An illustration of the bold attitude of critical philosophers toward the authorities is offered by Philostratus in his story of Apollonius of Tyana and the emperor Domitian.[27] In antiquity the philosophers gave special instruction in "dialectics," or the art of argumentation. The intellectual self-confidence which the readers apparently possess through their philosophical training is categorically rejected by the author. Boasting of such dialectic wisdom and shrewdness is contradictory to the truth, inasmuch as the pretended wisdom is not real.

This wisdom which results in aggressiveness and insolence is not heavenly, vs. 15, as is truly Christian wisdom, but earthly; it is not spiritual but carnal or sensual; and it is not divine but demonic. It is understood in vs. 16 that this false wisdom is used to oppose the existing order of society. Anarchy[28] and every foul matter[29] will be the result of the attitude of the readers.

In contradistinction to this, heavenly wisdom is pure, vs. 17, and furthermore peaceful, reasonable, etc. Characteristic of it is a positive, generous attitude toward the authorities and fellow men, without any partiality (cf. ii 1) or hypocrisy.[30] It must be noted that neither the epistle of James nor other New Testament writings recommend this patient and peaceful wisdom because of a conservative respect for the government or the state. In the eyes of the author these possess no value in themselves. The exhortation in behalf of a constructive approach is prompted by the concern that the mind of the believers may be preserved from envy, bitterness, and filth. It is further emphasized that the fruit of righteousness is sown only by those who work for peace, vs. 18, that is, only these lay the foundation of the eternal reward of righteousness. The fruit or reward in question is said to consist of "peace,"[31] or heavenly blessedness. Here the author is in agreement with Isa xxxii 17: "And the fruit of righteousness will be peace, and the effect of righteousness quietness and trust forever."

The contrast presented in this passage between earthly and heavenly wisdom is analogous to the difference between knowledge and love presented by Paul in I Cor xiii 4–7. Love is described there in phrases similar to the characteristics of heavenly wisdom enumerated in the present verse: "Love is long-suffering, kind; love is not aggressive; love is not boastful, not puffed up, not insolent; it does not seek its own advantage," etc.

## 8. THE COMBATIVENESS OF THE RECIPIENTS
### (iv 1–12)

**IV** 1 Whence do fights and quarrels arise among you? Is it not from this: from your lusts which are in conflict in your bodies. 2 You desire but do not acquire [anything]. You kill and are fanatics but are not able to obtain [anything]. You fight and strive; you do not gain [anything], because you do not pray. 3 You pray but receive nothing, because you pray wrongly, in order to dissipate it in your lusts.

4 You adulterers, don't you know that friendship with the world is enmity to God? Whoever wishes to be a friend of the world turns out to be an enemy of God. 5 Or do you think the epigram speaks in vain: "Even with jealousy does he claim the spirit which he settled in us"? 6 So much greater is the grace which he gives. Therefore it says[a]: "God resists the arrogant, but he gives grace to the humble." 7 Then submit yourselves to God. Resist the devil, and he will flee from you. 8 Draw near to God, and he will draw near to you. Cleanse your hands, you sinners, and purify your hearts, you double-minded. 9 Be miserable and mourn and wail. Let your laughter be turned into mourning and your joy into gloom. 10 Humble yourselves before the Lord, then he will exalt you.

11 Do not defame one another, brothers. Whoever defames or judges his brother, defames and judges the law. And if you judge the law, then you are not a doer of the law but its judge. 12 One is the Lawgiver and the Judge, who is able to save and destroy. But who are you to judge your neighbor?

[a] Prov iii 34, according to LXX.

Comment

The present passage is a typical "parenesis," or series of admonitions. Such passages occur throughout the epistle, but this one is more characteristically hortatory than the others.

It is evident that the minds of the readers harbored rancor and malice, along with tendencies toward violence, which erupted in open bickering and fights, vs. 1. We have no right to explain away or tone down the author's statements about these troubles, as though he exaggerated or did not mean to be taken seriously (as some expositors do out of respect for the early church, or for other reasons). Historical honesty demands that we acknowledge the situation as it was, rather than re-create it as we or others should like it to have been. On account of the cravings and desires of the readers, they become involved in quarrels and struggles. According to the following verses this is because they strive to acquire what they claim as their due by violence and intrigue.

In spite of all their efforts they do not succeed in obtaining their fill, as vs. 2a points out. They are even accused of murder, vs. 2b. This charge must be taken seriously, but it is difficult to interpret it as simple killing, just as the verb "kill" in v 6 can scarcely denote individual homicide. Probably the accusation may rather have a figurative meaning in as much as the more belligerent of the readers are thought of as driving Christians to martyrdom and death through their aggressive or provocative behavior. To the words "You kill" the author adds "and you are fanatics."[32] Undoubtedly there is a direct connection between these statements. The sentence may be interpreted as follows: "You drive people to death by being zealots." Thus the thought is parallel to a contemporary passage of great importance, I Clem. 4:7–6:3, in which "zeal"[33] is said to cause the death of innocent, pious men. So the expression "you are fanatics" probably has reference to a provocative and violent self-assertion, similar to that of the Jewish zealots. That such a provocation is meant is indicated in the same verse of James, where the readers are accused once again of struggling and fighting. No military enterprise is meant, but the strong words suggest that the readers are engaged in certain hostile activities, such as riots, sabotage, and the like. Through their fanatic and violent self-assertion the readers may be thought of as driving their Christian brothers to death, since the authorities react to this behavior by suppression and persecutions. Thus we may understand the drastic charge of murder against the readers in a historically acceptable fashion. James the Righteous may have uttered similar words against Palestinian zealots in the sixties. But here the discussion concerns Christian congregations in the dispersion which are not striving for national independence, but for material advantage.

Why don't the readers, in spite of their vigorous efforts, succeed in obtaining anything? According to vs. 2c it is because they do not pray. The necessity of petitioning God for what we need and desire was underscored in the comment on wisdom in i 5f. Here in iv 2c it is more a question of material things. It may be that prayers are offered, the author concedes in vs. 3, but the recipients of the epistle pray quite poorly, for they desire possessions only to be able to squander them in sumptuous living. Their desire for the good things of this world leads the author in vs. 4 to call them "adulterers," an expression that often denotes idolatry. Love of the world not only means unchastity, but enmity toward God (compare the words on God and Mammon in Matt vi 24). A proverb of unknown origin referred to in vs. 5 is further designed to illustrate this; in the Greek it seems to form a hexameter which, like i 17, is not entirely regular.[34] The meaning is that God, as the creator of man's spirit, demands the exclusive right to control it. He does so "even with jealousy," that is, with no less than absolute possessiveness or passionate intolerance.[35] Just for this reason, vs. 6 adds, he is more merciful toward those who submit to him and who do not show arrogance, but are humble. The exhortations in vss. 7–8a to submit to God, to resist the devil, and draw close to God logically follow these observations. James here gives expression to his solemn concern for the eternal salvation of the recipients which is risked by their attempts to assert themselves in the world. The same is true of the admonitions to the readers in vs. 8b to cleanse their hands, to keep their hearts pure, not to be double-minded, dividing their interests between God and the world (compare again Matt vi 24). According to vs. 9 they should lament over their sin. Yet they are not aware that anything is out of order, but glory and rejoice in their extravagance. This, in accordance with ancient custom, was probably expressed in excessive eating and drinking (cf. II Pet ii 13; Jude 12). With prophetic emphasis the author admonishes them rather to mourn and grieve over their unworthiness. They ought to humble themselves before the Lord, and then he will exalt them, vs. 10. It is a fatal self-deception to suppose that they can elevate themselves.

In vss. 11–12 some comments are appended about the readers' reprehensible practice of speaking evil of one another. To malign and judge one's brother is tantamount to maligning and rejecting the law. As above in i 25, ii 8–12, "the law" here denotes the word, or the gospel. Since the gospel is directed to all people and invites all into the fellowship of the church without distinction, whether the person is Jewish or Greek, clean or unclean, rich or poor, wise or ignorant, rejection and condemnation of a brother is a contradiction of the gospel. Whoever engages in this practice becomes a self-confident judge of the law rather than its humble doer (cf. i 22–24). This is an insult to God, who is the only one who has the right to make law and to judge.

## 9. BUSINESS ETHICS
### (iv 13–17)

**IV** 13 Come now, you who say: "Today or tomorrow we will go to such and such a town and spend a year there to trade and make a profit," 14 you who do not know what your life will be like tomorrow. For you are a vapor which appears for a little while and then disappears. 15 Instead you ought to say: "If the Lord wills and we live, we shall do this or that." 16 But now you boast about your presumptuous plans. All such boasting is evil. 17 To anyone who knows how to act rightly but does not, it is sin.

### COMMENT

Throughout the epistle, James condemns those who hanker after riches and worldly advantages, i 10 f., ii 1–7, v 1–6. In the present passage he turns against the commercial schemer, vs. 13. The style and character of this material conform closely to a pattern familiar in the Bible, and it is difficult to escape the impression that this utterance was inspired by if not modeled on the prophetic pronouncement of doom (cf. for example Isa v 8: "Woe unto you who add house to house"; I Enoch 94:6–95:7; Luke vi 24: "Woe unto you, you rich men"; Rev xviii 11–xix 23). What the author objects to specifically is the blithe self-confidence with which businessmen make their complex plans and count anticipated profits, as though times and places and events were subject to their calculations. In fact, God controls their enterprises and will frustrate schemes contrary to his will. According to vs. 14, no one knows with certainty what tomorrow will bring (as stated in Prov xxvii

1), and the rich man is after all only a vapor that fades away in this world (cf. the picture of the flower in i 10 f.). The only right thing is humbly to place one's life in the hand of God, vs. 15. Above all, these capitalists should not boast so conceitedly of their plans and achievements, vs. 16. All such boasting is out of place. In conclusion vs. 17 states: To anyone who knows how to act rightly,[36] but neglects to do so, it is sin. Failure to act correctly before God is counted as a serious transgression for anyone who knows better. This was also emphasized in Jewish ethics. Probably the author is thinking of certain successful businessmen who have come in contact with either Jewish or Christian biblical instruction. Such people are without excuse when with lofty self-assurance they leave God out of their plans for commercial expansion and success. This verse apparently contains a traditional maxim regarding sins of omission, which the author quotes to give emphasis to his admonitions. It must be admitted that logically it does not fit well into the context.

The attack on those engaged in worldly enterprises is continued in the following passage.

## 10. JUDGMENT ON THE UNRIGHTEOUS RICH
## (v 1–6)

**V** 1 Come now, you plutocrats. Lament and wail over the calamities, which are coming upon you. 2 Your wealth has rotted, and your garments have become moth-eaten. 3 Your gold and silver have corroded, and their corrosion will be a witness against you and devour your flesh. As a fire you have gathered it for the last days. 4 Behold, the wages withheld by you from the laborers who mowed your fields cry out; and the cries of the harvesters have come to the ears of the Lord of Hosts. 5 You have lived lavishly and sumptuously upon the earth. You have fattened your hearts for the day of slaughter. 6 You have condemned, you have killed the righteous one. He does not resist you.

### COMMENT

This passage is a continuation of iv 13–17, and like it conforms to the pattern of the prophetic oracle of doom; it may well reflect a traditional type of apostolic preaching (cf. the comments given above as introduction to iv 13). In the present case there is a close resemblance to the second chapter of the Wisdom of Solomon, in which in similar language the ungodly are said to oppress the righteous person. The style is also characteristically Jewish-Hellenistic.

While previously the self-confident schemers of business enterprises were censured, criticism is now leveled against the rich in general. These are said in vs. 1 to have reason for lamentation rather than for self-satisfaction, for many causes of sorrow await them. And in vss. 2–3 some of the coming misfortunes are enumerated. In mentioning these the author puts the verb in the perfect tense, as if the anticipated misfortunes had already occurred. He thus uses a mode of expression peculiar to prophetic pronouncements, but which is psychologically easy to understand. In the eyes of the author peering into the future, the garments of the rich, their gold and silver have already been destroyed, and their own bodies have been consumed. He thinks it is as if in their covetousness they had merely gathered fire[37] for the last days.[38] That is, they have stored up the fire of the underworld (cf. iii 6) to be annihilated by it when the end comes.

As employers, especially in their position as feudal lords, the rich cheat their laborers of their wages, vs. 4. It is pointed out that the wages "cry" (as Abel's blood cried, Gen iv 10), and that the cries of the laborers come to God's ears (cf. I Enoch 47:1; Herm. *Vis.* 3:9:6). The oppressed laborers must seek redress from God, and he will champion their cause against the employers who stand as condemned sinners before him (as Deut xxiv 15 had emphasized). God is here called "the Lord Sabaoth," a characteristic Old Testament and particularly a prophetic term which means "the Lord of Hosts," that is, of the heavenly forces. According to vs. 5 the luxury and gluttony of the rich have only contributed to making their hearts heavy for the day of slaughter (Jer xii 3).[39] The illustration of the heart that is growing fat through sumptuous living is not based on anatomical observations, but on the usual conception of the heart as the seat of the will, and in this case of the lusts or desires. By having made their hearts fat in this way, the worldly rich will become a magnificent prey for the destroying powers on that day of slaughter. Nonetheless, as vs. 6 indicates, their misuse of the poor goes far beyond withholding wages. They have also brought the innocent or "righteous" one, as the author describes him, into court for trial, so that he has been condemned (cf. ii 6). In this way they have even driven him to death by judicial murder, as the text literally reads; this statement may in turn be compared with iv 2. Yet the righteous one does not oppose them. The last remark appears to be a direct polemic against the words that the ungodly rich speak about the righteous one according to Wisdom of Solomon 2:12: "He is troublesome to us and opposes our undertakings."

The two related passages iv 13–17 and v 1–6 both contain

attacks on businessmen and rich people. Here the author displays a general aversion toward such persons and takes the side of the poor completely, as has been evident throughout the epistle. These threats against the rich are turned directly against a whole group of society, for the author speaks in the second person plural. After all there may have been little possibility of reaching the ears of the rich and powerful in society with these fulminations. But the actual listeners were the Christians who, by recognizing the objectionable nature of financial scheming, were to learn to avoid imitating the money-hunters of this world, and to be patient and hopeful in spite of the self-indulgence of the mighty.

## 11. PATIENT WAITING FOR THE LORD'S RETURN
### (v 7–11)

V ⁷ Therefore be patient, brothers, until the coming of the
Lord. You know the farmer waits for the precious fruit of the
earth and is patient for it until it has received the early and late
rains. ⁸ You be patient also. Strengthen your hearts, for the
coming of the Lord is near. ⁹ Do not grumble at each other,
brothers, so that you may not be judged. You see, the Judge is
standing at the door.

¹⁰ Take the prophets as an example of long-suffering and
patience, who spoke in the name of the Lord: ¹¹ "Indeed, we
regard as blessed those who endure." You have heard of Job's
perseverance and the Lord's final dealing [with him], because the
Lord is compassionate and merciful.


#### COMMENT

In spite of all vexations and disappointments in the world, the
Christians ought to wait patiently for the coming of the Lord, vs.
7a. During the early days of Christianity it was easy to become
impatient over the delay of Christ's return. There were conflicts
and disorders in certain places, as some fanatics tried to anticipate
the heavenly blessedness by earthly means. The problem is referred to in a number of New Testament books beginning with
Paul's letters to the Thessalonians and extending to the General
epistles. In James, the author finds it necessary to intervene in
similar instances of disorderly conduct, rooted in the widespread
dissatisfaction with the oppressed status of the Christians in the

world (i 2–8, 12–16, 20 f., etc.), and to warn against excessive zeal for reform or revolution. Because of the circumstances these admonitions to patience constitute a basic theme in the epistle.

Making apt use of an illustration from agriculture, vs. 7b, the author further encourages his readers to persevere in patient waiting for the day of victory. As a farmer waits patiently for his crops to be nurtured by the beneficial early and late rains—these terms were well known from Deut xi 14, an expression of trust in the faithfulness of God—so the leaders of the congregations ought to wait patiently for the fruit of the implanted word (i 21) eventually to mature at the coming of the Lord. Possibly the author has in mind here a first and a second coming of the Lord, as in Rev xx 4, 11, but the figure of the two rains does not absolutely require this interpretation. The whole illustration is parallel to the Lord's parable of the growing seed (Mark iv 26–29); one may also compare the parables of the mustard seed and the leaven (Matt xiii 31–33). It should be recognized that the kingdom of God or the church will finally triumph under God's supervision without the intervention of men. It is important therefore to remain constantly patient and to strengthen the heart, vs. 8, that is, to have courage, for the coming of the Lord is not far off. There is also an added measure of responsibility in attitude and behavior, vs. 9: The members of the church must not complain about each other or judge one another, for the Judge is already standing at the door.

In the discussion of forbearance and patience the Old Testament prophets may serve as models, vs. 10. What they said was in the name of the Lord, that is, on behalf of the Lord Jesus (as I Pet i 11 also emphasized). When the author continues in vs. 11a, "Indeed, we regard as blessed those who endure," he apparently cites an example of this prophetic message. The "we" probably refers to the prophets, as the author usually does not speak of himself in this way. Furthermore, the sentence is perfectly suitable as a summary of what the prophets might have announced for the comfort of the Christians. The citation does not correspond exactly to any known prophetic utterance, but it is reminiscent of Dan xii 12: "Blessed is the one who endures." Here the wording has been changed slightly, which may be due to a faulty memory or the use of an otherwise unknown version of the passage. The author may include Job among the prophets, as vs. 11b refers to him. In any case, the experience of Job should be a source of comfort to Christians, in view of his patience under suffering and his final restoration by the Lord,[40] who is always merciful.

## 12. MANUAL OF DISCIPLINE
### (v 12–20)

*No swearing, but praying, singing,* v 12–13

V 12 Above all, my brothers, do not swear, either by heaven or the earth, or any other oath. But let your yes be yes and your no be no, so that you may not come under judgment.

13 If anyone of you suffers, let him pray. If anyone is happy, let him sing hymns.

COMMENT

In vs. 12, the readers are warned to avoid every form of swearing. This is essentially in agreement with the words of Jesus in the Sermon on the Mount (Matt v 33–37). James, however, expresses himself more briefly and mentions only heaven and earth as common objects invoked in oaths, not such details as Jerusalem or the head of the oath taker. The author is probably not dependent upon the gospel of Matthew for this teaching, but preserves another tradition of the early church. What is the intention in this admonition? It is undoubtedly to emphasize the preceding instruction to be patient. The connection with the previous statements is clear from the introductory words, "above all." Among the recipients of the letter, swearing appears to have been a means of expressing impatience with their lot and bitterness at the oppressive social order. They should not rebel but remain loyal and trustworthy, letting their "yes" and "no" be definite (in Matt v 37, the emphasis is rather on not being verbose). If they hedge, they will be punished. According to vs. 13, the proper comfort and help in suffering is not resentment but prayer to God. If, on the other hand, a joyous and hope-filled mood prevails, it ought to be manifested in spiritual songs and hymns. The analogy with Eph v 18 f. suggests that the author has in mind the joyous atmosphere which commonly obtained when the church members came together to eat. Instead of the arrogant and salacious songs that were characteristic of banquets and similar celebrations, the Christians ought to use pious words and chaste tunes. Here it is worth noting that Christian singing is supposed to be the medium of light and joyful as well as more serious sentiments.

## The healing of the sick, v 14–18

14 If any one of you is sick, then let him call the elders of the congregation, so that they may pray for him and anoint him with oil in the name of the Lord. 15 Then the prayer of faith will save the sick person, and the Lord will make him rise. And if he has committed sins, he will be forgiven. 16 Therefore confess your sins one to another and pray for each other, so that you may be healed.

The vigorous prayer of a righteous man is very effective. 17 Elijah was a man with experiences similar to ours. He prayed fervently that it might not rain, and it did not rain upon the earth for three years and six months. 18 He prayed again, and the heaven gave rain and the earth produced its fruit.

### COMMENT

In case of sickness the elders of the congregation ought to be called, vs. 14a. By "elders" or "presbyters" are meant the leaders of the community, not just the older members of the church who might be accorded special recognition on that account. Compare I Pet v 1 f., where the elders are treated as shepherds responsible for their congregations. "Bishops" are not mentioned in James, though such ministers were known to Paul. Here apparently the concerns of the congregations are cared for by elders alone.

The institution of "elders" was taken over from the Old Testament, in which the elders appear as representatives of the important families responsible for the government of cities and villages. As to the immediate Jewish background of the New Testament it is to be observed that such laymen of rank were members of the Jerusalem senate, i.e., the Sanhedrin, and that committees of elders governed the synagogues. In the Christian congregation of Jerusalem the apostles were the first to exercise authority, but their ministry was unique and does not correspond to the normal activities of elders. When the Twelve, about A.D. 35, suggested the election of the Seven who should be responsible for the maintenance of the growing Hellenist groups of the congregation (Acts vi 1–6), this move may be regarded as introducing a committee of elders into the structure of the church. The basis of this development may well have been the system of elders in the Hellenistic synagogues. Now the committee of Seven had only a provisional existence. But in the forties and the fifties we find that elders have a permanent place in the Jerusalem congregation alongside the apostles (Acts xi 30, xv 2, etc., xvi 4, xxi 18), and this precisely in the church where James the Righteous played a leading role. It is possible that they were elected and ordained like the Seven, but as there is no direct evidence of this, it is perhaps safer to assume that they were the men of rank in the community corresponding to the Jewish elders in the synagogues. On the other hand we are expressly told that Barnabas and Paul selected and ordained elders in the congregations of Asia Minor (Acts xiv 23). It is within this area that elders appear in later contexts as those responsible for community administration (Acts xx 4, 28; I Pet v 1–5), ordination (I Tim iv 14), preaching and teaching (I Tim v 17–19). The writers of some epistles addressed to Asia Minor even call themselves "elders" (I Pet v 1; II John 1; III John 1), which proves that it was a title of honor in that district. Generally the elders seem to have been laymen in the sense that they were engaged in ordinary professions and occupations. It was some time before the individual congregations were able to employ full-time ministers. Yet the elders mentioned in Acts and the later epistles are not exclusively laymen. They are supposed to be appointed and ordained by apostles or disciples of apostles (Acts xiv 23; Titus i 5). Their functions partly correspond to those of modern congregational ministers. In the present passage in James, the elders are described as having extraordinary spiritual gifts, which enable them to heal the sick. Thus it would not be correct to regard these elders as simply laymen, even if no sharp distinction is to be made between laymen and ministers. Though every believer may in principle have a share in the same gifts and functions, Paul nevertheless pointed out that in the church there are varieties of talents and services (I Cor xii 4 f.).

James emphasized the importance of the elders in connection with illness. Since sickness was attributed to sin, as in the Old Testament and contemporary Judaism, it posed a serious problem to the early church. At the sickbed, vs. 14b, it is the task of the elders to pray for the sick person and to anoint him with oil in the name of the Lord, i.e., on behalf of the Lord Jesus Christ. Here the oil is apparently regarded as a kind of life elixir, in accordance with the Jewish idea that the precious fruit of the olive tree possessed life and spirit. This concept is found for example in the Apocalypse of Moses 9, and the Book of Adam and Eve 36 in which the paradisaic tree of life is described as flowing with healing oil (cf. the Gospel of Nicodemus 19). It was a Jewish custom to anoint with oil not only at a king's coronation (I Sam x 1, etc.), but also in the treatment of wounds (Isa i 6; Luke x 34), at the healing of the sick (Talm. Jer. Ber. 1, 3a, 9, etc.; Mark vi 13), and in the preparation of the dying and the dead for a new life (Mishn. Shabb. 23:5, etc.; Matt xxvi 6–13; Mark xvi 1). James's instruction to anoint the sick with oil is rooted in traditional Jewish conceptions and has a point of contact with a suggestion by Jesus himself (Mark vi 13). The practice sanctioned here later developed into the custom of anointing the dying to prepare them for eternal life. In spite of popular beliefs and superstitions concerning the oil, there is no hint of magic in this passage. For the anointing is performed on behalf of the Lord. The healings of Jesus are thought to be perpetuated and effected through the officials of the church, as a result of intercessory prayer confirmed by the use of the holy oil. In vs. 15a it is stated that it is not because of the oil but because of the prayer to the Lord that the sick one is expected to recover from his illness. Though questions relating to the practical possibility of these miracles cannot be answered, there is little reason to doubt that the elders of the early church, as the apostles before them, really performed such healings. In any case the author lived in a community where such miracles of faith occurred and could be expected to occur.

According to the biblical view, sickness was regarded as a consequence of sin (I Kings xv 4 f.; Matt ix 2 with parallels; I Cor xi 30). In order to terminate a sickness it was necessary to confess one's sins and to receive forgiveness for them, a procedure likewise prescribed here by James. More specifically the elders are instructed in vs. 15b to forgive on behalf of the Lord the sins of the sick who repent. Then in vs. 16a the author stresses the duty of all to confess their sins to one another and to pray for one another so that illness may be overcome. This statement generalizes the theme of mutual confession as an obligation of the congregation as a whole, without differentiating between elders and laymen. It does not conflict with or supersede the specific instance mentioned above, of confession before the elders.

The effect of intercessory prayer is great, vs. 16b, if the praying person is a righteous man and the prayer is offered with power. In this context, the word "righteous" has a rather specialized meaning related to the biblical concept of the holy. In the example that follows, it is not a matter of intercessory prayer by any honorable or faultless man, but specifically by the righteous one, who because of his righteousness is able to intercede effectively.

For in vs. 17a no less a person than Elijah is referred to as an example of a "righteous" man and of the efficacy of prayer. It is made clear that Elijah was no superhuman being but a man. Nevertheless Elijah cannot be called "righteous" in any commonplace sense, but should rather be described as a "martyr (witness)," a "holy one," or something comparable. This is evident from the expression "with experiences similar to ours." On account of the Greek word used,[41] the "experiences" should be understood primarily as comprising occasions of suffering. The supernatural power of Elijah's prayer derives from his righteousness or holiness, as a man intimately associated with God. As evidence of Elijah's effectiveness in prayer the author, in vs. 17b, cites the story of the drought mentioned in I Kings xvii–xviii, when at Elijah's word the rain ceased for three and a half years. And at the end of this period, vs. 18, he prevailed upon the heavens to open and the earth to produce fruit.

Some of the details given here differ from the account in I Kings: it does not mention Elijah's first prayer in connection with the drought (see I Kings xvii 1). With regard to the duration of the latter, I Kings states only "in the third year" (xviii 1), whereas James specifies three and a half years. This number, while only a slight change, may have a special import since it is exactly half of a seven-year period, or week of years, a concept characteristic of Jewish eschatology (Dan ix 27; Rev xi 2 f.). Elijah's second prayer is the one uttered on Mount Carmel (I Kings xviii 36 f.; in xviii 42 it may be noted that the prophet humbly waited for the fulfilment of his prayer); the reader is expected to reconstruct the order of events for himself.

By linking these passages from I Kings xvii and xviii the author focuses attention on Elijah's power over the rain, secured through his prayers. Jewish traditions of a similar kind can also be cited (Sir. 48:3 and IV Ezra 7:109). It may be objected that the miracle of the rain is hardly relevant to the argument for prayer at a time of sickness, which is the subject under consideration here. But James does not understand Elijah's effective intercession simply as a model prayer for rain. Rather his main interest is to show that a righteous man praying effectively can delay or hasten the saving grace of God which is symbolized by rain, as also in vs. 7. Thus the three and a half years may be interpreted as a period of waiting for the final manifestation of God's grace. This idea is also found in Revelation, which mentions how two prophetic witnesses (one of whom may be Elijah) withheld the rain (Rev xi 6) during a corresponding period (xi 3). Because of its connection with the eschatological timetable, the Elijah story could be used to comfort the faithful of the church who were living in the last days. Thus by taking into account the various thought patterns that may be associated with the story of Elijah's prayer, we can more easily understand why the author used this episode to illuminate the present passage. If that man of God could hold back and call forth heavenly grace through prayer, then a righteous and holy man of the church can also by his prayer call down God's healing power on a sick person. In this connection the sick person may be compared to the dry earth that needs rain from heaven in order to recover and yield fruit.

## The salvation of apostates, v 19–20

19 My brothers, if any one of you goes astray from the truth and someone else converts him, 20 consider that the one who turns a sinner from the error of his way will save his soul from death and cover a multitude of sins.

### COMMENT

James emphatically condemns all laxness in the faith and practice of believers, all unchristian traits and attitudes in the life of the church. His ultimate intention, however, is not to reject and condemn, but to reprove and set right. This purpose appears very plainly in the last verses of the epistle.

As the author, throughout his message, wishes to save his readers from deception and destruction, so in vs. 19 he affirms that it is the duty of every Christian to lead an erring brother back to the right path. Like i 18 and iii 14 this verse uses the expression "truth" as a designation of the gospel, which is also the case in the writings of John and Paul (John i 17, v 23, viii 32; Rom i 18, 25, etc.). Thus, according to vs. 20, if a Christian succeeds in converting an individual who, like the people generally criticized in this epistle, has forsaken the truth and begun to walk in paths of error, then the soul of the latter is saved even from death. In the same way it is emphasized in Jude 22 f. that erring brothers ought to be snatched out of the burning fire, i.e., the fire of the realm of death.

According to several Jewish and early Christian texts it was a great merit to save a soul from destruction (e.g., Pirqe Aboth 5:18; II Clem. 15:1).

It might appear that the expression "covers a multitude of sins" refers to the sins of the individual who rescues an erring brother. But this is not likely in view of the emphasis placed on the multitude of sins in the community. Close study of the context suggests a more appropriate interpretation: The reference is to the erring persons and their community, so that the salvation of those who err prevents the perpetration of numerous sins in society. This is also the meaning of Prov x 12, which is the source of James's statement, for there love, in opposition to hatred, is said to prevent others from committing sins. The same interpretation is applicable to I Pet iv 8, which is likewise based on Prov x 12.

Clearly it is James's deepest wish that as many as possible may be saved from destruction. In spite of the severe pronouncements of judgment in the earlier parts of the epistle, the writer recommends mercy (ii 13) and desires his readers to follow the example of Jesus in seeking out and saving the lost (compare for instance the three parables in Luke xv 1–32). This is also the ultimate concern of Jude (see vss. 22–23 of his epistle), who is otherwise extremely rigorous with regard to the errant.

# Textual Notes

1. Greek, *dokímion*.
2. Greek, *haplôs*, an adverb meaning, "outright." The corresponding adjective is *haploûs*, "simple," "undivided," exactly opposite to the attitude for which the querulous man is rebuked in i 8: *dípsychos*, "double-minded."
3. The verb *peirázō* here means both "to test" and "to tempt."
4. Greek, *apeírastos kakôn*, "one who is not tempted by evil." The expression seems to have this passive meaning because of its contrast with what follows.
5. Mention may be made of the collection of hexameters called Pseudo-Phocylides, which belongs to the body of Jewish-Hellenistic gnomic poetry. The verse is not flawless as to form since an ictus must fall on the last syllable of *dósis* which is short. In spite of this irregularity it may be regarded as a hexameter.
6. Greek, *tropḗ*. In several places referred to by lexicographers, this expression is used with reference to the winter solstice and the declination of heavenly bodies.
7. Together with the following verb, the participle *boulētheís* is probably determined by *hēmâs* as its direct object. Then it may conveniently be rendered on the analogy of passages in which *boúlomai* or *thélō* with objects has the meaning "to have good will toward," as in Arist. *Pol.* 5:9; II Sam xx 11; Ps xl 12; Matt xxvii 43; Ign. *Magn.* 3:2; Ign. *Rom.* 8:3. If the participle is understood in an absolute sense and is translated, "after his own will" etc., then the interpreter ascribes to the passage a thought which is quite unsuitable in the context, and is simply a truism, inasmuch as it cannot be said that God brought the believers into newness of life except by his own will or decision.
8. Greek, *oîda*.
9. Greek, *íste*.
10. Greek, *dé*.
11. Greek, *hóste*, instead of *íste*.

12. Greek, *parakýptō*, "to bend forward over."

13. Greek, *tês dóxēs*. We understand this as a qualitative genitive, not referring to "our Lord," but to the preceding "faith." For the word "Lord" is already determined by "our."

14. Greek, *échō tinà en*, "to make someone or something the object of," as in Rom i 28.

15. Greek, *prosōpolēmpsíai* (pl.). Compare the LXX expression, *prósōpon lambánein*, "to pay attention to a person."

16. The words *dialogismôn ponērôn* appear to be a qualitative genitive.

17. Here, *graphē* means a passage of Scripture, as in ii 23.

18. Greek, *katakaucháō*, "to triumph over."

19. Greek, *graphē;* cf. note 17.

20. Greek, *hýlē*, which means "wood," and also "matter."

21. The expression *ho kósmos tês adikías* is probably predicative.

22. The pronoun *tís* here is equivalent to *hóstis*.

23. Greek, *tà érga autoû*.

24. The word *sophías* may be either a qualitative genitive or a genitive of limitation.

25. Greek, *zêlos*, "zeal," here in a critical sense.

26. Greek, *eritheía*, denoting too much ambition in political affairs, etc.

27. Philostr. *Vit. Apoll.* 7:4–42 *passim;* 8:3, 16, 26, etc. Besides the usual text editions, cf. Philostratus, "Life and Times of Apollonius of Tyana," rendered into English by C. P. Eells, *Stanford Univ. Publ. Univ. Ser. Lang. Lit.*, II (1923), pp. 1–263.

28. Greek, *akatastasía*.

29. Greek, *prâgma*, "affair."

30. The two final adjectives of vs. 17, which form a rhyming pair: *adiákritos* and *anypókritos*, are connected with *diakrínō*, "to separate," and *hypokrínomai*, "to be an actor."

31. Greek, *en eirēnē*, "consisting of peace," like *en dógmasin*, "consisting of ordinances," Eph ii 15. The translation "is sown in peace" does not provide a good concrete meaning for the expression, whereas the translation "is sown through peace" makes the phrase "by (or for) those who work for peace" a tautology.

32. Greek, *zēloûte*. Cf. notes 25, 33.

33. Greek, *zêlos*.

34. Like the quasi-hexameter of i 17 (cf. note 5), this rhythmic quotation is reminiscent of the hexameters of Pseudo-Phocylides. The form of the verse is not regular in so far as the first syllable of *epipotheî* receives an ictus although it is short.

35. Greek, *pròs phthónon,* literally: "as far as jealousy," that is, "even with jealousy," "with nothing less than jealous zeal."

36. Greek, *kalòn poieîn.* As in II Cor xiii 7, etc., the question here is of good behavior, not of good works.

37. The words *hōs pŷr* may possibly belong to the preceding phrase, but are more suitably connected with *ethēsaurísate,* which otherwise would stand alone. Some old manuscript traditions as well as ecclesiastical authorities like Oecumenius support this interpretation.

38. The adverbial expression *en eschátais hēmérais* seems to mean "for the last days," since a similar phrase in vs. 5 probably means "for the day of slaughter." An explanation of the latter is offered in note 39.

39. Greek, *en hēméra sphagês.* As this expression may be traced back to Jer xii 3, it is presumably to be understood as meaning "for the day of slaughter." Cf. note 38.

40. The word *kyríou* must be a subjective genitive, because in what follows the merciful activity of the Lord is mentioned.

41. The expression is *homoiopathês,* which includes the idea of *páthos,* "suffering."

# THE FIRST EPISTLE OF PETER

# Introduction

The epistle traditionally known as First Peter is a message to Christians in the northern, central, and western provinces of Asia Minor admonishing them to be meek, patient, and ready to endure suffering in times of tribulation.

The problem of the identity of the *author* is raised by the text itself. Whereas the greeting, i 1, is in the name of Peter, one of the concluding verses, v 12, indicates that another man had an important part in the epistle: "By Silvanus, the faithful brother . . . I have briefly written to you. . . ." Was this faithful Silvanus Peter's secretary, his collaborator, or, as many scholars believe, the author of the epistle?

It was not uncommon in antiquity for letters to be dictated. Scribes could write rapidly, and systems of shorthand were known. Paul normally used technical assistants to write out his epistles (I Cor xvi 21; II Thess iii 17), and once the scribe is mentioned by name (Rom xvi 22). Such a dictated message was generally in the author's own words. The fact that Peter did not write the epistle in question with his own hand does not of itself cast doubt on his authorship.

What, however, if v 12 implies that Silvanus was more than a technical stenographer? Paul sometimes wrote his epistles in collaboration with others. Among them was a man also called Silvanus (I Thess i 1; II Thess i 1). Can it be the same man in First Peter, and can he be regarded as co-author of this epistle?

Silas or Silvanus (in Aramaic probably *Še'ilā*, corresponding to the Hebrew name Saul) is fairly well known from Acts and the Pauline epistles. He was chosen by the Jerusalem congregation in A.D. 48 to inform the Antioch church of the settlement between the Jewish and the Gentile Christians (Acts xv 22). Later he was invited to accompany Paul to Asia Minor and Greece (xv 39, etc.).

He also served as co-author of Paul's epistles to the Thessalonians (see above). Obviously he knew Greek very well, and was in fact a Roman citizen (Acts xvi 37). There is actually reason to identify this well-known assistant of Paul with the Silvanus mentioned in First Peter. No other Silvanus is known in the early church. And when his important position in the Jerusalem congregation led by Peter is remembered (Acts xv 22), it is plausible to suppose that he later came into contact with Peter in Rome where the epistle was composed (see above).

The theological character and the language of First Peter confirm the assumption that Paul's fellow-traveler Silvanus gave its content and form a personal stamp.

a) As to its theological character First Peter reminds us to an astonishing degree of Paul. Not only is the line of thought characteristic of Gentile Christianity, but a considerable number of phrases correspond to similar expressions in the Pauline epistles; long lists of parallels to the whole Pauline corpus can be produced. That the epistle is intimately related to the Pauline theology and message is inescapable. It is difficult, however, to picture Peter as such a thoroughgoing adherent of Pauline thinking. That would mean a complete abandonment of the Jewish-Christian position which, according to Gal ii 11–14, he held during a visit to Antioch sometime in the fifties. A shift from a Jewish-Christian position to a marked Gentile-Christian way of thinking is certainly possible. But would Peter have adjusted himself to Paul's message and manner of writing so completely as to become an echo of his fellow apostle? This conclusion is not probable in view of what is otherwise known about the relationship of the two men (I Cor i 12, iii 22, xv 5; Gal i 18, ii 1–14). It is more reasonable to attribute the striking Pauline characteristics of First Peter to a disciple of Paul, who like Silvanus may later have joined Peter.

b) Turning to the language we find additional support for this hypothesis. First Peter is written in correct and rather elegant Greek without any striking Semitisms. Citations from the Old Testament are to a great extent in the Greek of the Septuagint. The unlettered Galilean fisherman Peter would hardly have been the master of this Greek style. It is simpler to assume that he had a collaborator steeped in Greek culture, like the Hellenistic Silas-Silvanus, to frame the phrasing of the letter.

Some scholars have gone to the other extreme and credited Silvanus with sole authorship of First Peter, holding that it was simply attributed to Peter for prestige. But as a matter of principle Peter should not be eliminated from the picture. Had there been no association with Peter, one would expect Silvanus to write either in his own name or in that of Paul, the apostle whose disciple he was. Provided that the epistle was composed before the death of Peter (as indicated by i 1), it is natural to believe that it was written with the knowledge and consent, or even at the direct request of the great apostle.

Regarding the *time* of composition different possibilities offer themselves.

The present writer joins those who prefer an early date, that is, before the death of Peter around A.D. 64. He holds this view for the following reason. If the epistle were not written before Peter's death, then it would have been unwise of Silvanus so directly, and without qualification, to admonish the recipients in the name of an apostle whose death must already have been a well-known fact. It is true that other epistles may have been published after the death of their alleged originators, as seems to be the case with James and Second Peter. But here the assumption of pseudonymity would imply that the reference to Silvanus was also fictive, and this is not likely.

The opposite view, that is, that the epistle was written after Peter's death, is commonly based upon the references to current persecutions in iv 12–19, v 6–9. It is stated that such persecutions did not occur in the sixties. Nero attacked the Christians in connection with the burning of Rome, but this was a local manifestation. In fact, no official persecution of the Christians in Asia Minor, where the recipients of this epistle reside, is attested in historical documents until about A.D. 95, toward the end of Domitian's reign. Some scholars therefore date First Peter in this period. Others place it as late as A.D. 112 because at that time Pliny the Younger, in his letters to the Emperor Trajan (Nos. 96 and 97), describes certain measures taken against the Christians in Bithynia which are reminiscent of the description in First Peter and which were carried out in one of the provinces mentioned by Peter.

Nevertheless, the historical circumstances do not require such a late dating of First Peter. It is true that no persecution of Christians

in Asia is mentioned in any secular documents from the time of
Nero. But this is not decisive. The epistle does not speak about
the extermination of the Christians by imperial decree, but only
about slanderous accusations made by heathen leaders, and some
routine police investigations by the authorities, ii 12, iii 16, iv 14 f.
Such commonplace matters may easily have occurred during Nero's
time without attracting the attention of historians.

To this should be added the very important fact that sacrifices
to the emperor are not mentioned in First Peter as a problem
confronting the Christians. If the epistle had been written during
Domitian's persecution, that well-known, grave issue could not
have been passed over (cf. Mart. *Epigr.* 13:4; Plin. Min. *Ep.* 10:
96:5). That this is not the case speaks for an early date of the
epistle. Furthermore, as the Pauline character and the use of
Peter's name are most naturally explained by dating First Peter
in the time of Nero, the conclusion is that the epistle was probably written shortly before Peter's death around A.D. 64.

The *recipients* of the epistle are mainly Gentile Christians inasmuch as they, before their baptism, fulfilled the will of the heathen,
iv 3. Probably some former Jews and proselytes were numbered
among them. They are scattered throughout five Roman provinces,
i 1, which are situated in the northern, central, and western parts
of Asia Minor and occupy the larger portion of the peninsula north
of the Taurus mountains. Apparently the church of Rome, in the
name of which the epistle was written, v 13 (cf. the comments on
that passage), already had a certain authority in addressing Christians in these provinces, whereas the rest of Asia Minor or the
southeastern part most likely was still under the influence of Antioch.
But the ecclesiastical leadership of these provinces evidently centered in Ephesus, which maintained several connections with Rome
(cf. Eph i 1; I Tim i 3; II Tim i 18, iv 12, passages which represent
Paul as writing from Rome to Ephesus). As Christianity first gained
a footing in the large cities and reached the rural regions only later,
it is probable that the recipients of the epistle lived in the most
important cities of the provinces mentioned. Although the popula-
tion of the whole territory, apart from certain portions along the
coast, was in itself non-Greek, the cities had been Hellenized to a
large extent. In these cities there was considerable tension between
the rich industrial and commercial magnates on the one hand, and

the laborers and slaves on the other. And in addition there was a long-standing opposition to Rome's political hegemony. That the author is especially anxious for his readers to manifest loyalty both to Rome and the local magistrates, ii 13–iii 6, is evidently due to the fact that the adherents of the gospel were largely made up of people belonging to the poorer classes, who were easily stirred by revolutionary aspirations. It is to be observed that no members of the upper classes, whether employers or wealthy people, are addressed in the maxims for daily living, ii 18–iii 7, whereas in the other New Testament epistles such exhortations are directed to different classes of society. Here only laborers or slaves are urgently admonished to submission and meekness, ii 18–25. From the study of this list an instructive picture is gained of the social status of the churches.

The author's *purpose* is not, however, to protect the worldly interests of the rich and of the secular power. His only desire is to prevent the believers from ruining the precious gift of the gospel by bitterness and strife. He does not glamorize the state and its power or the influential people among the heathen. On the contrary, he makes no secret of the fact that on principle these are unfriendly to and suspicious of Christians, ii 12, iii 15 ff., iv 4, 14–18, v 8. But if the Christians will live honestly and incorruptibly, if they will act loyally and patiently toward the hostile and suspicious non-Christians, the latter will ultimately turn both to understanding and repentance, ii 15, iii 16, and even to positive conversion, ii 12, iii 1. Through this the God-pleasing disposition of Christians is not only preserved, iii 8–12, but the opportunity of conversion is also opened to non-Christians during the short time remaining before the last judgment, iii 20, iv 5 f. The conversion of the non-Christians is one of the main interests of the author and he will not hear of misgivings about its success. Believers are to confess their Christian hope without fear of the secret police and other agents of the autocratic society, iii 15. In doing so they must remember that after his death Christ himself preached to the abominable spirits of the flood who are the most potent source of inspiration for paganism, iii 19 (cf. iv 6). This theme is taken from the books of Enoch and applied to Christ by the author in order to initiate unlimited confidence in the supernatural efficacy of the gospel for mission work among the heathen (cf. the commentary on iii 19).

In order to insure the salvation of their own souls and to contribute to the repentance and conversion of non-Christians, Christians ought to be prepared to suffer as did Christ, i 6 ff., 11, ii
19–25, iii 13–18, iv 1 f., v 1. Persecutions threaten and are even
at hand, iv 12–19, v 6–9. But the Christians ought to rejoice over
them as over a test of faith, i 6 f., an opportunity to share with
Christ in his sufferings, i 12, ii 21–25, iii 18, iv 1, 13 f., v 1,
a welcome anticipation of the final assize, iv 17 ff., v 6, 10. In
connection with this encouragement to fearless suffering and martyrdom the over-all purpose of the epistle is revealed, v 12: "By
Silvanus . . . I have briefly written to admonish you and to testify
that this is a true grace of God. In view of this remain steadfast."

The *form* in which the author has chosen to present his message
is outwardly that of an epistle. It is introduced and closed by the
forms of greeting common to epistles, i 1 f., v 12 ff. On closer
examination it is evident, however, that First Peter is really a baptismal sermon in the form of an epistle, first directed to newly
baptized people, i 1–iv 6, and after that to the congregation as a
whole, iv 7–v 14. Baptism is alluded to in i 2 as shown by the
reference to election "in the sanctification of the Spirit to obedience
and sprinkling with the blood of Christ." This alludes to the communication of holy spirit at baptism, the promise of obedience
given by the baptismal candidates, and their participation in
Christ's atoning death through the waters of baptism. From that
point on the awareness of the recent conversion of the hearers is
maintained through the entire text until iv 6; it is only after this
verse that the speaker addresses himself to Christians generally.
In the earlier section, which constitutes the main portion of the
epistle, the baptismal procedure is expressly affirmed in iii 21, where
baptism is said to save the believers "now."

It was probably the author's intention to have this general letter
to Christians in the northern, central, and western provinces of Asia
Minor presented at the baptismal services of the churches as a
greeting from the apostle Peter. The epistle is meant to replace the
spoken admonitions to the newly baptized, which Peter himself
would have delivered if he had been present. Perhaps, on the other
hand, the speech should be called a confirmation sermon. In the
early church the confirmation sermon was presented by some church
official immediately after baptism. This was already the case when

Peter and John, according to Acts viii 14–25, visited Samaria in order to confirm with apostolic authority the Christian baptism that had been performed. On account of this, First Peter is comparable to Paul's epistle to the Ephesians, which also gives the impression of being an apostolic sermon to recently baptized Christians.

The object of this baptismal or confirmation sermon is to strengthen the faith of new Christians and to help them recognize the infinite value of the gift which they have received through the gospel. Its *contents* may be divided in the following way:

I. THE RESPONSIBILITY OF THOSE BAPTIZED FOR THE GRACE RECEIVED, i 1–iv 6

1. *Words of greeting,* i 1–2
2. *Thanks for the gift of a living hope,* i 3–12
3. *Admonition to holy living,* i 13–25
4. *The avoidance of malice,* ii 1–12
5. *Loyalty to the authorities,* ii 13–17
6. *Maxims for daily living,* ii 18–iii 12
   *Laborers ought to manifest patience,* ii 18–25
   *Wives ought to honor their husbands; men ought to show consideration for women,* iii 1–7
   *General humility inside and outside the congregation,* iii 8–12
7. *Fearlessness and evangelical open-mindness toward all,* iii 13–22
8. *Readiness to suffer,* iv 1–6

II. THE LOVE AND STEADFASTNESS OF THE WHOLE CONGREGATION, iv 7–v 14

9. *Love, hospitality, and co-operation,* iv 7–11
10. *Joy and perseverance in persecution,* iv 12–19
11. *The devotion of the elders toward the flock,* v 1–5
12. *Trust in God and steadfastness,* v 6–11
13. *Summary, greeting, a wish for peace,* v 12–14

# Translation and Comment

## 1. WORDS OF GREETING
### (i 1–2)

I  1 Peter, apostle of Jesus Christ, to chosen immigrants of the dispersion in Pontus, Galatia, Cappadocia, Asia, and Bithynia, 2 [chosen] according to the providence of God the Father, through purification by the spirit, for obedience and sprinkling with the blood of Jesus Christ. Grace be with you, and may peace abound.

### COMMENT

The epistle opens in vs. 1 with approximately the same form of greeting which commonly introduces the Pauline epistles. None of the other General epistles, however, are as personal or detailed with regard to the audience. In this greeting Peter ascribes to himself a specific authority as an apostle of Jesus Christ. The recipients are characterized as chosen immigrants or foreigners in the dispersion. Evidently they are expected to compare themselves with the Jews of the dispersion who, in the Greco-Roman cities, were legally treated as resident aliens without the rights of citizenship. By analogy, Christians are elected to live as strangers in this world. And as the hearers of the epistle live rather far from either Jerusalem or Rome, they are said to belong to the dispersion (the *diasporá*). They are further said to live in five provinces of Asia Minor. Pontus was located in the northeast, and Galatia and Cappadocia in the

central portions of the peninsula; the province of Asia occupied
the western region, while Bithynia was located in the northwest.
The enumeration of the provinces thus follows a circle from the
northeast to the northwest. Galatia, however, is mentioned before
Cappadocia in spite of the fact that it was located west of Cappadocia. The reason for this sequence in the listing is not clear. In
any event the provinces mentioned are those whose Christian communities cherished respect for Peter and the Roman congregation. One may suppose that the Christians of the southern provinces
were more closely related to the church at Antioch, and that this
is why they are not mentioned here.

The recipients had been chosen a long time ago by God the
Father himself to receive the grace in which they now participate,
vs. 2a. Peter is referring to God's providence and to Christian baptism, i.e., the believers were predestined by God to receive his
grace through baptism. The references to sanctification of the spirit,
obedience, and sprinkling with the blood of Jesus Christ are best
explained in this way. At their baptism the believers received the
sanctification of the spirit (cf. Titus iii 5); they also pledged themselves to obey God (cf. vss. 14, 22, and "pledge" in iii 21).
And on that occasion they were cleansed with water which contains
the blessing of Christ's atoning blood (cf. Rom vi 3). Cleansing
with blood was also used at the Jewish sacrifice for a person converted from heathenism to Judaism (see the comments on i 19).
That baptism is of pivotal importance is also shown by what
immediately follows, concerning the new birth of the believers.

The greeting is concluded in vs. 2b by a wish for peace which
appears in a similar form in Second Peter and Jude (II Pet i 2;
Jude 2).

## 2. THANKS FOR THE GIFT OF A LIVING HOPE
### (i 3–12)

I  3 Blessed be the God and Father of our Lord Jesus Christ who, according to his rich mercy, has begotten us anew to a living hope through the resurrection of Jesus Christ from the dead, 4 to [give us] an imperishable, unspotted, and incorruptible inheritance which is preserved for you in heaven. 5 You are protected by the power of God through faith to [gain] a salvation which is ready to be revealed in the end-time.

6 Therefore, rejoice, even if you must now suffer a little under trials of many kinds, 7 so that the testing of your faith, many times more precious than gold—which is perishable, though also tested by fire—may be found worthy of praise, glory, and honor at the manifestation of Jesus Christ.

8 Although you have not seen him, you love him. At present you do not observe him, but having faith in him, you rejoice over him with inexpressibly glorious pleasure, 9 as you are about to reach the goal of your faith, the salvation of your souls.

10 Concerning this salvation, the prophets, who prophesied of the grace intended for you, searched and studied. 11 They were inquiring about the date and circumstances to which the spirit of Christ within them referred, when he foretold the sufferings of Christ and the glories to follow. 12 To them it was revealed that they were not serving themselves but you in these matters, which have now been announced to you by those who proclaimed the good tidings to you through holy spirit sent from heaven. Into these things angels long to look.

## COMMENT

When, in vs. 3, the author begins to praise God for the new birth to a living hope, his manner is both solemn and appealing. His objective is to help the hearers to recognize the infinite value of the gift that they have received: the gospel and their faith. For this purpose the author makes use of an elaborate style of Greek rhetoric, which was highly regarded in ancient times, but which is hardly suitable for modern speech. He constructs long, boldly sketched lines of thought, joining one clause to another by means of prepositions and relative pronouns. Actually, vss. 3–12 in the original constitute a single lengthy sentence. In translating, it seemed wise to break up this imposing series and present each idea as a separate unit. Present-day readers have not been trained to retain the line of thought as were the listeners to a speech in ancient times. But in this, as in many other cases, the long periods of the Greek language are not a sign of unwieldiness or tediousness: they are rather an expression of inspiration approaching ecstasy.

In the first instance, the author praises God who, in his rich mercy, has brought the Christians to a new birth in a living hope. Here is no abstract image, but an actual experience made real through baptism. Compare the expression "washing of regeneration" in Titus iii 5 where, as in the present passage, both baptism and God's mercy are involved. The basis of the new birth through baptism is the resurrection of Jesus from the dead. The consequence of the same regeneration is the gift of a living hope. By "living hope" is meant a hope by which one may live. It sustains the soul after the new birth with the nourishment needed for a higher life.

According to vs. 4 it is a matter of hope for or concerning[1] an imperishable inheritance, namely, eternal salvation with God. This treasure, in a wonderful way and unrelated to the merits of man, has been preserved in heaven through all eternity, solely for the Christian believers. In the same way God holds his mighty hand over the believers, vs. 5, so that through faith they may be preserved from all dangers and in due time receive their inheritance, the awaited salvation.

In anticipation of their glorious inheritance Christians ought to rejoice in this world, vs. 6, even if suffering overtakes them.[2] No one should think that he is forsaken by God when faced with such trials, or regard them as a limitation of his power. Rather, these also are part of God's providence, vs. 7, inasmuch as they have a definite purpose. Their object[3] is to afford the Christians an opportunity to demonstrate the quality of their faith. More specifically the testing of the faith is said to be many times more precious than gold,[4] for the latter is perishable, although tested by fire as the Christians are by persecution. This illustration reveals the author's realistic and even tactile mode of thinking. Faith is a substantial element in the Christian which must remain unshaken in the midst of difficult trials. The more successfully it endures trials, the greater is the honor and glory it will give the Christians at the final manifestation of Jesus Christ.

In vs. 8 two verb forms appear, "to love" and "to rejoice," which logically might be thought of as imperatives. The thought expressed would then be as follows. The Christians must love Jesus Christ, even if they really have not seen him, as has Peter: The apostle's testimony as an eyewitness is later stressed in v 1 (and also in II Pet i 16). In addition, they ought to rejoice over Jesus with inexpressibly glorious joy, although they probably do not[5] see him now with their eyes, but simply believe in him. For soon they will reach the goal of their faith, vs. 9, the salvation of their souls, that is, victory and participation in Christ's glory.

There is reason for infinite thankfulness toward God when it is remembered that he has reserved the gift of salvation through all past time in order to grant it only to those who enter into fellowship with Christ. Not even the prophets of the Old Testament, vs. 10, the most pious among the people of earlier generations, were able to do more than foretell the grace that has now come to the Christians. According to vs. 11, they investigated at which time and at what sort of time, that is, under what conditions, the sufferings related to Christ and which had been predicted to them by the Holy Spirit, were to take place. The prophets of the Old Testament are here looked upon as having supernatural knowledge of the eschatological events, but still being obliged to discuss the problems of their historical fulfilment. Similar concepts are found in the Old Testament itself (Dan ix 2, xii 4) and in the Qumran

literature (1QpHab ii. 9–10, vii. 1–5). In the present case, however, interest centers on the messianic travails or the sufferings
of Christ which are virtually expressions of divine grace. The faithful investigation of these problems by the prophets was not con-
ducted for their own sake, vs. 12a, but it was their commission
to serve the coming age of Christian believers thereby.[6] This is
further evidence of the fact that the Christians are in an exceptionally favored position, vs. 12b, as God-sent messengers preach to
them the joyous gospel of salvation. Not only were these noble men
of past generations prevented from having these glorious experiences
which, in the midst of all trials, contemporary Christians enjoy, but
even angels, vs. 12c, burned with desire throughout the ages to see
into[7] the mystery that is now being revealed to the believers. They,
however, have not been granted this privilege, which is an honor
reserved for Christ's disciples on earth. A similar view that angels
are kept outside the mysteries relating to the Messiah is found
in I Cor ii 8. The line of thought in First Peter is likewise analogous
to the well-known words that immediately follow in I Cor ii 9:
"What no eye has seen, and no ear heard . . . the things which
God has prepared for those who love him." So incredibly great is
the gift which the Christian believers have received, that not even
angels were permitted to observe the mystery connected with the
coming of Christ and his salvation.

## 3. ADMONITION TO HOLY LIVING
### (i 13–25)

I  13 Therefore gird up the loins of your mind. Be sober. Place your hope completely in the grace which is offered you through the revelation of Jesus Christ. 14 As you are committed to obedience, do not be conformed to the desires which governed you previously in your ignorance. 15 But like the Holy One who has called you, be holy yourselves in your whole manner of living. 16 For it is written[a]: "You shall be holy, because I am holy."

17 And if you invoke as Father the One who, without regard for persons, pronounces judgment according to the deeds of each individual, then live out the time of your sojourn [here] in fear. 18 Consider that it was not by perishable things such as silver or gold that you were redeemed from the vain manner of life inherited from your fathers, 19 but through the precious blood of nothing less than the blameless and stainless lamb Christ. 20 He was predestined before the foundation of the world, and was manifested at the end of the times for your sakes. 21 Because of him you are believers in God who raised him from the dead and gave him glory so that your faith and hope might be in God.

22 Since you have, by obedience to the truth, purified your souls for guileless brotherly love, then from the heart you ought to love one another with constancy. 23 You have been born again, not from a perishable but an imperishable seed, through the living and abiding word of God. 24 For [it says]:

[a] Lev xi 44 f., xix 2

All flesh is like grass
and all its glory like a flower of the grass.
The grass withers away,
and the flower falls.
25 But the word of the Lord remains forever.[b] That is the word
which has been preached as a gospel to you.

[b] Isa xl 6–8

### COMMENT

The illustration of girding up the mind in vs. 13 is reminiscent
of the words of Jesus in Luke xii 35. In that text the disciples
are admonished to keep their loins girded and their lights burning
in order to be prepared to meet their Lord at the end of the wedding.
To gird one's loins involved the pulling up and the tightening together of the long wide outer garment so that it would not cause
the wearer to stumble in the line of a march or a race. According
to an ancient tradition, the children of Israel were to celebrate
the Passover in this fashion to show that they were ready for
imminent departure (Exod xii 11). This tradition may have influenced First Peter. It is even possible that this figure of speech
reflects the author's awareness of the custom of arranging baptismal
services at Eastertime, the exodus and the passing through the
Red Sea being prototypes of Christian baptism (I Cor x 2). The
admonition to gird the loins would then rest in part on the assumed
baptismal situation. Baptism was also celebrated in the early church
by symbolically dressing in a certain costume (as probably reflected
in Gal iii 27, where baptism is compared to the putting on of
Christ, and in Eph vi 11, 13–17, with its description of the Christian's armor). However, even without the support of such thought
associations it is evident from the illustration that the admonition
relates to the preparedness of the Christians for the journey that
faces them.

On account of this the speaker then admonishes the listeners
to be sober, which is to be understood in a spiritual sense as an
expression of steadfastness in the faith. Further he wishes them to
set their hope once and for all[8] on the coming revelation of the

Lord and his accompanying grace. The recipients of this message are to be regarded as recently converted. The same conclusion may be drawn from vs. 14 which, in the original, is introduced by the words "as children of obedience." This is a Semitic expression, "children" being used to indicate the group's dependence on or connection with a certain quality or characteristic. Accordingly, the sense may be rendered, "as having committed yourselves to obedience." The phrase is especially applicable to newly baptized individuals who, soon after baptism, would have their faith confirmed by apostolic authority (cf. Acts viii 14–17, on Peter's and John's confirmation of the baptisms performed in Samaria). Inasmuch as the believers have vowed to obey Christ and the gospel, they are no longer allowed to accommodate or fashion themselves according to the lusts that formerly controlled them in their ignorance as unconverted heathen.

Just as He who called the Christians is holy, vs. 15, they must also be holy in all their living. This is underscored in vs. 16 by a citation from the Levitical law of holiness (Lev xix 2 in conjunction with xi 44 f.). Holiness is not an attribute of man, and man cannot attain it by himself, nor progressively sanctify himself, and then triumphantly present the result to God. Rather, holiness belongs to God; he is the only Holy One. Inasmuch as he is holy, his people must live a holy life before him. This God-centered doctrine of sanctification differs from the view that man, through holy living, can develop a holy personality.

Having been accepted into church fellowship the believers may now call God their father, vs. 17. But they must recognize that God is not only kind, good, and forgiving toward his children, but is also severe toward the disobedient when this is necessary. For it must be remembered that God will judge all for their deeds without respect to persons. It is imperative therefore not to settle down, trusting solely to the grace received. God must also be feared. During their entire sojourn here as strangers[9] the believers must fear God so as to escape the visitation of his wrath. God's holiness may express itself in consuming wrath as well as in fatherly love. The divine mystery is ambivalent. It is repellent because of its awe-inspiring majesty and attractive because of its fascinating love. This may also be illustrated by the well-known words of Luther's catechism which express man's proper approach to the divine holiness in its continual ambivalence: "We should fear and love God."

A special circumstance is pointed out in vs. 18 which ought to instill and encourage a wholesome fear in the presence of God's majesty. It is the infinite value of the grace received. The thought concerns the price by which the Christians have been redeemed from their earlier corruptible way of life derived from the pattern of their fathers. Here the illustration of redemption rests on ancient custom. Private philanthropists or temples might redeem slaves from their masters and let them henceforth live as free men. God has in a similar way redeemed his followers from their earlier slavery in inherited heathenism and corruption. And what constituted his payment for this deliverance? It was not silver or gold, or any perishable substance. But it was something of eternal value, vs. 19: the precious blood of nothing less than[10] the blameless and stainless lamb Christ.[11] Through an infinitely precious sacrifice God has redeemed the Christians from slavery to the world. Here the sacrifice was Christ himself who, according to the Christian understanding of the prophecy of the Suffering Servant in Isa liii 7, was to be brought forth and slaughtered like a lamb. In a formal sense the sacrifice of Christ is also thought of as a higher counterpart of the Jewish offering for proselytes. Jewish rabbis taught that the proselyte might attain to complete sacramental rights through baptism, circumcision, and the shedding of the blood of atonement. The last was justified by reference to Exod xxiv 8, which speaks of the blood of the covenant shed for Israel at Sinai. With regard to Num xv 14–16, where the stipulations of the law are said to be applicable to strangers who desire to join Israel, this passage was enlarged to include the admittance of proselytes into the Jewish congregation. Consequently, in Judaism sacrificial blood was supposed to complement circumcision and baptism, so that the uncleanness of the proselytes derived from heathenism might be removed and expiated. This practice explains the line of reasoning in the present verse, though circumcision is no longer of importance. Baptism is thought to be effective in combination with the shedding of Christ's blood, when new believers are received into the church. This way of thinking also explains why in vs. 2a baptism was presented as a sprinkling with the blood of Christ (see our commentary on that passage). It is to be admitted that the recipients of the letter were only in part Jews and Jewish proselytes. Yet the author here, as also in other passages, boldly employs Old Testament and Jewish arguments. Peter's epistle, in spite of new principles of interpretation, is essentially influenced by the Jewish background of the first disciples. The author is a Jew himself, and like Paul he is confident that his readers are familiar with basic Jewish concepts, both through observation of the Jews in their own communities and through Christian instruction based on the Old Testament. And so he expects to be understood by his readers, as he emphasizes that they have been redeemed from heathenism through the sacrificial blood of Christ. The thought of this costly ransom ought to incline the newly baptized members to serious consideration of their responsibilities. Above all, the gift of liberty must be handled with the greatest care so that a relapse into the temptations of heathenism does not occur, by which the sacrifice of Christ would be made worthless. If this happened, the punishment, as may easily be imagined, would be appalling.

In vs. 20 the author reverts to a thought already touched on in vss. 4 and 10–12, namely, that the gift of grace has been reserved for the Christians from the very beginning of the world. Here it is a matter of the pre-existence of Christ in God's providence and his incarnation in the last days for the eternal salvation of the believers. Christ originated the faith of the believers, vs. 21a, for "through him," or through the gospel emanating from him, they have attained to their faith in God. He is finally the guarantee of their faith and hope in God, vs. 21b, through his resurrection from the dead and subsequent entrance into glory (the last-mentioned reason is given again as an argument for the saving power of baptism in iii 21 f.). In view of such wonderful gifts, it behooves the believers to be full of faith and hope in God.

In vs. 22 it is pointed out that the believers, in obedience to the truth, which is here the gospel, have purified[12] their souls for mutual love. Undoubtedly this is another reference to baptism. It is to be assumed that this cleansing or purification involves deliverance from evil lusts. For its result is said to be a guileless or sincere brotherly love which is not possible to the old carnal nature. Whoever has thus had his soul purified by being baptized is truly able to love his brothers, and will do so from the heart with perseverance. The new birth through baptism is then illuminated more fully in vs. 23. In the Introduction it was pointed out that Titus iii 5 contains an instructive parallel to the concept of "the new birth" presented here. There baptism is spoken of as "the washing of regeneration and of renewing of the Holy Spirit." In the present epistle, however, the author is more interested in the power that is behind the sacrament and makes it a bath of regeneration. That power is the word of God, the gospel. Peter wishes to emphasize that it is not a perishable but an imperishable seed which has brought the believers to newness of life. By "seed" the author signifies a certain teaching or message, as the seed in Christ's parable about the sower denotes the word of God. No earthly or temporal propaganda accounts for the conversion of the believers and their new birth, but God's own word which is eternal. This contrast between human and divine seed is further illuminated in vss. 24–25 through a citation from Isa xl 6–8 (cf. Ps ciii 15). The human or carnal is only like grass, "its glory" or its most exalted manifestations like a flower in the grass; before the Lord's breath it withers. But the word of God remains forever. And it is exactly this word which has now been "evangelized," that is, proclaimed as a message of joy, to the recipients of the epistle. They depended previously on perishable "flesh" and its seed, that is, on human interests and propaganda. Now they have been born again through the eternal seed, God's word. Why does the author go to such lengths to bring out this point? The reason is that in vs. 22 he has admonished the recipients to persevere in love. He who is born merely of human "flesh" and is subject to the "flesh" with its evil proclivities cannot truly love his brother. But he who is born again through the eternal seed, God's eternally abiding word —the inmost nature of which is love—he will be able to love his neighbor with unfailing constancy, especially since he has now participated in a new and higher fellowship with all those who are born again.

# 4. THE AVOIDANCE OF MALICE
## (ii 1–12)

**II** 1 Put away therefore all wickedness, all deceit and hypocrisy, envy and all kinds of slander. 2 As newborn babes you should crave the undeceitful milk of the word so that by it you may grow up to salvation, 3 inasmuch as you have "tasted that the Lord is good."[a]

Come unto him, 4 the Living Stone, who was rejected by men but before God is "chosen," "honored."[b] 5 And you yourselves will be built up as living stones into a spiritual house, a holy priesthood to offer spiritual sacrifices, well pleasing to God through Jesus Christ.

6 For it stands in a Scripture[c]:

"Behold, I am placing in Zion a chosen stone,

a precious cornerstone,

and he who believes in him shall not be put to shame."

7 Thus the honor is for you who believe. But to unbelievers [it says]: "The stone which the housebuilders rejected—this has become a cornerstone,"[d] 8 and "a stone of stumbling and a rock of offense."[e] They stumble in disobeying the word, for which they were destined.

9 You are, on the other hand, "a chosen race,"[f] "a royal priesthood, a holy nation,"[g] "a people to be [God's] private posses-

[a] Ps xxxiv 8
[b] Isa xxviii 16
[c] Ibid.
[d] Ps cxviii 22; Matt xxi 42
[e] Isa viii 14
[f] Isa xliii 20
[g] Exod xix 6

sion, in order that you may proclaim the glorious deeds"[h] of the one who has called you out of darkness into his marvelous light. [10] You once were "No-People"[i] but are now the people of God; you were "Not-Pitied"[j] but have now received mercy.[k]

[11] Beloved, I exhort you as pilgrims and immigrants to abstain from the fleshly lusts that war against the soul. [12] Let your conduct be good among the Gentiles so that, while slandering you as evildoers, they may observe your good deeds and glorify God on the day of visitation.

[h] Isa xliii 21
[i] Hos i 9
[j] Hos i 6
[k] Hos ii 23

### COMMENT

The basic concern of this passage is with the duty of Christians to be holy in their conduct. In the same way that newly converted believers ought to put off the old man and his deceptive lusts (cf. Eph iv 22), those addressed in vs. 1 ought to put aside every kind of evil, deception, and malevolence. It is to be noted that the lusts enumerated are expressions of a negative attitude toward society. This is connected with a special desire on the part of the author to arouse his readers to an awareness of the duties of every Christian toward society. Before their conversion the readers were subject to certain antisocial tendencies but these must now be left behind. With the baptismal situation in mind, the author is eager to show how completely the evil inclinations are to be "put away." They must be surrendered, as at baptism the candidate takes off his old clothes and puts off his old self. So the recipients are in vs. 2 spoken of as "newborn babes." In this capacity they are encouraged to concentrate on a single objective: to crave the "milk of the word." For this is nourishment for innocent souls, being undeceitful in contradistinction to the subtle and twisted forces dominant in heathenism. Christians ought to long eagerly for this spiritual nourishment, in order to grow up to salvation. For,[13] vs. 3, they have now tasted that the Lord is good (Ps xxxiv 8). The author presumably alludes here to a custom connected with the rite of baptism in the early church, according to which the newly baptized individuals, as they came out of the water, were given some milk to drink. This milk, together with honey, was regarded as paradisaic and even messianic food (cf. Exod iii 8; Isa vii 15), leading to a sacramental connection with Christ. Here, however, it is primarily a symbol of the word, for which the Christian from this moment on must hunger and thirst, so that he may grow in the spirit. Then attention shifts, as it were, from the baptismal font to the altar of the sanctuary. For the believers are no longer spoken of as newborn babes, but as the priesthood of the chosen people gathered for sacrifice.

In vs. 4a the Christians are admonished to come to Christ who is to be the "living stone" for them. The illustration of the stone, also used in vs. 6, is chosen in conformity with Isa xxviii 16, which refers to a foundation stone laid by God in Zion. In this connection it is not necessary to decide whether the thought originally was of a cornerstone or the keystone over a door. At any rate the stone served to hold the building together. It is against this background that Christ is called the living stone, "living" in the sense of "life-giving." The thought of the Christian preacher, however, is more immediately centered upon the "stone" which the newly baptized Christians are to approach, namely, the altar. It is hardly conceivable that at the time of the composition of this epistle the congregations had big altar stones. But probably the church had a table for the celebration of the Lord's supper (I Cor x 18, 21; Heb xiii 10). Soon afterward the author describes the Christians as a counterpart to the Jewish priesthood who present offerings in the temple, vss. 5, 9. Thus it is reasonable to think of the stone mentioned here as a spiritual altar to which the Christians come, and on which they place their offerings. The illustration of the living stone consequently has a dual meaning: it is a life-giving and essential stone in the building, but at the same time it serves as an altar for offerings. If it is remembered that it represents Christ and his significance in the church, then this duality becomes understandable.

This representation is confirmed by vs. 4b, where, in accordance with Ps cxviii 22, the stone is said to have been rejected by men, but chosen and honored by God as emphasized again by vs. 7b (see below). Undoubtedly the reference is to Christ's humiliation and rehabilitation. The illustration of the stone is then extended in vs. 5a, where it is applied to the Christians. It says that the believers, as living stones, ought to be built up into a spiritual house (in 1QpHab x. 1, the members of a community are also compared with the stones of a house, though it is the community of a despotic priest which is meant). The church is not to be made up of individuals who are cold and dead, but who enrich their environment with life-giving love. After this the figure is further shifted so that in vs. 5b the living stones become a holy priesthood which presents spiritual, well-pleasing sacrifices to God. This transition becomes understandable if we think of the altar stones as bearing offerings, like priests. These offerings are not of a material but of a spiritual nature (cf. the sacrifice of "the lips" in 1QS x. 6). When Paul speaks of such offerings in Rom xii 1, he has reference to the commitment of the whole life to God on the part of the believers, entirely independent of the conventional practices of the world. The author of First Peter probably also regards the offerings as holy living in the service of God. In this connection a comparison with vs. 9 is illuminating. Here the responsibility of Christians as a holy priesthood is mentioned again. The duty of the truly chosen people, according to this verse, is to proclaim the wonderful deeds of the God who has called them. As is also evident from vs. 12, this sort of proclamation is not so much oral as practical and consists in irreproachable conduct among the non-Christians. Both the parallel in Romans and the context thus make it probable that the spiritual sacrifices in vs. 5 are thought of as becoming manifest through holy conduct in God's service. In this way the Christians are built up as living stones into a spiritual house, the church of Christ, and through such "sacrifices," well-pleasing to God, they are worthy to be called a holy priesthood. Here it ought to be observed that, while the illustration of the house of living stones represents the intimate fellowship of the believers, the conception of all Christians as Levitical priests, that often misunderstood idea of a "general priesthood," represents their responsibility toward non-Christians.

In vs. 4b a thought was touched upon which is discussed in more detail in vss. 6–7, namely, that Christ as the living stone was rejected by men, but was chosen and honored by God. The author makes no secret of the fact that Christ was despised by men; compare for example vs. 12 with its allusion to the fact that the Christians in the Roman empire are known as lawbreakers. But he emphasizes that this despised "stone" is more valuable and more important than everything else in life.

As an illustration of this, Isa xxviii 16 is quoted in vs. 6. The prophetic utterance implies that God himself has placed a cornerstone[14] in Zion. It further states that the one who puts his trust in this stone shall not be ashamed. The application to Christ was easily arrived at, especially since the Targum tradition applied the statement to the anointed king. It is supposed by the author that Christ was designated long ago on the basis of the old covenant, as the foundation stone of a new house, made up of those who believe in him and so are saved. A well-known amplification of this idea occurs in Matt xvi 18 where the apostolic ministry, in the person of Peter, is designated the foundation stone of the church. On the other hand, Eph ii 20 regards Jesus himself as the chief stone while the apostles and the prophets make up a more general foundation of the church (cf. Rev xxi 14).

Then it is stated in vs. 7a that those who trust in Christ, the chosen foundation stone, also partake of the honor God has accorded to him. In vs. 9, they are further described as a chosen generation, a royal priesthood, etc. The glory and power intended for Israel have thus been transferred to the Christian community. But to the unbelievers, vs. 7b, the words of Ps cxviii 22 are applicable, which are cited by Jesus (Matt xxi 42 with parallels) and which speak of the stone rejected by the housebuilders. These "builders" are the Jews who are regarded as striving to build up the temple of Zion as God lays the foundation of a new house. For the Jewish scribes were known to lay claim to the name of "builders" (Targ. Ps. 118:22, etc.), and Jesus used this passage from the Psalms to point to the Jewish leaders and their responsibility in his death. To the Jews who resist the gospel, vs. 7c, Jesus becomes a "cornerstone."[15] More exactly,[16] vs. 8a, he becomes "a stone of stumbling and a rock of offense," that is, a stone on which people stumble and which infuriates them. This quotation is from Isa viii 14 according to which the Lord was to become such a stone to the children of Israel. Jesus had expounded the word about the cornerstone more severely, as he foretold that it was to crush all opponents (Luke xx 18). But in First Peter, vs. 8b, it is simply that the Jews take offense at the word about Christ, as they also do according to Paul in Rom ix 32 f., where the same passages of Isaiah are quoted. The word of the cross is generally a cause of offense to the Jews according to I Cor i 23.

The author of First Peter is always patient and mild in his views. Consequently he hastens to add in vs. 8c that the recalcitrants have acquired their negative attitude in accordance with the purpose of God. The author's thought is comparable to that of Paul in Rom xi 11, 25, in so far as the obduracy of the Jews would open the way for the conversion of the heathen.

It is also affirmed that the Christians have received the special privilege of appropriating the names of honor with which Israel was favored in the Old Testament. These titles are enumerated in vs. 9a: "a chosen race," etc. When the author speaks of a "royal priesthood," he is referring to priests in the service of a king, or perhaps to those of royal rank.[17] It is to be noted that all these titles are taken from Exod xix and Isa xliii, passages associated with Israel's election. Thus the Christian community is said to be the true Israel, the people who constitute God's possession. Special stress is also laid on the fact, vs. 10, that these honorific names belong to the Christians. Previously the Christians were heathens, or a "non-people" and "without mercy" as Hosea said (*Lō'-'ammī, Lō'-ruḥāmāh,* Hos i 9, 6). But now they have experienced divine mercy and become a people of God. On this account, a significant responsibility devolves on them, vs. 9b: Through blameless conduct (cf. vs. 12) they are to proclaim the glorious deeds[18] of the one who summoned them out of darkness into light. Here the author's emphasis is on the realization of the gospel in daily living. This must be a principal concern of those who, having been called, have tasted that the Lord is good, vs. 3, and are now to step out into a hostile and suspicious world.

No misfortunes, however, will overtake the believers if only they maintain a certain reserve with regard to the world and at the same time, conduct themselves irreproachably as Christians. On the one hand, vs. 11, the Christians are expected to see themselves as foreigners and strangers without citizenship in the world (cf. i 1, 17), and to abstain from the desires which characterize "the flesh" —that is, the lower levels of life—and which war against the eternal well-being of the soul. On the other hand, vs. 12a, it is neces-

sary to "let their conduct be good," to live a disciplined life among
the heathen. The latter are strongly suspicious of the Christians and
slander them readily as lawbreakers. New religious movements were
outlawed in the Roman empire on the basis of charges that they
were hostile toward society; in certain instances this was actually
the case. The Christians were exposed to such accusations from the
time it was discovered by the authorities that Christianity was not
identical with Judaism, which had legal status and enjoyed special
privileges in the Roman empire. Recognition of this distinction is
first attested during the reign of Nero, who persecuted the Christians
in Rome, accusing them of being evildoers (Suet. *Vit. Ner.* 16:2).
It is with reference to the danger of being persecuted as enemies
of society that the author admonishes the Christians to lead absolutely blameless lives before the heathen. In doing so he is not
particularly anxious that the Christians escape all conflict and suffering. According to numerous statements that follow, the Christians
should make no effort to escape martyrdom. On the contrary, vs.
12b, the author is thinking of the benefits that the heathen may derive from seeing the honorable, patient, and loyal manner of life
of the Christians. In this way they may be moved from their present
attitude of suspicion to good will toward Christianity. Although they
customarily regard Christians as evildoers or criminals,[19] they cannot fail to be impressed when they see their good deeds, and loyalty
to the social order. Thus they may be led to a genuine conversion
"on the day of visitation" when God comes to them.[20] Here, the
epistle's remarkable theory of missions is expressed. The gospel will
be promulgated to the extent that the believers everywhere show
such extraordinary patience and loyalty, in spite of the ill will of
the non-Christians, that every observer will be astonished and
converted. This is also one of the basic thoughts in the Sermon on
the Mount (Matt v 16, 47). What follows in First Peter is largely
characterized by an unshakable confidence in the success of such
a practical demonstration of Christianity.

## 5. LOYALTY TO THE AUTHORITIES
### (ii 13–17)

II  13 Submit to all human authority for the Lord's sake, whether to the emperor as being supreme 14 or to the governors as being appointed by him to punish evildoers and to praise those who do right. 15 For this is God's will, that in doing right you may silence the ignorance of senseless people. 16 Although you are free, yet without using your liberty as a cover for evil, but as God's servants, 17 show respect for all men, love the brotherhood, fear God, honor the emperor.

### COMMENT

The author is anxious that the recipients adopt a positive attitude toward state and society. In this regard he completely agrees with Paul who expressly recommended submission and loyalty to the civil authorities (Rom xiii 1–7; cf. Titus iii 1). According to vss. 13–14, it is necessary to be subject both to the emperor and to the "governors," the representatives of the civil authority in the different provinces. These are appointed to discipline those who do evil, that is, criminals (cf. vs. 12), but encourage those who do right, that is, good citizens. It is vitally important for the Christians to do right or behave well,[21] vs. 15. In this way they may silence uninformed people who expose their ignorance by casting unwarranted aspersions on the Christians. Certainly the feeling of solidarity with society is not to lead to servility, vs. 16. In principle the Christians are free from the bonds of society, and need not have respect for the social order as such. But they must not use their freedom as an excuse for perpetrating "evil," or cherish a hostile attitude to

society. Obviously there were concrete reasons for the author of
the epistle to emphasize this. During the early period of the empire,
several organized attempts at revolt occurred in Asia Minor, especially among the numerous industrial workers. The author seeks to
prevent Christian liberty from being used in a similar manner as a
cover for subversive activity against society. On this account he
emphasizes that the Christians are God's servants and ought not
to have any part in "evil." Rather, vs. 17, they ought to assume a
respectful attitude[22] toward all. Besides loving the Christian fellowship and fearing God, they may still show respect[23] for the emperor
with a good conscience, though in reality they are free. In the eyes
of the author, the state has no permanent value in itself, but he is
anxious that Christians avoid evil deeds and instead, through good
civil behavior, gain the favor of society. By doing so they serve
the cause of Christian missions (cf. I Tim ii 1–4).

## 6. MAXIMS FOR DAILY LIVING
### (ii 18–iii 12)

*Laborers ought to manifest patience, ii 18–25*

II  18 You workers, be submissive to your masters with all respect, not only to the good and reasonable ones, but even to the difficult ones. 19 In fact, this is a grace, if with God's approval somebody bears afflictions while suffering unjustly. 20 For what credit is it, if as transgressors you are punished and endure it? On the other hand, if while doing right you suffer and endure it, that is a grace in the eyes of God. 21 For to this you have been called, because Christ suffered for you, leaving you an example so that you might follow in his footsteps. 22 Sin "he did not commit, nor was deceit found in his mouth."[a] 23 When he was reviled, he did not revile in turn; when he suffered, he did not utter threats but committed [his case] to the one who judges righteously. 24 He himself carried our sins[b] in his body on the tree so that we might die to sins and live to righteousness. "Through his stripes you have been healed."[c] 25 For "you strayed like sheep,"[d] but now you have turned to the shepherd and supervisor of your souls.

[a] Isa liii 9
[b] Isa liii 12
[c] Isa liii 5
[d] Isa liii 6

COMMENT

In vs. 18 the rendering "workers" and "masters" has been chosen deliberately, instead of the more traditional "servants" and "lords." The latter expressions evoke for the modern reader the archaic world of the patriarchs, rather than the contemporary Greco-Roman society. The reader may overlook Peter's reference here to one of the burning social problems in the Hellenistic world: the plight of the slave-laborers.[24] In the empire the majority of workers were slaves. In the present discussion, it is their status as workers, rather than as slaves, that is emphasized, and in particular the right of Christian workers to participate in strikes and sabotage against ruthless employers—at that time a critical problem in the industrial cities of Asia Minor, where the slave-workers were especially numerous. An apparently modernizing translation is required here, if the concrete meaning of the passage is to be properly understood. Regardless of provocation, Christian workers should not rebel or fail in respect toward their employers. This admonition is not due to the political or social conservatism of the author, or out of respect for the rich. His interest centers exclusively on the eternal well-being of the Christian workers.

The particular problem described in vs. 19 concerns the mistreatment of Christian workers by their employers, and the ill will to which they have been exposed. The author's judgment does not pertain to all labor conflicts, nor does he express his views on socio-economic problems in general. He deals only with the question as to whether the Christian workers should react to persecution with violence, in the same way as non-Christian laborers. The author warns against such behavior for the sake of the gospel and salvation. In the event that they are persecuted on account of their faith in God, then the Christian workers are to regard it as providential. Suffering for faith is always a grace, as previously indicated in i 6–11. But this rule only holds true when Christians endure suffering "with God's approval."[25] They must not cause suffering themselves by any provocative behavior. And their persecution must be undeserved in the sense that they suffer "unjustly."

Furthermore, vs. 20a, suffering is not meritorious if the abused laborers are guilty of actual transgressions, making their Christian liberty an excuse for doing evil (cf. vs. 16), and so becoming slaves of the evil power (cf. Rom xii 21). In this case their suffering is of no value, no matter how fanatically it may be endured for the purpose of provocation. On the other hand, vs. 20b, if the workers endure suffering for the sake of their Christian faith even though they "do right," that is, work loyally and honestly, it is a privilege in the eyes of God. For, as vs. 21a points out, the believers are called to endure this suffering for the sake of Christ.

Above all, the Christians ought to remember, vs. 21b, that Christ also suffered for their sins. By doing so he left an example for them to follow. Since he was the Suffering Servant spoken of in Isa liii, Christ should be the model of every suffering slave-worker. Christian workers should know that it is through patient suffering they receive grace to be followers of Christ. This experience in turn leads to eternal honor and salvation. Christ was innocent of evil and deceit, vs. 22—that is, he did not take part in political and social intrigues. He did not stoop, as many oppressed people on earth, to reviling and threatening, vs. 23, but committed his case to the righteous Judge. No striving after personal liberty or antisocial behavior or opposition to the existing order can be allowed to impair the Christian workers' imitation of Christ. According to vs. 24, such conduct is no longer possible for the Christian. Christ carried their sins in his body on the cross. For he took upon himself all human iniquity and brought it to an end by his innocent death (Isa liii 6), so that his believers have already departed from their sins and must live to righteousness. They are no longer common, weak human beings, but have through Christ's wounds been healed of all frailty. Previously they strayed like sheep from one interest to another, vs. 25, but now thay have turned to the real shepherd and supervisor of their souls, and have no excuse or occasion to follow false leaders and seditionists into rebellion.

It may be repeated that the author's admonitions to meekness and patience are not prompted by any special deference to the rich and powerful, but only by his interest in the eternal welfare of the Christian workers. He applies to that class of society the peaceful social program which runs through the entire New Testament and radically rejects all violence. In First Peter there is the imminent expectation that the rich and mighty will be converted to the gospel of peace and love (see e.g. iii 1 f.), with the result that pressing social problems will simply disappear. Christianity will bring about a social revolution, but it is to be accomplished through spiritual means. In our days Gandhi tried in a similar way to achieve a social revolution through "non-violence." Jesus and the apostles, however, even rejected attempts at passive resistance to the social order. The extraordinary optimism of the New Testament as to the effects of non-resistance is a permanent legacy. It is expounded in the present passage with a clarity, directness, and modernity that are unsurpassed.

*Wives ought to honor their husbands; men ought to show consideration for women, iii 1–7*

**III**  1 Likewise, you wives, be submissive to your husbands. If some disobey the word, they may be won over without preaching through the behavior of the wives, 2 when they observe your respectful and chaste conduct. 3 Not proper for the wives is outward self-adornment by plaiting their hair, putting on gold jewels, and wearing grand robes, 4 but rather the hidden person of their heart decked by the imperishable adornment of a mild and quiet spirit,which is very precious before God. 5 So once the holy women who hoped in God used to adorn themselves through submission to their husbands, 6 as Sarah showed obedience to Abraham and called him "lord."ᵃ Her daughters you have become, when you act rightly without fear of intimidation.

7 You husbands, likewise, conduct your family life with understanding. As it is a weaker element, you ought to have esteem for womankind, since they are coheirs of the grace of life, so that your prayers may not be blocked.

ᵃ Gen xviii 12

COMMENT

The principle of evangelization through loyal and patient behavior toward fellow human beings is applied in vss. 1–6 to mar-
ried women. Here the reference is primarily to so-called "divided"
marriages. In these, one party was a Christian, while the other was
a heathen or simply indifferent (I Cor vii 12–16). Such marriages
have again become common in our days, but differences in faith
played a far greater role in the world of the early church than
in modern society. According to vs. 1a, it is necessary in such instances for a Christian wife to be submissive to her husband, even
if he is disobedient to the word. For if she behaves in this fashion, vs. 1b, there is hope for his conversion. Such a conversion is
made possible not so much through oral persuasion, at which not
every woman is necessarily adept, as by exemplary conduct, vs.
2, which will arouse the husband's admiration and respect. More
specifically, a Christian wife's conduct ought to be "with respect,"
that is, "respectful," and "chaste," characterized by full awareness of
her duties to Christ and her husband. In this way a wife becomes
beautiful and attractive to her husband, not through the exterior
decoration of the body, vs. 3, but through the interior adornment of
the heart in a meek and peaceful spirit, vs. 4. Thus a Christian wife
ought to believe and hope for the best from her husband, although
he appears utterly indifferent to the gospel. Even he must sooner
or later respond to a gentle spirit, which in the eyes of God is a
truly precious ornament for a woman.

The imperishable value of obedience in marriage is then underscored in vs. 5 by reference to holy women of the Old Testament
whose glorious ornament was submission to their husbands. As an
example, vs. 6a, the author mentions Sarah, the venerable wife of
the patriarch Abraham who showed obedience to her husband and
called him "lord." Here the author refers to Gen xviii 12 in the
Septuagint translation. According to this verse Sarah was prepared,
in spite of her advanced age, to bear children to Abraham, as she
only said: "My lord is rather old." The wives who believe in Christ
have become her daughters, vs. 6b. Abraham and Sarah were
the progenitors of the chosen people and, more particularly, of the

Messiah. According to this epistle her election rested on her obedience (in Heb xi 11 reference is made to her faith; cf. Rom iv 19, ix 9). By "acting rightly," that is, in accordance with their duty,[26] the Christian wives become partakers of her election and holiness. Consequently they need not fear any threat.[27] The author has in mind here that the wife might incur the husband's ill will, and so be charged before the authorities for violation of the religious laws —an all too common occurrence in the Roman empire. A Christian wife ought, however, to fear nothing. She should wholeheartedly perform her duties toward her family and society, and at the same time remember that she belongs to a kingdom which is not of this world. Instead of being daughter and wife to earthly men, she has become the daughter of Sarah, the ancestress of the chosen people.

Among the maxims for daily living, there are corresponding words of instruction for the men, vs. 7a. The wives having just been counseled to submit to their husbands, it is entirely in order for the speaker here to say something to the husbands about their relationship with their wives. However, he broadens the discussion to include all the women in the home. He does not speak directly about the wife, but in a more abstract way about "the female element."[28] Of course, the wives must be looked upon as the principal object of attention; nevertheless the discussion generally deals with the relationship of the men to the more delicate element of their households.

The husbands are not to take advantage of the superiority which the wives, according to the preceding passage, must render to them, but should participate in domestic life[29] with "gnosis," that is, understanding. Christian knowledge in this sense is different from that "gnosis" which the representatives of Gnosticism claimed to possess. Paul had already discussed the question, although he did not have to deal with the elaborate Gnostic systems, known only from the second century. According to I Cor viii 1–13 Christian knowledge does not consist in the egoistic spirituality characteristic of Gnosticism, but in consideration for those who are weak. In the present case the word "gnosis" is used with a similar implication, as shown by the subsequent elaboration of the idea of considerateness. We may reasonably detect here the hand of Silvanus, Paul's disciple.

Gnostic teaching represented a quite different view. Women were despised as lower, carnal, and unclean beings. Our author does not deny that the female is a weaker element. However, the frailty of the woman must not lead to contempt for her. Just because she is weaker,[30] the husband is permanently obligated to show her esteem and consideration.[31] For according to the well-known instruction of Paul (I Cor xii 23 f.), those members of the church who appear lower and weaker in the social and hierarchical order should be the objects of greater consideration. Similar thoughts are expressed in the gospels, as when Jesus warned the disciples not to despise "these little ones" (Matt xviii 10), for their angels, who constantly behold the face of God the Father, rank among the highest angels, the "angels of the presence." These analogies help the reader to grasp the significance of the understanding and consideration which, according to First Peter, ought to characterize the behavior of men toward the weaker element in their homes.

On the whole, vs. 7b, men ought to remember that women also are heirs to the grace of life. Men are not sole heirs, but share the inheritance equally with women, even though men, according to vss. 1–6, must fill the dominant role in society. The equal right of both men and women to the gift of salvation was also emphasized by Paul (I Cor xi 11 f.; Gal iii 28; Eph v 23–33). Within the realm of salvation a re-evaluation of inherited conceptions about social rank has taken place. Gnosticism's lopsided contempt for women must be avoided.

If men do not recognize and follow this precept, vs. 7c, their prayers will be "blocked."[32] The author is speaking about "your" prayers, that is, the prayers of the men. United prayers of marriage partners may have been practiced, but here the reference is to prayers of men only (cf. I Tim ii 8). Probably the "blocking" of prayer means that the prayer loses its power and does not reach God. This is the well-known circumstance referred to by Paul (I Cor xiii 1): "If I do not have love, I have become as sounding brass," which means that his prayer becomes lifeless and meaningless like the empty sound of a gong. Similar thoughts about the danger and worthlessness of an egoistic service of God and of prayer in which no consideration is given to others are found in several New Testament passages (Matt v 23; Luke xviii 9–14;

I Cor xi 20–29; James iv 3). Behind the present verse there is above all the conception of the organic unity of the different members of the family and of the church.

*General humility inside and outside the congregation, iii 8–12*

8 Finally, all ought to be of the same mind, sympathetic, full of brotherly love, compassionate, humble.

9 Do not repay evil with evil, or reviling with reviling. On the contrary you ought to bless; for to this you were called, in order that you might inherit blessedness.

10 For he who wishes to be devoted to life and to see good days,

ought to withhold his tongue from evil and his lips from speaking guile.

11 Let him turn away from evil and do right;

let him seek peace and pursue it.

12 For the eyes of the Lord are upon the righteous

and his ears [are turned] to their prayer;

but the face of the Lord is against those who do evil.*

*a* Ps xxxiv 12–16a

#### COMMENT

The maxims for daily living applicable to the different Christian classes are concluded with some admonitions to the congregation in general. In this section of the epistle, the apostle is represented as speaking first to one group and then to another of the newly converted Christians who may be imagined as being assembled for a baptismal service, and finally to the congregation as a whole.

He is first concerned with their inner unity, vs. 8. Same-mindedness, love, and humility ought to characterize the relationships of all the brethren toward one another. In vss. 9–12 attention is focused on the quality of meekness which is necessary for believers in their dealings with each other as well as with those on the outside.

From the context, which mentions the reactions of the heathen in view of the blamelessness and the patience of the Christians, it is evident that the author is primarily concerned with their relationship to non-Christians.

More specifically, vs. 9 admonishes the believers not to be disturbed by the ill will that often meets them. Whatever the cost, evil must not be repaid with evil, nor reviling with reviling. Rather, everyone in society ought to be blessed. Furthermore, Christians are called to distribute blessings, since they themselves will in due time inherit eternal blessedness. The earnestness of the author in warning against temptations to seek revenge and indulge in bitter recriminations does not stem merely from a general awareness of man's unruly nature. It must also be remembered that the majority of the believers were poor laborers. The social conditions of Asia Minor could easily arouse Christians to criticism of society and animosity toward those in power. Any display of ill will on the part of non-Christians would have given rise to further bitterness. Recognizing the dangers inherent in the situation, and the development of attitudes which were harmful to the spirit of the gospel, the author particularly warns against that fretfulness which leads to the rejection of non-Christians. Paul expresses the same concern (Rom xii 17; I Thess v 15).

In vss. 10–12 the author emphasizes the importance of the matter by a citation from the Scriptures, Ps xxxiv 12–16. This passage is quoted with certain deviations from both the Hebrew text and the Septuagint, although the quotation conforms more nearly to the latter. "The one who wishes to be devoted to life" is in the eyes of the author the Christian who earnestly seeks after eternal life. The expression is tantamount in meaning to "the one who desires to be a Christian." As this implies suffering, the expression "to see good days" must be understood with reference to eternal life and cannot be referred to earthly living in calm and peace, as was the ideal of the old Hebrews. In order to have assurance of eternal life, the Christian must restrain his tongue from speaking anything evil and malicious. He must also refrain from intrigues, perform honest deeds, and strive after peace. For the Lord is with the righteous, but against those who perpetrate evil. It is thus made clear that David, the supposed author of this Psalm, had already warned against the desire for revenge and reviling mentioned in vs. 9.

## 7. FEARLESSNESS AND EVANGELICAL
## OPEN-MINDEDNESS TOWARD ALL
### (iii 13–22)

III  13 And who is there who will harm you, if you become zealots for what is good? 14 Yet even if you should suffer on account of righteousness, you are blessed. "Do not fear or be disturbed by their frightful appearance, 15 but hallow the Lord" —Christ—in your hearts.[a] Always be ready to give an answer to anyone who asks you for an account of the hope you have. 16 However, [do this] with gentleness and respect, cherishing good will, so that when you are defamed, those who revile your good conduct in Christ may be completely ashamed.

17 For, if the will of God should so require, it is better to suffer while doing right than while doing wrong. 18 For even Christ once died [as a sacrifice] for sin, in the capacity of a righteous man for the sake of unrighteous men, in order to bring you to God, suffering death in the flesh, but being made alive in the spirit.

19 On that occasion he went and preached even to the spirits in prison, 20 those who had once been disobedient, when God, in his long-suffering, kept waiting in the days of Noah. An ark was then constructed, into which a few people—that is eight persons—were saved by means of water. Just this [is the] analogous baptism [that] now saves you. 21 It does not involve putting away the filth of the flesh, but is a pledge of good will to God.

[a] Isa viii 12 f.

[And it saves you] through the resurrection of Jesus Christ,
22 who is at the right hand of God; since he ascended into
heaven, angels, magistrates, and powers have become subject
to him.

## COMMENT

The Christians need not encounter any real danger, vs. 13, if
only they behave correctly in society and become "zealots for what
is good." Particularly during the first part of the sixties, there was
in Judaism that anti-Roman movement whose adherents were called
zealots or "eager ones," and who used violence as an instrument
of policy to gain their goal of liberty (see the General Introduction).
If, as seems probable, First Peter was written during this period,
then the author undoubtedly has in mind these Jewish fanatics and
warns against their terroristic methods as he advises the Christians
rather to be zealous for what is good. The remarkable expression
"zealots" is best explained in this way. In other places also there
are indications that some Christians were being carried away by
the revolutionary activity of the Jewish zealots against the existing
order (Rom xiii 1–7, xvi 17–20; Philip iii 18–20). According to
vs. 14a, however, the authorities may still become suspicious and
take measures against the Christians no matter how blameless their
behavior. In such cases the believers are to realize that suffering
for the sake of Christ is bliss. As had been indelibly stressed in
Isa viii 12 f., they are not to be afraid of the frightful appearance[33]
of the heathen, vs. 14b, but in their hearts ought to sanctify the
Lord who is understood here to be Jesus Christ, vs. 15a. This means
that they ought to fear Christ and take him as their example, a
theme which is further developed in vss. 19–22. If the Christians
are questioned by the authorities, the police, or meddlesome ac-
cusers, vs. 15b, which often happened under the Roman government,
they are to answer openly and give an account of their Christian
hope (cf. Matt x 3 f.). They have nothing to hide.

However, according to vs. 16, the Christians must not answer the
Romans insolently after the manner of both Jewish and Greek

martyrs (as is evident from Fourth Maccabees and the so-called Acts of the Pagan Martyrs from Alexandria). They ought rather to manifest due respect for the authorities, and a good attitude or will.[34] In this way the individuals who molest[35] them for their good conduct in Christ will be put to shame. The authorities will also be obliged to acknowledge the blamelessness and worth of the Christian message and way of life, as soon as they realize what the evangelical hope really involves. Therefore believers ought to be confident and open in their conduct. Even if they should be compelled to appear for examination before the representatives of the Roman empire, which was not at all tolerant in religious matters, there is still a good chance that nothing evil will befall them. They are rather to utilize this opportunity for spreading the gospel and converting the heathen.

Verses 17–22 furnish theological evidence to validate and strengthen the admonitions given in vss. 13–16. This means that a parenthetic section is followed by a theological passage which logically supports the exhortations just pronounced.

In vs. 17 the thought broached in vss. 13–16 is taken up again, namely, that it behooves the Christians to be zealous for what is good and that suffering for Christ's sake in reality leads to blessedness. It may sound like a truism when the writer says that it is better to suffer for doing good deeds than for perpetrating evil ones. The observation, however, is made with reference to those who tried to gain the glory of martyrdom through stubborn opposition to the power of the state. It is unworthy of Christian believers to court martyrdom through deeds of violence, as for instance, the Jewish zealots did. Thus, as just stated in vs. 13, they became zealots for what is evil instead of good. So this superficially trite statement serves the purpose of safeguarding Christian martyrdom from provocative tendencies. It is therefore no tautology but a profound warning, owing to an urgent need.

The basic premise is further justified by a reference to Christ's suffering or death, vs. 18, which ought to be an example for every sincere believer. Christ once suffered (some manuscripts prefer the reading "Christ once died for us," or "for you," which has approximately the same meaning) as a sacrifice for sin.[36] He endured this suffering as a righteous man on account of unrighteous men, that is, for the sake of those who are now Christian believers, to be able to present them to God. The recognition of this ought to make the Christians willing to endure comparable suffering for the sake of others, as righteous people suffering for the unrighteous. Certainly this suffering is not comparable to that of Christ, which was unique in achieving universal atonement and redemption. Christians may follow Christ partially, however, by sharing his innocent suffering to the extent that they will be able, through unmerited suffering, to bring other people to belief in God. This is an obligation that devolves on all Christians. Besides, such innocent suffering for the sake of sinners contributes to the acquisition of blessedness (cf. vs. 14). For as Christ suffered death in the flesh but was made alive in the spirit, so his followers, after enduring suffering, will likewise be made alive in their spirits.

In vs. 19 there follows a widely disputed remark about Christ's preaching to the spirits in prison, with a series of short reminders of the circumstances connected with this event. Some scholars have found the verse so difficult to explain and so strange in the context that they regard it as an interpolation or a somewhat irrelevant digression. This opinion is not at all justified. In view of the conceptions prevalent in Judaism and early Christianity, everything is quite logical and reasonable in sequence. The reader must only be aware of the fact that the verse has a permanent connection with the preceding admonitory passage, vss. 13–16. One has to recognize that Christ is the model for the Christians who received these admonitions and then the matter becomes clear.

The author indicates that Jesus went and preached to certain "spirits." He did this at the time of his death and resurrection.[37] It was a preaching before the most dreadful sinners—those spirits that were in prison since they had been disobedient in the days of Noah. This undoubtedly refers to the angels mentioned in Gen vi 1–4 who fell into sin and thus were responsible for the flood. Probably the people who perished in the flood are also numbered with these "spirits." They were the descendants of the fallen angels, and in the story of Gen vi received the punishment meted out as a consequence of the sin of the angels with the daughters of men. In speaking about persons of remote antiquity, no sharp distinctions were made between angels and men (cf. Jude 6 f.). Human beings often assumed superhuman proportions, in particular those who were exceptionally evil (several examples of this kind are found in the books of Enoch and the apocalypses of Baruch, Jewish works of the last pre-Christian and first Christian centuries). Despite their remoteness in time these biblical figures had not lost their current importance. Many vivid and imaginative stories about these sinful spirits of the time of the flood circulated in late Judaism and early Christianity, picturing them as captives in the deepest darkness. The books of Enoch contain gruesome descriptions of them, but there are Christian traditions as well (like II Pet ii 14). In First Enoch (i.e., the Ethiopic Book of Enoch) appearances of the patriarch Enoch to the imprisoned spirits are mentioned. They may have been regarded as a pattern of Christ's coming before these same spirits. Jesus, his apostles, and the early church were undoubtedly well acquainted with the Enoch traditions also represented at Qumran. The fact that First Enoch is quoted as holy prophecy in Jude 14 f. is partial evidence of this. Since that epistle has close resemblances to the epistles of Peter (especially Second Peter), the author of First Peter in all likelihood was either directly or indirectly dependent on the picturesque descriptions contained in the books of Enoch, when he referred to the captive spirits from the days of the flood. He took it for granted that his readers were acquainted with the story of the disobedient spirits. Otherwise he would hardly have made this passing allusion to them.

What significance then did these ancient spirits possess according to the books of Enoch? They were important as patrons of the kings and mighty men of the world and as such constituted the origin and source of heathenism. Several passages in First Enoch make it clear that their punishment in the flood was thought of as a prototype of the coming judgment of the heathen rulers and oppressors. Note, e.g., I Enoch 67:4–69:1, and 67:12 especially: "This judgment wherewith the angels are judged is a testimony for the kings and the mighty who possess the earth."

In the present verse the author thus recalls a tradition known to his readers, namely, that Christ at his death went and preached to those arch-sinners and sources of inspiration for heathenism and its mighty rulers. No emphasis is placed on details or specific information as to time and place. A variety of conceptions have been and can be entertained with regard to this matter. It may be simplest to assume the lower regions as the place, and death as the time for Christ's preaching. But the text does not expressly state (as does the Apostles' Creed) that Christ descended into the realm of death. Interest is restricted to two particular facts: 1) that Christ *preached,* and 2) that his preaching was for these *spirits.*

The essential point is this: Just as Christ after his death preached to the demonic patrons of the heathen rulers, so Christians ought to preach to the heathen rulers in their communities, even if this brings death to them. Ever since the spirits in prison listened to the preaching of Christ, the power of paganism has been broken. Whether they heard a message of freedom or of eternal judgment at the occasion mentioned is not stated. In either case they learned the secret of Christ and his suffering which was to lead to his eternal exaltation. For this secret is part of all preaching concerning Christ, and when it is said that Christ "preached," it is evident that the author means he has proclaimed the same messianic secret which was essential to the preaching or the "kerygma" of the church.[38] Christ's preaching to the spirits in prison is the prototype of the preaching of Christian messengers. Therefore it is emphatically the duty of every Christian to proclaim the message of Christ in the midst of suffering and death to all heathen peoples, regardless of their power and the dangers involved.

It was just this fact that vs. 15 had enjoined upon the believers: the Christians are to sanctify Christ in their hearts. By taking him as their example, they will be prepared to defend the gospel before the heathen magistrates. Thus it is only at first glance that vs. 19 appears peculiar. Its meaning becomes clear when the admonitory context is kept in mind, and the conceptions which the writer's contemporaries normally connected with the spirits in prison are taken into account. The verse simply confirms the exhortations to general evangelization so characteristic of this epistle and emphasizes the limitless extent of the gospel of suffering.

In the following verses, several items are cited from the history of the flood which likewise are intended to be applied to the present experience of the believers and the church. What happened at the violent end of the preceding age is applicable to the imminent catastrophe of the present world, expressly mentioned in iv 7 (cf. II Pet ii 4–10).

According to vs. 20a, the spirits in question had once been disobedient in the days of Noah. Whether their disobedience was to God himself or to the message of righteousness proclaimed by Noah

(cf. II Pet ii 5), it constitutes a significant prototype of the indifference of the heathen in the present setting of the church. The
fact of pagan indifference troubled both author and readers, as we
know from several passages (e.g., ii 8, iii 1, iv 17). Here, however,
it is attributed to the spirits from the time of the flood, and the
point is argued that Jesus, through his preaching to these spirits,
broke the roots of heathenism so that the current indifference of
the heathen should not cause discouragement. After this the readers
are reminded of the fact that "God, in his long-suffering, kept
waiting" before the destruction of the antediluvian world. For according to Gen vi 3, God gave the people a respite of 120 years.
In the same way the destruction of the present world, iv 7, has been
delayed solely on account of God's patience (cf. II Pet iii 9).

It is further pointed out in vs. 20b that when the old world
was threatened by inundation, Noah's ark was constructed for the
elect as a means of escape. It is mentioned here as a prototype of
the church which is conceived as a lifeboat launched upon the sea
of time. An allusion to the cross is also possible, but less probable.
Like the ark of old, the church now, in anticipation of imminent
disaster, is being built up (note the emphasis on this point in ii 5).

A few people only, a chosen group, were saved in the ark. This
is the case even now, although the actual number to be saved at
present is larger. The author finds significance in the fact that those
in the ark numbered exactly eight souls, if Noah and his wife are
counted, together with three sons and three daughters-in-law. In
those days the number eight was often regarded as a symbol of
completeness and perfection, and is so applied here to the people
of the church, the whole group destined for salvation. The basis
for this view was the sacred number seven (compare in the Old
Testament, the seven days of creation, the seventh year, etc.). Since
it was also the number of the planets, seven was anciently thought
to comprise the whole universe. Gradually the notion gained support, however, that the number eight was even more important,
because the sum of seven was counted as an eighth number, expressing their unity and totality. In the evolved numerology of the
contemporary world, eight thus emerged as the number of perfection. The coincidence of the number in the story of the persons
saved in the ark provided an ideal opportunity for this symbolic
interpretation. Noah and his family are therefore a type of the

perfect totality to be saved through the new ark, the church. The analogy was facilitated by a specific Christian application of the number eight: Sunday was called the eighth day. It is to be noted that the setting of the epistle appears to be a baptismal service, usually celebrated on a Sunday.

Additionally it is stated that Noah and his family were saved "through water." In the next verse this is explained as a counterpart of the waters of Christian baptism. Here it is of minor importance whether the expression "through water" is to be understood as having local or instrumental meaning. The emphasis is placed on Noah's salvation from a godless environment. He is not thought of as having been saved "from" the water, as in the Genesis narrative, but "through" water from the evil of man. In the same way the Christians should understand that they are saved from the evil of man through the waters of baptism (cf. Acts ii 40, 41; II Pet ii 5, 7). So they should be willing to stand before the heathen without fear and proclaim the gospel by word and deed in accordance with the preceding admonitions, vss. 13–16.

The pattern of idea associations exemplified in the present verse was of special value to the people of the church. For the more imaginative the combinations, and the more esoteric the word-pictures, the more convincing and comforting they were to those engrossed in the world of the Bible. They cared little for a strictly logical sequence, since it was a matter of God's wonderful dealings with man and the world, which are not comprehended by the limited knowledge of the human mind, but only through the wisdom of the spirit and the receptiveness of the heart.

Following the reference to Noah's salvation through water, vs. 21a continues with the explanation that it is exactly this[39] "antitypical" or analogous baptism[40] which now saves the Christian believers. Here the author wishes to emphasize that the flood was an Old Testament counterpart to Christian baptism. The combination of these concepts does not rest solely on the fact that water was the means of salvation in both instances. Just as in the Old Testament the flood signified the death of the old world and the birth of the new, so the New Testament Christians connected baptism with the death of the old man and the birth of the new (Rom vi 13; Eph iv 22; Titus iii 5). Furthermore, the suffering and death of Christ were regarded as a baptism (Mark x 38; Luke xii 50), and, in turn, the individual was thought of as being baptized into the death of Christ (Rom vi 3). This remarkable association of Christ's suffering with baptism may reflect passages in the Old Testament Psalms, in which the suffering of the Elect One is described as a struggle in the surging waves of the underworld (Ps xviii 5–8, 17, xlii 8, lxix 2–4, etc.), which is also found in Qumran Hymns (1QH iii. 6–18, 19 f., 25–27, v. 6, vi. 22–24, x. 33 f.). Ps xlii 8 may be quoted as representative: "Deep calls to deep at the noise of thy cataracts. All thy breakers and thy waves have gone over me." The thought of Christ's struggle in the waves of the lower regions, brought forcibly to mind in the rite of baptism, may have suggested a further connection with the dark waters of the flood, and so with those evil spirits that were regarded as being held captive somewhere under the turbulent waters. In view of the current ideas concerning Christ's death and baptism, the idea associations of Peter are therefore understandable.

When it is stated that baptism "now" saves the Christian believers, it is most natural to understand the time reference as part of an actual baptismal service. The expression itself need only mean that baptism is always a present reality in the life of the Christian, but such an indefinite, generalized interpretation does not do justice to the contents of the epistle. Here the believers, throughout the early chapters, are treated as recently converted individuals. Furthermore, in the characterization of baptism which follows, emphasis centers upon a specific deed or event rather than on a persisting condition or state. We conclude, with reference to the first part of the epistle, that a baptismal ceremony is about to be celebrated, or has just taken place.

In vs. 21b the nature of baptism is described. This sacrament does not consist in putting off the uncleanness of the flesh, as purifications were occasionally regarded in Judaism (cf. Matt xv 1–20, with parallels; Col ii 23; Titus i 14–16). The effect of the latter might easily be to isolate a man from his environment. What the author wishes to emphasize is that such is not the case with Christian baptism, for the Christian is to live and work among the people in his community. For this reason, baptism is said rather to be an agreement[41] before God with respect to good will or a positive attitude.[42] The emphasis is on the confession and the promises connected with baptism. Thus the import of baptism is not negative, as

one might suppose from the figure of putting off the garment of
the old man which, tangibly or symbolically, preceded the descent
into the waters of baptism (cf. Eph iv 22; Col iii 9). On the contrary its significance is positive, inasmuch as the most important
part of it concerns the acquisition of new virtues, following the
ascent from the waters of baptism (cf. Rom vi 11–23). What saves
the Christians from destruction is not a hostile separation from society according to the pattern of sectarian Judaism, but a confession made before God and a promise of loyalty comprising good
will, a positive attitude toward people and a serious effort to pro-
mote their well-being. If the baptismal promise is kept, the individual will really walk in the footsteps of Jesus. And so, vs. 21c,
he will become a partaker of the inner power of baptism to
achieve salvation: the resurrection of Jesus Christ.

Speaking of the baptismal confession, the author is led to complete his reference to Christ's resurrection by recording additional
christological items, vs. 22. Judging from various indications, such a
confession had apparently begun to develop in the church and was
used in connection with baptism even if the precise form had not
as yet been fixed. In the present case the confession is not simply
an enumeration of general articles of the faith. On the contrary,
it is the author's intention to relate each point to his main theme,
namely, to convince the recipients that they have nothing to fear
from contact with their heathen surroundings. The expressions used
here, including the reference to the resurrection in vs. 21c are designed to validate the preceding admonitions, vss. 13–16. In all
there are four main points: 1) Christ's resurrection; 2) his place
at the right hand of God; 3) his ascension; 4) his authority over
angels, magistrates, and powers. Among these four testimonies, the
first and the third deal with Christ's exaltation, and the second and
the fourth with his authority over all things. From the context the
Christian reader is to draw the conclusion that he, through fellowship with Christ, is saved for life eternal and need not fear or be
subject to any earthly powers, even if these are partly supernatural
and demonic.

## 8. READINESS TO SUFFER
### (iv 1–6)

**IV** 1 Inasmuch as Christ has suffered in the flesh, you also ought to arm yourselves with the same mind. For the one who suffers in the flesh has ceased from sin. 2 Thus it should no longer be to obey the lusts of men, but the will of God that you live out the rest of your days in the flesh. 3 For it is enough that in time past you accomplished the purposes of the heathen, and lived in brutalities, lusts, wine orgies, riots, drinking bouts, and unlawful idol cults. 4 On account of this, they are surprised that you do not run to join them [any more] for the same licentious outbursts, and speak evil of you. 5 But they will render account to Him who is ready to judge the living and the dead. 6 For to this end the gospel was preached even to the dead, that they might be judged according to the nature of men in the flesh, but live according to the nature of God in the spirit.

### COMMENT

Thus the newly converted, vs. 1a, must be ready to suffer for Christ in the flesh as Christ suffered for them in the flesh. In some manuscripts, the expression "for us" or "for you" is found but the clause has the same meaning even without that addition. The admonition ties in with what has preceded, particularly iii 19. But the author is speaking more exactly about equipping oneself with the kind of mind which Christ had. The reference to girding on spiritual armor or weapons probably comes from the baptismal ceremony, in which there occurred a real or symbolical putting on of

certain items of clothing. One may compare this passage with Eph
v 13–17 where the illustration of clothing oneself in Christ's spiritual armor is most easily understood as a reflection of certain baptismal acts. The recommendation of a way of thinking in agreement
with Christ's may be compared with Philip ii 5 which introduces the
well-known hymn on Christ's appearance in the form of a servant.
According to vs. 1b, the immense advantage of such Christian suffering in the flesh is that one has no further connection with sin.[43]

On account of this, vs. 2, the newly baptized members must
henceforth live according to God's will rather than following the
lusts of man. If suffering does come, they are to regard it as a
welcome means for the mortification of sinful flesh. They are not
to seek consolation in the enticements offered by their fellow men.

A serious matter is referred to in vs. 3, namely that the recipients of the epistle, for a long time prior to their conversion,
participated in the debaucheries of heathenism. In a catalogue of
vices, the speaker provides information about the dissipations of
the heathen environment to which the Christians had previously
succumbed. General brutalities[44] and lusts are mentioned first; then
follow three designations of typically Dionysian debaucheries, wine
orgies, riots,[45] and drinking bouts; finally unlawful idol cults[46] are
alluded to. These heathen practices are not a general characterization of human depravity. If this were the case, we would hardly
have the present list with its peculiar details. We are rather compelled to regard this enumeration of vices as reflecting actual conditions prevailing in the communities of Asia Minor in which the
recipients of the epistle lived. The description must pertain to organized gatherings or even regular clubs in which the shameful
activities described were carried on. In such gatherings the recently
baptized individuals had evidently been participants. On this assumption it is possible to explain why the heathen, according to vs.
4, now manifest surprise and speak evil of those who have been
converted to the gospel, inasmuch as they no longer run to join
the heathen and participate in their excesses of licentiousness. The
surprise of the heathen would scarcely make sense unless they had
regular gatherings, in which the Christians had formerly participated.

Such celebrations, marked by violence, Dionysian dissipations,
and "unlawful" idol cults, were common among the heathen in

Asia Minor. In fact, they were sponsored by the important social clubs of the early days of the empire, particularly among the Greeks. These clubs were prohibited on principle by the Roman emperors, since their members, often as a result of excessive drinking, were easily stirred by revolutionary sentiments against the state. Usually these clubs were under the protection of some Oriental or Greek deity (often Dionysus), the worship of which was inimical to the interests of Rome. This was especially true of Asia Minor where social discontent was widespread and the people were eager to throw off the yoke of Rome. How dangerous these organizations were in the eyes of Rome is evident from the correspondence between Trajan and Pliny the Younger, the governor of Bithynia (Plin. Min. *Ep.* 10:33). The emperor did not even permit the establishment of a fire brigade, as such a group might be involved in seditious activity. Pliny also discusses the Christians, in view of their possible opposition to the empire, and the imperial laws dealing with organizations of this kind (*ibid.* 10:96–97).

The specific enumeration of vices in the present verse fits well into this historical framework. It is apparent that prior to their conversion the Christians had participated regularly in the activities of certain organizations in Asia Minor, where excessive drinking and unlawful worship of Oriental or Greek deities took place and hostility to the Roman state was aroused. Now their former companions wonder why the Christians no longer frequent their gatherings but have adopted a way of life which does not allow them either to enjoy Saturnalian excesses or to oppose the Romans. On account of this, they speak evil of the Christians.

Often the effort is made to relate the dissipations mentioned to festal meals connected with emperor worship. Thus the heathen of the environment are thought of as being surprised that the Christians no longer wish to participate in the officially authorized cult. But that view is clearly untenable, for the author of the epistle is anxious to instill a loyal attitude toward the emperor and his representatives and expressly advises his readers to be submissive to them (ii 13–18). This would not have been possible in a situation where emperor worship, against which Peter would certainly have reacted, was already compulsory. Accordingly, the epistle must have been written before the emperor cult was forced upon the Christians, which is first known to have happened during the reign of Domitian.

And the heathen dissipations mentioned cannot have had any connection with earlier voluntary emperor worship either. The words "brutalities" and "unlawful idol cults" used in the verse immediately show that it is a matter of extravagant feasts hostile to the state. Henceforth the newly baptized members of the church must abstain from them and maintain a positive attitude toward society, even if their old drinking-companions despise them for their apostasy.

Moreover, vs. 5, these revilers are soon to render an account to the one who is ready to judge both the living and the dead. Whether the judge is God or Christ is not stated. By "the living and the dead" undoubtedly are meant all the people who ever lived, or are still living when the judgment comes. That the final judgment is imminent, vs. 6a, is also evident from the fact that the gospel has already been preached to the dead. Exactly how this was done is not stated. It is possible to imagine Christ's descent into the lower regions after his burial as the time for this preaching of the gospel, but explicit information is not given. A certain relation to iii 19 and to Christ's preaching to the spirits in prison may be assumed, although the spirits in prison are not to be equated with all the dead. On the other hand these people are really dead, as is evident from the analogous expression in vs. 5. About them it is further stated in vs. 6b that they received the message about Christ in order to be judged in the flesh and made alive in the spirit. No one escapes judgment, which takes place "according to men," that is, it belongs to the very nature of men, which is sinful. Even for the dead there will be a judgment in the flesh, through the resurrection of the body. And the result for each individual will depend upon his relationship to Christ. On account of this all must hear the message of salvation through Christ, the dead as well as the living. The judgment, however, is not the last thing, but a necessary prerequisite for eternal life, which is in accordance with God's nature and comprises eternal fellowship with his life. As it is received through the spirit of God, it means life in the spirit.

Throughout this passage the author's concern is the universality of the final judgment. But whereas in vs. 5 he reminded his readers of the coming judgment with special reference to the scoffers, the center of interest has been shifted in the present verse. The extension of the judgment to the dead is mentioned here in connection with the universal scope of the gospel. As even the dead have heard the gospel and will be judged according to their varying responses to it, so it must be recognized that the heathen are subject to judgment on the same basis. It is therefore the responsibility of Christians to co-operate confidently in the preaching of the gospel everywhere, as was repeatedly emphasized earlier in the epistle. Theological details are referred to only so that the readers may apply them to their own situation. Furthermore, they are to recognize that through their suffering they are already experiencing that judgment in the flesh. Compare vs. 17, where the persecution of God's house or the church is said to be anticipative of the judgment. Everyone must be judged in the flesh: This is part of the very nature of man, and it has been extended even to include those who have died. Only thereby is the possibility afforded to live according to God's nature in the spirit. Now since this judgment partly comes to the Christian believers during their earthly life, they must not be discouraged by suffering but should rather look upon it as a gift of God's grace leading to salvation (cf. i 6, iii 14, iv 12–14, v 12).

## 9. LOVE, HOSPITALITY, AND CO-OPERATION
### (iv 7–11)

IV  7 For all, however, the end is near. Therefore be prudent and sober so as to bring about prayers. 8 Above all you ought to let your love for each other remain intense, for "love covers a multitude of sins."ᵃ 9 Show hospitality to each other without murmuring. 10 Just as each has received a gift of grace, you ought to dispense it to each other as good managers of God's manifold grace. 11 If anyone speaks, [take it] as God's words. If anyone serves, [regard it] as coming from the strength which God grants. Thus in everything God is to be glorified through Jesus Christ, to whom belongs the glory and the power forever and ever. Amen.

ᵃ Prov x 12

### COMMENT

In this section, the perspective is widened to include not only the recently baptized members but the congregation at large. For vs. 7 speaks expressly of "all," and in vss. 9–10 the writer speaks about the different gifts of grace and offices, as in v 1–5 "the elders" of the congregation are specifically addressed.

The mention in vss. 5–6 of the judgment of the living and the dead leads the speaker in vs. 7 to remind the hearers of the imminent termination of everything. The awareness of this must prompt all believers to prudence and soberness, so that it may bring about prayers[47] (variant reading: "prayers for us," or "for you"). Noth-

ing else should be of concern to the Christians. Experience had
otherwise shown that the anticipation of the victory of the kingdom
of God frequently led to disorder or sensuality in the life of the
church (e.g., I Thess iv 11–v 11; II Thess iii 6–16; I Cor xi 21).
According to vss. 3–4, the newly converted Christians had recently
forsaken certain heathen activities involving drunkenness and "brutalities." It is with reference to these dangerous possibilities that
the readers are flatly instructed to practice self-control and sobriety.
Then they may properly understand that humble prayer is the only
correct means of preparing oneself for the imminent judgment
(cf. Jude 20).

In the same way, according to vss. 8–11, it is necessary for the
church during the time of waiting to live in unity and orderliness
following the ways of love. This is a very common theme in the
New Testament epistles and clearly implies that in many instances
the young congregations lacked order. As always, love is recommended as the only effective remedy, vs. 8, with an appropriate
citation from Prov x 12: "Love covers a multitude of sins." The
meaning is probably that the unifying power of love (Col iii 14)
prevents sins and weaknesses from manifesting themselves. It is
pointless to ask whether the "covering" pertains to one's own sins
or to those of others. Undoubtedly it has both meanings since the
author speaks of the Christians as a community of reciprocal loyalty.
To this love of the believers also belongs the duty of hospitality,
vs. 9, which is to be offered without murmuring. Here the writer is
probably thinking of evangelists and leaders of the church, like
Peter and Paul, who were often traveling among the different congregations. Thus he comes in the following verses to the gifts of
grace. As also indicated by Paul (Rom xii 3–13; I Cor xii 4–31),
these easily became occasions of pride and jealousy. Therefore vs.
10 emphasizes that these gifts are not to be an occasion for self-
exaltation, but ought to be used for reciprocal service in the church;
in their different manifestations they are the expressions of God's
manifold grace and not of any special ability of the individual.
In vs. 11 this line of thought is illustrated by several examples.
Those who possess the gift of preaching, as those engaged in practical service, are to realize that both inspiration and the power
to effectuate have their source in God. Everything is for the glorification of God through Jesus Christ. There is no basis for personal

pride or envy on account of the gifts of grace. It is to be noted
that the author does not enumerate the gift of tongues or other extreme manifestations as illustrations of this grace, but only such
basic church activities as preaching, stewardship, and works of
mercy. Common practices and ordinary deeds are regarded by the
author as holy gifts of God's grace.

## 10. JOY AND PERSEVERANCE IN PERSECUTION
## (iv 12–19)

**IV** 12 Beloved, do not be surprised at the fiery ordeal which you must undergo in order to be tested, as if something strange were happening to you. 13 But as you share the sufferings of Christ be of good cheer, so that at the revelation of his glory you may also gladly rejoice. 14 If you are reviled because of the name of Christ, you are blessed, for the spirit of glory and of God*a* rests upon you. 15 Let none of you suffer [punishment] as a murderer, a thief, a malefactor, or as a depositary of foreign assets. 16 But if [he suffers] because he is a Christian, then let him not be ashamed but glorify God through this designation. 17 Indeed, the time is at hand for the judgment to begin at the house of God. But if it begins with us, what will be the end for those who are disobedient to God's gospel? 18 And "if the righteous man narrowly escapes, what will happen to the godless and the sinner?"*b* 19 Therefore let those who suffer according to God's will commit their souls to the faithful Creator in doing right.

*a* Another reading: "the spirit of glory and strength and of God."
*b* Prov xi 31, quoted from LXX.

### COMMENT

According to an eschatological conception which was alluded to in i 7, the expected destruction of the universe will take place through fire, vs. 12. For this reason it is understandable why the current persecution of the Christians is here called an ordeal by fire.

For the persecution is anticipative of the final judgment and destruction (cf. vs. 17), though so far it consists mainly in revilings. The believers therefore ought not to be surprised that the fire of the final judgment is already burning them through the persecutions of the non-Christians. In fact its purpose is to test their faith (compare i 6 f.). Furthermore, persecution means participation in the sufferings of Christ, vs. 13, which ought to produce immediate joy in view of the prospect of exulting with joy at the definitive coming of Christ's glory. In the same way Peter and the apostles in Jerusalem rejoiced because they had been permitted to suffer ignominy for Christ's sake (cf. Acts v 41). There is immediate blessedness, vs. 14, for anyone who is reviled or in disgrace because he bears the name of Christ. The glorious spirit of God already rests on him (Isa xi 2), as he shares the experience of Christ who was himself scoffed at by men (cf. ii 23).

In vs. 15 the speaker adds that no Christian, however, should court suffering as punishment for any criminal activity. He must not provoke the authorities to interfere by becoming a murderer, a thief, a malefactor, or as a "depositary of foreign assets."

Our translation "depositary of foreign assets" is an effort to render an especially difficult Greek word, *allotriepískopos*. In the whole of Greek literature this word is only found here, if citations of the present text by later church writers are excepted. Like the other expressions in the list, "murderer," etc., it appears to designate unlawful and not simply immoral activity. In this connection two meanings present themselves, as *allótria* may be either "other men's concerns" or "other men's property." Either the word means, 1) "one who watches over foreign concerns," which can be said about a sycophant, or an informer; or 2) "one who watches over foreign capital," "a depositary of foreign assets," that is, of money paid by strangers. The latter interpretation fits the person whom the Romans called a *sequester*. He received money from a candidate for political office, as a deposit to be held for distribution to the members of an association or guild, should the candidate be successful in his quest through their efforts and votes. Both sycophancy and vote-buying, though opposed and punished by the authorities, were widely practiced. The latter practice is a principal concern of Cicero's famous speech in favor of Plancius. Now the Christians would hardly be inclined toward sycophant activity, and a warning against such involvement was certainly unnecessary. On the other hand, the deposit and transfer of money for votes undoubtedly constituted a grave temptation under the prevailing social conditions; this situation may well be reflected in two other General epistles (James ii 1–4; II Pet ii 12–22; see our comments on these passages). Thus it is possible to explain the text as a warning to Christians not to serve as depositaries of foreign assets, that is, of unlawful money. Yet the whole question remains unsolved because there is no illuminating parallel to the usage of this particular Greek word.

In any case the author wishes to prevent the believers from seeking the glory of martyrdom on any but a completely legal and honest basis. So if the believer suffers simply because he is a Christian, vs. 16, then it is no shame to him; and he will glorify God by being a Christian, that is, a bearer of the name of Christ.

The ill will of the heathen toward the Christians in reality shows that the last judgment has already begun, vs. 17a. For the current slander and suspicion are only anticipatory of the judgment as it pertains to the Christians. The judgment is to begin with God's house, the church, but the final judgment of the opponents will be much worse, vs. 17b. With a quotation of Prov xi 31 (according to the Septuagint), it is further stated in vs. 18 that the severity of the divine judge toward the righteous indicates that the godless must soon face a far sterner punishment. Here the reader might well think of Jesus' words about the narrow and the broad ways (Matt vii 13), and the comparison between the green and the dry tree (Luke xxiii 31).

The Christians who experience suffering because of God's will should commit their souls with confidence into the hand of the faithful Creator, vs. 19. It is he who has given them life on this earth, and he can demand it back from them. As he is faithful he will not surrender his own unto destruction. In the same way Jesus himself at his death committed his spirit into the hands of his Father (Luke xxiii 46), and God did not permit his soul to meet corruption (Acts ii 27). But a necessary condition for the salvation of the Christian witnesses is that they place their souls in God's hands while doing right and not as criminals (cf. Luke xxiii 40 f.). Christian martyrs should not be anarchists. This is stressed again in direct reference to vs. 15, but was also underscored several times in the preceding passages (ii 20, iii 14, 17).

## 11. THE DEVOTION OF THE ELDERS
## TOWARD THE FLOCK
### (v 1–5)

**V** 1 Now I exhort the elders among you, as your fellow elder and witness to the sufferings of Christ, and also as a partaker of the glory which is to be revealed: 2 Be shepherds of God's flock among you, not under compulsion but willingly after God's direction, not for the sake of money but with an eager mind, 3 not through domineering over the groups allotted [to you], but through being examples to the flock. 4 And when the Chief Shepherd appears, you will receive the unfading wreath of glory.

5 In the same way, you younger ones, submit to the elders.

All of you gird yourselves with humility one toward another, for "God resists arrogant persons, but unto the humble he gives grace."[a]

[a] Prov iii 34


#### COMMENT

Peter himself appears in vs. 1. The reason for this is that some words of admonition are now to be directed to the "elders" of the congregations. According to the following verses the elders are the leaders of their respective groups and are thus designated as shepherds (cf. the title "pastor") who are directly subordinated to Christ as the Chief Shepherd, vs 4. Peter, on the other hand, does not present himself as the chief shepherd of the shepherds. He places himself unpretentiously on a par with the elders of the churches, as he expressly calls himself "a fellow elder." The only special authority he claims is the privilege 1) of having been a

witness to Christ's sufferings and 2) of being a joint heir of
the coming glory. The meaning of this is undoubtedly that the reader
is to think of Peter as an eyewitness to Jesus' sufferings and glorification (cf. II Pet i 16–18). In addition these prior experiences
ought to be regarded as extending to the present time and con-
stituting current forms of contact with Christ. As during the earthly
sojourn of Jesus the apostle intimately experienced his suffering
and glorification, so he is even now a partaker of them by living
as a follower of Christ. This and nothing else gives Peter his place
of honor, as he now in humble terms goes on to instruct the
ecclesiastical officers among the recipients.

The elders or the leaders of the congregations are admonished
in vs. 2 to be shepherds and to take care of the groups within
the flock of the universal church which have been assigned to each.
This must not be done through compulsion but willingly, according
to God's direction. It may be noted here that there were not yet
any paid offices in the church. The care of the congregations was
assumed by voluntary functionaries reminding us of the laymen
who serve as elders or trustees in modern congregations. These
trustees are not to undertake their offices in the shameful pursuit
of financial gain, but with a ready mind and good will. It seems
as if the temptation was close at hand for the officers to secure
not only a reasonable financial reward for their labor (I Tim v
17 f.), but even a handsome profit (I Tim iii 3, 8, vi 5–10).
Apparently it was easy to take advantage of the generosity of certain members of the church, a danger against which Paul in particular was constantly on his guard (for example in Acts xx 33; I Thess
ii 5). The temptation to acquire dishonest income from those
outside, by receiving bribes, etc., might also be present (cf. the
remarks on iv 15). Finally Peter, or Silvanus speaking in his
name, warns the elders in vs. 3 against oppressing their "lots," that
is the groups "allotted" to them. How large these groups were is
not known, but the author may have in mind smaller groups within
a local parish. Analogies to this are represented by the Qumran
texts and the Damascus documents which are related to them; for
here, groups of ten persons are mentioned (1QS vi. 3; CDC
xiii. 1 f.). Further, the elders ought to guard against hierarchical
arrogance and rather be examples to the flock in humility and
unpretentiousness. The reward for their humbleness will be pro-

vided at the appearing of the Chief Shepherd, vs. 4. Then they
will be crowned with the honor and glory from which they must
abstain during their ministry in the earthly church.

In the same way the "juniors" of the congregations ought to
show respect to the "seniors," or elders, vs. 5a. The difference
between the groups referred to is more than a matter of age. According to vss. 1–4, the "elders" constitute the leaders of the church
or the shepherds, and in this position they are treated as colleagues
of the apostle Peter. The "juniors" thus represent the rest of the
congregation. If the leading men of the congregation are not to appear arrogant but humble, then the other members of the congregation ought to be willing to submit to their leaders.

All individual members of the church, both superiors and sub-
ordinates, ought to clothe themselves with humility, vs. 5b. The
necessity for this is reinforced by a citation from Prov iii 34
(according to LXX): God resists the arrogant ones, but to the
humble he proffers grace. Unpretentiousness on the part of the
individual is a condition of life for all the members of the church,
whatever their position in the hierarchy or social organization of
the church.

## 12. TRUST IN GOD AND STEADFASTNESS
## (v 6–11)

V ⁶ Humble yourselves therefore under God's mighty hand so that he may exalt you in due time. ⁷ Cast all your anxiety upon him, for he cares for you.ᵃ ⁸ Be sober and vigilant. Your adversary, the devil, lurks about as a roaring lion seeking someone to devour. ⁹ Resist him, firm in the faith, knowing that the same experiences of suffering confront your brothers in the world. ¹⁰ And the God of all grace who has called you to his eternal glory, after you have suffered for a little in Christ, will restore, support, strengthen, and establish you. ¹¹ To him belongs the power forever and ever. Amen.

ᵃ Ps lv 23

### COMMENT

Humility, vs. 6, is not only to characterize the relationship of the Christians one to another (as was emphasized in vs. 5), but it is also to be the manner of the whole church in meeting God's dispensations. The reward will be exaltation when the time comes. Consequently there is no occasion for anxiety now, vs. 7, but all earthly worries may be placed upon him, who in his fatherly care sustains and guides his faithful ones toward the determined goal. Along with this freedom from concern go soberness and vigilance, vs. 8a, for it is easy to become entangled in the world's temptations. Behind them stands the devil, vs. 8b, who lurks about like a roaring lion on the lookout for prey. His chief objective is to make Christians apostatize from the faith because of the strains and sufferings which he brings to them. It is on this account that the admonition to sobriety and vigilance is necessary. Thus the believers are urged in vs. 9a to resist the devil with firmness in the faith. They are also to remember, vs. 9b, that they do not suffer alone, for their Christian brothers in the world endure the same afflictions.

Finally, vs. 10 assures the reader in solemn phrases that God in his grace will strengthen and confirm the believers so that they do not fall. He has called them to his eternal glory, which they will share after they have suffered for a short time in Christ.[48] And the necessary strength comes from God, vs. 11, for he is all-powerful forever and ever.

# 13. SUMMARY, GREETING, A WISH FOR PEACE
## (v 12–14)

V  12 By Silvanus, the faithful brother, as I regard him, I have briefly written to you to exhort you and to testify that this is a true grace of God; in view of it remain steadfast.

13 The congregation in Babylon, chosen like you, and my son Mark greet you. 14 Greet one another with a kiss of love.

Peace be to you all, who are in Christ.


## COMMENT

Silvanus in vs. 12a is probably identical with the Silas of Acts xv 22–40 who accompanied Paul on his missionary journeys and, under the name of Silvanus, is designated along with Timothy as co-author of First and Second Thessalonians. In the Introduction it was pointed out that this disciple of the apostles probably wrote the epistle in Peter's name, at the apostle's request. A further testimony in support of this view are the words about the "faithful brother." The trustworthiness of Silvanus would hardly have been a matter of concern if he had served only as an amanuensis to the apostle. As a modifier of the adjective "faithful" he adds the words "as I consider him." By doing this in the name of Peter the author has avoided the impresson of self-praise.

In vs. 12b an epitome of the contents and purpose of the whole epistle is given. With the authority and support of the leading apostle of the church who is honored especially in Rome, the author wishes to admonish and comfort the Christians of Asia Minor in their troublesome situation, suspected of disloyalty and exposed to mistreatment because of their heathen neighbors. He wishes to certify the fact that their present difficulty constitutes a true grace of God.

Therefore he challenges the recipients, who are to a large extent recently converted Christians, to remain steadfast with reference to God's true grace,[49] so that they may in full measure receive it.

Then in vs. 13 a greeting is conveyed from "the co-elect congregation in Babylon," and also from the apostle's "son," Mark. Babylon must here be a symbol of Rome (as in Rev xiv 8, xvi 19, xvii 5, xviii 2, 10, 21); the Mesopotamian Babylon had no significance in the days of the early church. Mark is probably that John Mark of Jerusalem (known from Acts xii 12, 25, xv 37 ff.). Peter had connections with him even before he left Jerusalem (Acts xii 12, etc.). Later on Mark accompanied Paul and attended this apostle during his imprisonment (Col iv 10; Philem 24; cf. II Tim iv 11). If this refers to the imprisonment at Rome, then Mark was there during the first part of the sixties. According to an important tradition reported by Papias (ca. A.D. 135), however, Mark was a co-laborer of Peter during the last period of the apostle's activity and after his death composed the second gospel on the basis of Peter's preaching and instruction. Although the notice of Papias cannot be fully verified, and may have originated secondarily on the basis of the concluding verses of First Peter, it certainly speaks of the same Mark, who was a native of Jerusalem and served with both Peter and Paul in their work. At the close of the epistle he is called Peter's "son," in his position as a disciple and co-worker of this chief apostle. Greetings are addressed to the readers from the church at Rome, and from Mark as well as from the apostle himself. And in vs. 14a the recipients are urged to transmit this greeting by saluting each other with a kiss of love. The custom of holy kissing was common in the early church at the celebration of the Lord's supper. It is feasible to suppose that the readers are assembled for the celebration of this sacrament, after they have now, according to iii 21, attended and celebrated a baptism (cf. also the allusions to the Lord's supper in ii 3). An analogy to this thought association occurs in I Cor xvi 20, 22 (a holy kiss, and then a eucharistic key phrase, *Māranathā*).

The epistle ends with a greeting of peace, vs. 14b. This also gains in significance, as being the words of the chief apostle Peter and the Roman congregation. After the decline of the primitive church in Jerusalem at the beginning of the sixties, the church at

Rome acquired ever greater prestige and authority, not least because its members resided in the capital of the world. To this city the apostle Paul had come as a prisoner about the same time (Acts xxviii 16). Peter, too, probably arrived here toward the end of his life, as is assumed in vs. 13 ("Babylon"). Later traditions of the church definitely make this assertion (above all, I Clem. 5:2–4; cf. the General Introduction). So the Christians of Rome were justified in the claim that the foremost apostles were with them. The greeting and wish for peace, important as an expression of good will from the great church in the west, nevertheless conveys a more explicit significance. For as the many preceding admonitions to loyalty and soberness of judgment indicate, dangerous tendencies toward disturbance actually existed in the communities of the recipients. It is with special reference to this danger that a prayer of peace is offered in the name of the leading apostle and the great congregation of Rome. Thus in every detail the author of this marvelous epistle pays regard to the particular needs of his readers.

# Textual Notes

1. Greek, *eis*, probably dependent on *elpís*, not on *anagennḗsas*.
2. Greek, *ei déon*, "if it is required."
3. Greek, *hína*, "in order that."
4. The word *polytimóteron* is taken here as a modifier of *tò dokímion*. It might, however, be referred to *heurethê*.
5. In the preceding clause the negative is *ou* which has a more absolute sense; here it is *mḗ* which has a more conditional meaning.
6. Greek, *autá*, accusative of specification.
7. Greek, *parakýpsai*, literally "to lean over."
8. The speaker uses an imperative in the aorist tense, *elpísate*, to emphasize the singularity and integrity of the action.
9. Greek, *paroikía*, an expression denoting residence in a place without the rights of citizenship; cf. Hebrew *gēr*, "resident alien."
10. Greek, *hōs*, "as much as," here "nothing less than," as in John i 14.
11. "The lamb" is used here as an epithet rather than as a noun in apposition to "Christ." Compare "glorious King David" as against "David, the glorious king."
12. Greek, *hēgnikótes*, perfect participle of *hagnízo*, which means "to purify," and is used primarily in connection with ritual purifications.
13. Greek, *ei*, "if," but actually with a causal meaning, as in John xiii 14, 32; Acts iv 9; I Pet i 17.
14. Greek, (*líthos*) *akrogōniaîos*. In both the Hebrew and Greek texts of Isa xxviii 16, this expression is connected with the concept of "foundation," so that the meaning is undoubtedly "cornerstone" or "foundation stone," the stone upon which the house rests and which keeps the house together.
15. Greek, *kephalḕ gōnías*. Here, this word probably means "cornerstone." It may, however, also refer to the keystone over a door, since the context of the Psalm quoted speaks of doors or portals.
16. An explicative *kaí*, as for instance in Rom i 5.

17. Greek, *basíleios,* not *basilikós,* which appears to mean "being in royal service," in John iv 46, 49.

18. Greek, *aretaí,* in Hellenistic Greek often used for the wonderful deeds of a god.

19. Greek, *kakopoioí.* Compare the passage on Nero quoted above, Suet. *Vit. Ner.* 16:2, according to which the Christians were suspected of being "a kind of men given to a new and malefic superstition." Here, the Latin expression *maleficus* corresponds verbally to the *kakopoiós* of I Pet ii 12, which also occurs in ii 14, iii 16, and iv 15. This correspondence is certainly not accidental.

20. The Greek word, *episkopê,* "visitation," is here used in a favorable sense.

21. Greek, *agathopoieîn.* This verb is used throughout First Peter in contrast with *kakopoieîn.* For this reason it does not specifically denote pious deeds, but acting rightly in general with regard to society, proper civil behavior in contradistinction to criminality. Compare also Rom xiii 3 f.; II Thess iii 13; Titus iii 8 ff.

22. Greek, *timêsate,* aorist, by which the action is comprehended as a single fact.

23. Greek, *timâte,* present tense, so that the permanence of the action is emphasized.

24. Greek, *oikétai,* used not only of domestic slaves, but of slaves in general.

25. Greek, *dià syneidêseōs Theoû.* In this epistle the word *syneídēsis,* which occurs also in iii 16, 21, does not mean "conscience," but "consent," "positive attitude," even "intention," "will." For in these instances, as in many others, *syneídēsis* is not related to *sýnoida emautô,* but to *sýnoidá tini,* "I agree with somebody or something." In ii 19 the meaning can be rendered, "because of an attitude of mind belonging to God" (genitive of quality), or rather "with the approval of God" (genitive of origin). As to this and other problems of First Peter's vocabulary and theology, see the discussions in the present writer's book, *The Disobedient Spirits and Christian Baptism* (1946).

26. Greek, *agathopiûsai.* Cf. ii 15, 20, and note 21.

27. Greek, *ptóēsis,* "fear," evidently in an active sense, as in Prov iii 25, the text of which is quoted here. Cf. note 33.

28. Greek, *tò gynaikeîon,* scil. *skeûos.* On account of the order of words, the expression probably does not belong with the preceding but with the following participle. The word *skeûos* virtually means "vessel." It is used in Jewish sources to express a collective idea; this is also the case in Acts x 11, 16, xi 5; Rom ix 21 ff.; II Tim ii 20 f. Hence the translation "element," which fits the sense of the passage above, and is based

on several linguistic analogies. This is not true of the common translation, "sex."

29. Greek, *synoikéō*, "to live together," which is not used exclusively of a husband's relationship with his wife.

30. The context requires that *asthenésteron* be understood in the comparative sense, although so far as form is concerned it could be taken as an elative.

31. Greek, *timé*, which also has this meaning in the important analogy to vs. 7 quoted in the next clause of the text above, I Cor xii 23 f.

32. Greek, *enkóptesthai*, often used of making a road impassable by means of barricades and pit-holes.

33. Greek, *phóbos*, used here with active force of something that causes fear. Cf. note 27.

34. Greek, *syneídēsis agathé*. As was pointed out in note 25, *syneídēsis* in this epistle has the meaning of "consent," "positive attitude," or "will." Cf. ii 19, iii 21. Here the context indicates that it is a question of a positive attitude or good will toward society. This is also the case in Acts xxiii 1 (*pásē syneidései agathé pepolíteumai*), xxiv 16; Heb xiii 18.

35. Greek, *epēreázō*. The verb is related to *ará*, "curse," and *aré*, "violence"; compare the name of Ares.

36. Greek, *perì hamartiôn*, a technical term for "sin offering" taken over from LXX.

37. Greek, *en hô*, "on which occasion," i.e., at Christ's death and resurrection. It is incorrect to connect *en hô* with the preceding "spirit," for it makes no sense to state that Christ's spirit or soul was made alive, and then to add, "in which he went away." The difficulty is avoided, however, as soon as it is recognized that *en hô* is always a conjunction in First Peter. Besides iii 19, it also occurs in i 6, ii 12, iii 16, and iv 4. In the present case it is quite natural to understand *en hô* as a temporal conjunction referring to Christ's death and resurrection, which have just been mentioned. "On that occasion," "in that connection," he went away to preach.

38. The verb used to indicate Christ's "preaching" to the spirits is *kērýssō*. In the New Testament this is the technical expression for announcing the "kerygma," i.e., the proclamation of the Christian preachers that Jesus is Christ, that the Suffering Servant is the Lord. This is probably also the content of Christ's preaching to the spirits in prison.

39. Greek, *hò kaí*. As is often the case in the New Testament, *kaí* may be regarded here as modifying the relative pronoun. Furthermore, as the clause is an example of "relative connection," the pronoun is best rendered as a demonstrative.

40. Greek, *antítypon báptisma*, which is most easily understood as an appositional antecedent drawn into the relative clause.

41. Greek, *eperótēma*, literally "inquiry," but often used as a designation for a contract. This is based on the fact that agreements were confirmed through a solemn procedure of questioning and answering.

42. Greek, *syneídēsis*, with the basic meaning of "consent" or "positive attitude," as in ii 19, iii 16 (see notes 25 and 34). Cf. *énnoia*, "mind," iv 1, and the characteristic expression *báptisma metanoías*, "a baptism involving a change of mind," Mark i 4.

43. The conjunction *hóti* introducing this clause probably means "for" and not "that," since it is hardly possible to attribute to Christ any special consideration as a reason for his suffering.

44. Greek, *asélgeiai*. The adjective *aselgés* has an obscure origin, but is used with the meaning "unmanageable," etc.

45. Greek, *kômoi*, originally used for village festivities at which people went about reveling and dancing.

46. Greek, *eidólolatríai*, in the plural.

47. In the expression *nḗpsate eis proseuchás*, the preposition appears to have a consecutive meaning: "Become sober so as to [bring about] prayers," "so that it leads to prayers."

48. Greek, *en Christô*. On account of the rhythm of the clause, this expression is suitably joined to the following participle.

49. Another form of the verb "to stand," represented in later manuscripts, implies the following meaning: "God's true grace, in which you are standing." Linguistically this is simpler, but probably it is a secondary reading, just because it is more convenient.

# THE SECOND EPISTLE OF PETER

# Introduction

The second epistle attributed to Peter is a message to Christians in general. In view of his approaching death and Christ's return, the apostle warns them to be steadfast and to avoid corruption.

Undeniably the epistle presents the apostle Peter as its *author*. It opens with a greeting from Symeon Peter (i 1); it refers to his personal experience of the Lord's transfiguration (i 16–18); and it emphasizes that after First Peter this was the second epistle he wrote (iii 1).

Nevertheless it must be recognized that here, still more than in the first epistle, it is reasonable to suppose that a follower of Peter composed the writing in the name of this great man. The prophecy concerning the death of the apostle (i 14) does not absolutely confirm the Petrine authorship. Of course Peter, especially if writing at an advanced age, may well have had presentiments of his departure. But when it is said that Jesus had already foretold this, the utterance may as easily have been reproduced by somebody who had either heard Peter speak of it, or was aware of a tradition corresponding to that found in a late appendix of the fourth gospel (John xxi 18). Another questionable point is the writer's anxiety that his readers continue to recall the apostolic instruction after the decease of the leading apostle (i 15; cf. iii 2). Such an exhortation may have been ascribed to Peter after his death by a follower, writing in the apostle's name and eager to preserve the apostolic tradition. The account of Jesus' transfiguration (i 16–18) does not supply specific details, and so may also be due to the author's having heard the story from Peter or from the Evangelists. On the whole the epistle contains no information about Jesus and the apostles which might not also have been available to a follower of Peter. If finally the strongly Hellenistic

language and imagery of Second Peter are considered (see the remarks below), it becomes extremely difficult to ascribe this epistle
to Peter, the Galilean fisherman. Because of these obstacles, it is
more likely that a follower of Peter was the author, though his
identity is unknown.

Provided that another man wrote the epistle in the name of the
apostle, the *date* of composition must have been after Peter's death.
Circumstances do not, as in the case of First Peter, justify any
earlier dating. For on the one hand the earliest possible date
of the first epistle is shortly before Peter's death around A.D. 64
—the chronology adopted in the present work. On the other hand,
this very writing is referred to by the second epistle as being already
recognized Scripture (iii 1), a status which it cannot possibly have
reached until some years after its composition. Thus the second
epistle was probably written a considerable time after Peter's martyrdom.

Many scholars have assigned Second Peter to a date as late as
around A.D. 150. This has been done on insufficient grounds.
References to Gnosticism and other movements are not conclusive,
as these were already present in the first century. Another argument
often advanced is that Second Peter is dependent on the epistle
of Jude, which is also believed to be one of the latest books of
the New Testament. The case for such literary dependence has by
no means been established (see also the Introduction to Jude).
But even if it were, there is still no reason to date either epistle
so late.

The present writer is inclined to date Second Peter about A.D. 90.
For if one takes into consideration the positive attitude toward
the magistrates and society expressed in Second Peter as well as
Jude (II Pet ii 10; Jude 8), then a suitable background for both
of these epistles is to be found some years before the end of the
reign of Domitian (A.D. 81–96). During his last two years this
despot instigated a persecution of the Christians because of their
refusal to pay respect to the emperor. After this experience it would
be quite impossible for Christians to speak so appreciatively of the
magistrates, as in Second Peter and Jude. On the contrary, the state
now became a cruel and unpredictable adversary of the Christians,
as it is presented in the book of Revelation. It is not likely, therefore,

that Second Peter and Jude were composed later than Domitian's persecution of the Christians around A.D. 95. The preceding years of Domitian's reign, however, provide an ideal historical setting for these epistles. Obviously their authors wish to oppose certain propaganda for political freedom, propaganda which they regard as hostile to the social order, and to which the Christians have been exposed by the magnates and their parties. This fits especially well into the latter half of Domitian's reign, during which the aristocrats and the senators of the empire fought with desperation against Domitian's tyranny (Suet. *Vit. Dom.* 10).*

During this period also the First Epistle of Clement of Rome was written. Clement likewise seeks to quiet unrest among his readers and admonishes them to maintain law and order. Of course these disturbances might be attributed to other causes, since Clement urges primarily upon his readers in Corinth loyalty toward the authorities of the church. Nevertheless, the desire to avoid conflict with the state is prominent here as well. Clement also warns against disturbances and prompts his readers to maintain peaceful relations with the state, 60:4–61:2. This similarity between Second Peter and First Clement strengthens the case for dating Second Peter during the years preceding Domitian's persecution of the church, or about A.D. 90.

The actual *place* of origin does not greatly matter, but since the author wrote in the name of Peter, he must have desired his readers to associate the letter with Rome. And in this way he could easily capitalize on the authority of the Roman church. It is altogether possible that he was justified in doing so, just as the author of First Clement had the right to speak in the name of the Roman congregation.

The *recipients* of the epistle are addressed in general terms as "those who have for their share a faith as precious as ours" (i 1). Later it is said that this is Peter's second epistle to them (iii 1). Thus it appears as though the author is addressing the same readers in Asia Minor who are referred to in I Pet i 1 (see the Introduction and the commentary to that epistle). But failure to designate a specific audience rather indicates that the second epistle is intended

---

* Compare the references given in our commentary on James, which seems to reflect the same political situation.

for the church in general. Gentile Christians seem chiefly to be thought of as the readers, which is evident from the fact that Jewish traditions are referred to with a certain caution, while it is taken for granted that Paul is a recognized authority (iii 15 f.).

In *form* Second Peter is a so-called "testament." Among the Jews this was a popular type of literature based upon such farewell speeches as those of Moses in Deuteronomy. An originally Jewish, and later Christian, collection known as the Testaments of the Twelve Patriarchs is the classical example of this literary form. The characteristic setting depicts a man of God as he bids farewell to his intimate associates. He speaks about his imminent death and offers admonitions and edifying words, specifically pointing out that his survivors will have to endure the calamities that are about to come upon them without the support of his presence in their midst. The New Testament contains examples of this literary form in Jesus' farewell speech (John xiii–xvii), in Paul's farewell to the Ephesian elders (Acts xx 17–38), in Second Timothy, and in this epistle. Compare the characteristic mention of the speaker's imminent death (Acts xx 25; II Tim iv 6; II Pet i 14 f.), and his distress that after his departure false teachers will come to unsettle the congregation (Acts xx 29 f.; II Tim iii 1–9; II Pet ii 1–22, iii 3 f.). All this justifies the designation of Second Peter as a "testament," rather than as an epistle. The epistolary pattern appears only in the indefinite salutation in the first two verses. No greeting at all appears at the end.

The *diction* of Second Peter is peculiar and hard to understand. Long sentences are joined together with disregard for the balance and clarity required by classical taste. Elaborate and exquisite constructions are used by choice, instead of those simple, concrete expressions and colloquial features characteristic of the gospels and other New Testament writings. Several picturesque illustrations are used, strong, rhetorical metaphors such as ravenous beasts, and clouds chased by the storm (ii 12, 17), instead of traditional ideas from everyday life and agriculture. In view of this mode of presentation, the reader is apt to make comparison with European art and literature of the baroque period. Second Peter virtually embodies a school of Greek rhetoric which embraced an artificial style comparable to that of the baroque. This was the so-called "Asian-ism" that competed with strict Atticism. It was called "Asian" style because its foremost representatives came from Asia Minor, and it was characterized by a loaded, verbose, high-sounding manner of expression leaning toward the novel and bizarre, and careless about violating classic ideals of simplicity. An example is the grandiose inscription of the first pre-Christian century at Nemrud-Dagh in eastern Asia Minor honoring Antiochus I of Commagene.[1] Many stylistic analogies to it may be found in Second Peter. Our epistle was undoubtedly written in conformity with the rules of the Asianic school which was still important during the first Christian century.

This mode of presentation hardly conforms to the aesthetic con-cepts of modern readers, but when Second Peter is viewed against its own literary background, it is not as awkward in form as several modern expositors are inclined to make it. At the same time the author may have been writing out of an Aramaic or Latin linguistic background which contributed to the violation of the rules of Attic rhetoric. But more important is his adoption of a style then fashionable in literature. And he did not choose this style merely for its superficial effect. It was for him the natural medium for the expression of his richly variegated imagination. His intense feel-ing for the seriousness of the situation, and his fervent zeal in delivering his message should not be overlooked. Even if emotional intensity overrides proper literary form, with the result that the epistle takes on the quality of antique baroque, the reader cannot fail to be moved by the apocalyptic fervor of this "testament."

The *purpose* of Second Peter is to admonish the church to be steadfast and to warn it against deceivers. Of these two themes, chapters i and iii discuss the first, and chapter ii deals with the second.

More specifically, the *content* of Second Peter may be divided as follows:

I. ARDENT DEVOTION TO THE CALL AND TO THE HOPE OF THE RE-
TURN OF JESUS, i 1–21

1. *Words of greeting,* i 1–2
2. *Eager adherence to the gift of election,* i 3–11
3. *A reminder necessary in view of the imminent death of the
   apostle,* i 12–15
4. *Jesus' transfiguration as a guarantee of his return,* i 16–18
5. *Prophecy as a further guarantee,* i 19–21

II. WARNING AGAINST DECEIVERS, ii 1–22

6. *Seducers exploit the Christians,* ii 1–3
7. *The flood and Sodom and Gomorrah,* ii 4–9
8. *The seducers defame authorities,* ii 10–14
9. *Like Balaam the seducers receive money from non-Christians,*
   ii 15–17
10. *The seducers promise freedom,* ii 18–22

III. CHRIST'S COMING AND THE FINAL JUDGMENT REQUIRE BLAME-
LESSNESS AND STEADFASTNESS, iii 1–18

11. *Adherence to instruction,* iii 1–2
12. *The skepticism of the mockers,* iii 3–7
13. *Two mistakes about the delay of the end,* iii 8–9
14. *The day of the Lord,* iii 10
15. *Preparedness for the day of the Lord,* iii 11–18

The division of the epistle into three chapters, which dates back
to the Middle Ages, indicates its main sections. Its core is chapter
ii with the vigorous warnings against profligate teachers of heresy.
This chapter is commonly assumed to be nothing more than a
copy of Jude, with which it has many parallels. But it also contains
many independent thoughts. A mechanical dependence on Jude
cannot be proved, nor is it probable. The authors of the two epistles
probably relied on a sermonic pattern then current and which had
been formulated to resist the dangerous teachers of heresy of whom
this chapter speaks. In drawing on this common source, the author

of Second Peter has placed it in a more detailed setting, prefaced by chapter i and followed by chapter iii. A synopsis and a further discussion of the parallels between Second Peter and Jude will be found in the Introduction to the latter epistle.

# Translation and Comment

## 1. WORDS OF GREETING
### (i 1–2)

**I** [1] Symeon Peter, servant and apostle of Jesus Christ, to those who have for their share a faith as precious as ours, by means of the righteousness of our God and Savior Jesus Christ. [2] Grace be with you, and may peace abound through intimate knowledge of God and Jesus, our Lord.

### COMMENT

Exactly as in Acts xv 14, Peter's first name in vs. 1 has its Hebrew form Symeon (Heb. *Šim'ōn*). The author may have been a Jew. But he may also have wished to make the name appear especially venerable. In any case, Peter's authoritative position is underscored through the following appositional phrase "servant and apostle of Jesus Christ." The recipients are the Gentile Christians in general who are said to have gained a faith as precious as that of the apostle and his intimates. This has happened as a result of Christ's righteousness, or in other words, because of his gracious provision for and desire to save those far away. In this connection Christ is expressly called God and Savior. Though in the next verse God and Jesus are distinguished, here the second person of the Godhead is meant. For in the Greek text, the definite article links the two words, God and Savior.[2] Just as in Titus ii 13 ("our great God and Savior Christ Jesus"), Christ is presented as the divine Savior, a concept well known in the Hellenistic world. A wish for grace and peace follows in vs. 2. This wish agrees in form with I Pet i 2, except that certain words regarding knowledge are added. The hope is expressed that the readers may be filled more and more with peace through intimate knowledge of God and the Lord Jesus, who are here treated as two individuals. The expression "intimate knowledge" or "adequate gnosis" appears repeatedly in the epistle. But the emphasis is not on the mystic experiences characteristic of Gnosticism, the representatives of which were proud of their "gnosis" in the sense of ecstatic contact with eternity (cf. I Cor viii 1; II Cor xii 1–5). The author rather speaks polemically against the influence of Gnosticism (cf. Rev ii 14 f.). Here it is a matter of continuously deepening knowledge of God's words in the plan of salvation, the life in Christ, and the eschatological hope. The believers were instructed in these subjects, when they were accepted into church fellowship, and it is now their responsibility to improve and apply their knowledge in these matters.

## 2. EAGER ADHERENCE TO THE GIFT OF ELECTION
### (i 3–11)

I  3 His divine power has granted us everything that contributes to a life in godly fear, through the intimate knowledge of the one who has called us by his own glory and virtue. 4 Thereby, the priceless and magnificent promises have been granted us so that through them you may become sharers in divine nature, while avoiding that corruption in the world which is lust. 5 To this end exert all diligence so that by your faith you may further virtue, by virtue knowledge, 6 by knowledge self-control, by self-control perseverance, by perseverance godly fear, 7 by godly fear brotherly kindness, and by brotherly kindness love.

8 When these items are present and increase among you, they will make you neither idle nor unfruitful in the intimate knowledge of our Lord Jesus Christ. 9 Anyone without these is blind, shortsighted, and has forgotten that he was cleansed from his old sins. 10 Therefore, brothers, be the more eager to confirm your calling and election. For if you do this, you will never stumble. 11 In this way, entrance into the eternal kingdom of our Lord and Savior Jesus Christ will be amply provided for you.

### COMMENT

In the original text, vss. 3–4 form a genitive construction introduced by "as." The main clause follows in vs. 5 and is introduced by the expression "to this end." In the present translation, the complicated sentence has been divided into shorter principal clauses for the sake of clarity. Abstract substantival expressions have also been avoided in vs. 9. Here as well as in the following sections, a literal translation would sound too bombastic. The ancients were more used to rhetorical extravagance.

First the Christians are said in vs. 3 to have received their spiritual armor at the time of their call. This armor, which is needed for a continued life in godly fear,[3] consists in the knowledge of God who has called the believers to the glory and virtue (the same word that is used in vs. 5 to designate the commendable behavior of the believers) characteristic of him ("his own"). God's precious and magnificent promises given of old, vs. 4, have been fulfilled in the spiritual gifts which the believers have now received. Through these gifts the Christians become partakers of "divine nature," an expression that appears strange in a New Testament writing, but which may be understood as an accommodation to popular Greek philosophy, especially Stoicism (cf. the General Introduction and the comments on iii 7). In fact, the author here employs this concept well known in Hellenistic and particularly in Stoic circles in order to emphasize the same point that Paul expresses by relating how a convert is freed from the world through baptism, is clothed in Christ, and becomes a new man (Rom vi 5; Eph iv 22 ff.). But the believers will have to avoid that corruption, prevalent in the world, which is lust.

After establishing this, vs. 5a continues by urging the believers to strive diligently to be worthy of these wonderful gifts. Here occurs an interchange between the indicative and the imperative moods, which is characteristic of the New Testament. Compare for example Philip ii 12 f.: "Work at your salvation with fear and trembling . . . for it is God who works in you both the willingness and the deed." Another kind of interchange may be found in the transition from the first to the second person. Throughout, the writer is speaking about the believers in general and does not separate the apostles from the others. Inasmuch as the Christians have obtained the promised gifts of the spirit which impart divine strength and enable them to live in godly fear, they are diligently to strive so to live. More specifically according to vss. 5b–7 they are to let one gift "further" the other so that the basic gift of faith promotes virtue (cf. vs. 3), virtue promotes knowledge, etc. A detailed list of such ethical relationships is presented. Some of these constituted well-known Hellenistic ideals and were especially prominent in the propaganda of the Stoic philosophers; the author seems to have borrowed them from his contemporaries. However, they have been transplanted into the structure of Christian faith. The author did not wish to Hellenize the church, but only employed such expressions because they would be familiar to his readers. His enumeration of virtues may be arranged in the following manner, showing that the biblical ideals of faith, knowledge, and fear of God are fundamental, vss. 5b–7:

1) faith: virtue
2) knowledge: self-control, perseverance
3) godly fear: brotherly kindness, love.

The first virtue mentioned under 1, 2, and 3 respectively, concerns the Christian's relationship to God; the others relate him to society. Each virtue is presented as dependent on the immediately preceding one, and the whole series culminates in the two final virtues, brotherly kindness and love, which are especially vital to harmony in the church.

The believers are therefore to bear fruits worthy of the gifts received, vs. 8. In so doing they will attain to a real knowledge of Jesus Christ as well as fellowship with him. If on the other hand, the Christian is indifferent to the improvement of these virtues in life, vs. 9, he is blind, shortsighted, and forgetful. In such a case it is impossible to boast of knowledge and vision, as some teachers of heresy are trying to do. Their mistake is that they have forgotten the basic fact of their cleansing from sin received at baptism and acceptance into the church. It is necessary to retain this purifying experience, and consequently important to develop the power of salvation received at that time. As it is stated in vs. 10: work diligently to make your calling and election sure. Here the idea of confirming their election is not to be taken in a cognitive but in a practical sense: to make concrete progress. If the believers do this they will not stumble. Through such a growth of the gifts of grace already received, vs. 11, a grand road to eternal salvation is built and prepared.

## 3. A REMINDER NECESSARY IN VIEW OF THE IMMINENT DEATH OF THE APOSTLE
### (i 12–15)

I 12 Therefore, I intend to remind you constantly of these things even though you know them, and have been confirmed in the present truth. 13 But I think it right, as long as I am still in this tabernacle, to stimulate you by a memorandum, 14 since I know that I must soon lay away my tabernacle, just as our Lord Jesus Christ told me. 15 I am also eager, indeed, that after my departure you will always be able to recall these things to mind.

### COMMENT

The recipients of the epistle had enjoyed catechumenal instruction, vs. 12, but needed nevertheless to be continuously reminded of the basic power of Christian living. Before the apostle lays down his tabernacle, vs. 13, which is the body (cf. II Cor v 1), those who in the end may be sleeping must be awakened by a reminder. Peter knows, vs. 14, that he must soon leave this bodily tabernacle as Jesus had also hinted to him (cf. John xxi 18). Nevertheless the apostle states in vs. 15 that he will always be concerned that his readers be able to call to mind what they had learned. How could the speaker, even after his death, help keep the Christians awake and prepared? The answer is not hard to find: The author has attributed to Peter the same line of thinking which Jesus employed in the speech concerning the Comforter (John xiv 16f.), which, in form at least, may be regarded as a "testament." In both instances it is the Spirit, who rules over all preaching, that is responsible for the preservation of faith and hope.

# 4. JESUS' TRANSFIGURATION AS A GUARANTEE
## OF HIS RETURN
### (i 16–18)

I  16 For we did not follow any sophisticated myths, when we made known to you the coming of our Lord Jesus Christ in power, but it was because we had been eyewitnesses of his majesty. 17 He received from God the Father honor and glory, when the voice of the majestic Glory came to him as follows: "This is my Son, my Beloved one, whom I have approved."[a] 18 We heard this voice speaking from heaven, while we were with him on the holy mountain.

[a] Matt xvii 5

## COMMENT

In the preceding section the leading concern was the gospel and Christian teaching. In the present and following portions the author deals with fundamental aspects of this teaching, namely, the hope of Christ's return and of the consummation. He knows that some Christians have begun to waver in their faith in Christ's second advent and in the destruction and re-creation of the earth. This is evident from the more detailed presentation in chapter iii. But already in vss. 16–18 he addresses those who are doubtful about the last events and who have lost their hope. According to vs. 16 the message of Christ's return in power[4] is no slyly invented myth. It is rather a revealed truth, attested for the reader by Peter's own experience with Christ on the Mount of Transfiguration (Matt xvii 1–8 and parallels). At that time God himself expressly declared Jesus to be his Son, his Beloved one, vs. 17. By attributing to Jesus these well-known messianic titles (Ps ii 7; Isa v 1, xlii 1), God has affirmed that Jesus is the possessor of the greatest power and glory. When Peter, James, and John were with Jesus on the mount and witnessed the master's transfiguration, vs. 18, they themselves heard the heavenly voice delivering this message from God. Jesus' transfiguration must in turn be understood as an anticipatory sign of his coming glory. So the belief in Jesus' return in power and glory rests on attested historical events.

# 5. PROPHECY AS A FURTHER GUARANTEE
## (i 19–21)

I  ¹⁹ And we regard the prophetic word as most reliable. You do well to pay heed to it, as to a light which shines in a dark place, until the day dawns and the morning star arises in your hearts. ²⁰ Consider this in the first place, that no scriptural prophecy is the concern of private interpretation. ²¹ For no prophecy was ever uttered through human resolution, but it was men prompted by holy spirit who preached [what came] from God.[a]

[a] Some texts have, "It was holy men of God who preached."

## COMMENT

Like the testimony of the apostolic eyewitnesses, vs. 19, prophecy also confirms that the return of Jesus Christ in glory is imminent. As the author has Peter remark, the apostles agree in holding this word most trustworthy.[5] The readers ought to cling to that prospect of the future, painted by prophecy, just as a man traveling through a dark, desolate region may be guided by a light glimmering in the distance. Here is no danger of going astray. The day of Christ's coming will finally dawn. On that occasion the morning star will arise in the hearts of the believers, which means that their inner selves will then be completely illuminated (cf. Matt vi 23). According to vs. 20 it is important, however, to consider the danger of such an arbitrary exposition of the prophecies, as was practiced by certain apocalyptical troublemakers close to the church. The guarantee against that spiritual anarchy is the recognition that the

Holy Scripture must be interpreted by those who are properly qualified, who have been called by God and prompted by the Spirit,
which is true of the apostles and their legitimate successors. For
prophecy itself did not come into existence through the caprices of
private individuals, vs. 21, but through the preaching of men
prompted by holy spirit to bring announcements from God. Here,
the spirit is the divine power which stimulates the individual to
speak and to communicate superhuman wisdom. As for those who
revel in fantasies, their calculations of the end or denials of its
coming must be rejected as arbitrary. If the prophecies, on the other
hand, are used legitimately, they contain sure proofs of Christ's
return in glory.

# 6. SEDUCERS EXPLOIT THE CHRISTIANS
## (ii 1–3)

**II** 1 False prophets arose even among the people [of Israel], as false teachers will also be among you. These will smuggle destructive factional views in among you, and by denying the Lord who has purchased them, they will bring speedy destruction upon themselves. 2 And many will follow [them in] their brutalities. On account of these the way of truth will be defamed. 3 In their greed, under the guise of fictitious promises they will exploit you. But from of old their condemnation is not idle, and their destruction does not sleep.

### COMMENT

According to Deut xiv 1–5, false prophets were to arise among the children of Israel and would seek to entice the people into idolatry. In the same way, as stated here in vs. 1a, teachers of heresy are to arise among the Christians. "Teachers" in this context is not used in a strictly pedagogical sense, but has the more general meaning of "leaders."

The following items are characteristic of these false leaders:

a) Stealthily they introduce destructive factional views—party opinions—into the church, vs. 1b. The phrase is to be understood as referring to alien lines of thought, here of political stamp.

b) They deny the Lord who has purchased them, vs. 1c. The gist is that they have sold themselves to other masters. The context, and especially the comparison with Balaam in vs. 15, also shows that the issue concerns politically influential men who were anxious to have their opinions disseminated among the Christians. In order to attain this objective they used certain Christian leaders as their agents. As was pointed out in the Introduction, the epistle may suitably be dated in Domitian's reign, during which the senators and the aristocrats schemed against the power of the emperor (cf. also the commentary on Jude 16). The employers were probably some of these great men intent on revolution. Indeed, the supposition that they used church leaders as agents to gain as many adherents as possible among the Christians and thus further their political efforts is in conformity with a widespread practice in the Roman empire at that time. This was the custom technically called *ambulatio* and was vigorously opposed by the imperial power. It consisted in carrying on political and social propaganda with the help of the officers of flourishing religious and social organizations. The functionaries in question received financial remuneration for their services from their political employers. In view of this the remark that the false teachers denied the Lord who had bought them is easily understood. They permitted themselves to be bought by other employers, whose agents they became. For this reason, vs. 1d, they will bring swift destruction upon themselves.

c) These false leaders are further characterized, vs. 2, as having entangled many in their brutalities (cf. I Pet iv 3), so that Christianity or "the way of truth" is defamed. Propaganda for freedom, involving hostility to the existing government, easily attracts the multitude. Once the partisans have been incited to action, then violence is inevitable; thus the Christian faith is exposed to suspicion and defamation.

d) The movers of sedition are expressly said in vs. 3a to be motivated by covetousness (cf. 1QpHab viii. 11–13), and to exploit the Christians, making them an item of merchandise.[6] As was observed with regard to vs. 1c, this is understandable on the view that the seducers were political agents who, according to common practice, secured followers for certain magnates through bribes. Compare vs. 15 on Balaam. In doing so, these men are said to gain their ends on the basis of fictitious promises. In all likelihood the author refers to rosy promises of social freedom, something particularly attractive to the Christians, who, for the most part, were poor and very often maltreated and suppressed. This is confirmed by vs. 19: "promising them freedom."

But the condemnation of these false leaders, vs. 3b, was decided long ago. The author refers to Old Testament examples (see the following verses). One may also think of later Jewish traditions (like the passage on the spirits of iniquity in 1QS iv. 9–14, which contains many expressions reminiscent of the description of the teachers of heresy in Second Peter). And the actual judgment of these seducers is not far distant (cf. vs. 1d).

# 7. THE FLOOD
## AND SODOM AND GOMORRAH
### (ii 4–9)

II ⁴God did not [even] spare the angels who had sinned,ᵃ but cast them into hell to be kept in pitsᵇ of gloom, and thus abandoned them to judgment. ⁵And he did not spare the ancient world, but together with seven others he preserved Noah, a herald of righteousness, while bringing a deluge over the world of the ungodly.ᶜ ⁶He condemned the cities of Sodom and Gomorrah to destruction by reducing them to ashes,ᵈ and thus made them an object lesson for those who might turn to impiety. ⁷But he rescued the righteous Lot who was deeply troubled by the licentious conduct of the lawless. ⁸By what the righteous man saw and heard as he dwelt among them, he felt his honest soul tormented day after day because of [all] lawless deeds. ⁹Thus the Lord knows to save the pious from trial, but also to preserve the unrighteous for punishment until the day of judgment.

ᵃ Gen vi 1–4
ᵇ Another reading: "bonds" (cf. Jude 6).
ᶜ Gen vi 5–viii 22
ᵈ Gen xix 23 ff.

## COMMENT

In the original, vss. 4–9 form one long sentence. This consists of a series of clauses introduced by "if," with the connotation "as surely as," and a main clause beginning in vs. 9. In the translation above, the unit has been broken up into separate sentences for the sake of clarity. The passage draws upon examples from biblical antiquity to support the statement made in vs. 3b that the judgment and destruction of the contemporary teachers of heresy, decided long ago, are threateningly near.

Evidently the angels mentioned in vs. 4 are those described in Gen vi 1–4, and in more detail in First Enoch. They fell into sin on account of earthly women and were regarded as having caused war, violence, idolatry, and witchcraft. It is emphasized that even these heavenly angels were visited with the severest punishment. They were cast from heaven into hell, where they are kept in dark pits (cf. I Enoch 10:4) to be judged in due time. Because of the peculiar, even "Asianic" verb here meaning "to cast down," hell is surnamed Tartarus. As also in I Pet iii 19, the disobedient spirits are said to have been in prison from time immemorial. On the other hand there is no allusion to Christ's preaching, as in that passage. Concerning the duration of their arrest the author emphasizes that it will last until the day of judgment (as in I Enoch 10:12). Besides, he then observes in vs. 5a that the whole ancient world was destroyed on account of ungodliness (Gen vi 7), this being accomplished through a flood, vs. 5c (Gen vii 21). Sodom and Gomorrah were likewise visited with destruction because of their wickedness, vs. 6, on this occasion by brimstone and fire (Gen xix 24). What happened in ancient times, however, is properly a warning to the ungodly in the present time, for in the last days the events of primeval days will be repeated.

At the same time the disastrous events of antiquity provide a comforting pattern of salvation for the pious who live in the midst of ungodly surroundings. These prototypes are Noah, vs. 5b, and Lot, vss. 7–8. Noah is described as "the eighth" person among the saved ones, since he was saved with his wife, three sons, and three daughters-in-law (Gen viii 18). As in I Pet iii 20 (see the comments on this passage), the number "eight" suggests the idea of perfection and may be associated with such Christian institutions as the eighth day (Sunday), etc. Noah is further said to have been saved because he indefatigably preached righteousness in the midst of an ungodly world. Lot was deeply distressed by the godlessness and violence and licentiousness of his times, and was rescued because of his righteousness. Christians ought likewise to stand up against the tendencies of the seducers toward ungodly, violent, and lawless living.

The conclusion, vs. 9, is that the Lord saves his faithful ones but punishes the ungodly.

# 8. THE SEDUCERS
# DEFAME AUTHORITIES
## (ii 10–14)

II  10 [God] especially [punishes] those who, in filthy lust, follow what is flesh and despise authority. Impudent egoists, they are shameless enough to defame dignitaries. 11 Not even angels, who are superior in strength and power, bring a defamatory judgment against them before the Lord. 12 Those, however, are like brute animals, born primitive, to catch and destroy. By those whom they do not recognize, but defame in their corruption, they will also be destroyed, 13 thus deprived of the reward obtained for their unrighteousness. Finding pleasure in daytime revelry, they are blots and blemishes, reveling in their deceptions,*a* when they carouse with you. 14 Having eyes full of adultery and never ceasing from sin, they entice unstable souls. Having a heart expertly trained in covetousness, they are destined for damnation.

*a* Another reading: "at their love feasts" (Jude 12).


### COMMENT

In the foregoing passage examples were given showing that God punishes the unrighteous. This is now applied to the deceivers of the church.

Above all, the seducers distinguish themselves by deferring to influential subversive forces in society, and by reviling lawful authority. On account of this the author emphasizes in vs. 10 that

God especially punishes those who "walk after" or permit themselves to be controlled by "flesh," that is, human interests, and
despise all "majesty" or authority. This description fits those men
who, according to the view adopted here, are condemned by the
epistle: those who have offered their services to important men in
society, politically opposed to the existing order. The state of things
indicated at the beginning of the chapter (vss. 1–3) is thus made
the object of closer scrutiny. Furthermore, seducers of the Christians
are said to be defiant egoists, and to defame "glories," which may
be understood as dignitaries. The reference is probably to the magistrates of the society to whom several New Testament writings urge
obedience and respect, in particular the Pauline epistles (Rom
xiii 1–7; Titus iii 1 f.), but also First Peter (see the commentary on
I Pet ii 13–iv 6). In this connection the thoughts of the author
revert in vs. 11 to something that he probably gleaned from I Enoch
10:1–16, 12:3b–13:3, namely, that the archangels did not want
to present any defamatory judgment against their fallen brethren
among the angels. Moreover, according to I Enoch 64:1–69:1, the
fallen angels were regarded as standing behind the dignitaries of
the heathen state. So if the archangels did not wish to condemn the
fallen angels, the Christians ought not to defame the powers of the
state on which they depend. These powers are not to be detested,
as in Jewish apocalyptic literature, but regarded as preservers of
law and order (compare the widespread idea of a Pax Romana).
However, vs. 12, the teachers of heresy will be brought to ruin
by those whom they refuse to recognize and instead defame. This
is particularly true since the teachers of heresy are ravenous beasts
deprived of reason, even born "physical" which here is the same
as "primitive," and bent upon extortion and corruption. Such beasts
of prey are listed in more detail by another writing of the post-
apostolic period, the epistle of Barnabas, which shows that they were
a standard allegory for parasites (Barn. 10:1–8). The objects of
their rapacity are the Christians, whom they seek to win over to the
dubious purposes of their employers. But they will be destroyed by
the same authorities whom they defame and refuse to acknowledge.

As reward for their efforts, vs. 13a, the deceivers probably received part of the funds which the political agent had allocated for
distribution to accomplish his propaganda purposes. This would be
in accordance with a practice undertaken in antiquity by political

candidates. As unlawful *ambitus,* it was prosecuted by the authorities—likewise the activity of the intermediaries known as *sequestores.* However, the deceivers will forfeit this reward; compare the comments below on Balaam, vss. 15–17. Part of the accepted procedure was the incitement of the people through elaborate meals; this practice is probably referred to in vs. 13b. The teachers of heresy are said to distinguish themselves through revelry and gluttony at the meals that they celebrate with the Christians. In the principal New Testament manuscripts the meals in question are indicated as "deceptions." A variant reading, "love feasts," is meant to retain the line of thought which is preserved in Jude 12a. It is possible, though not so likely, that "deceptions" is a later correction made in order to avoid the expression "love feasts," which had become an object of suspicion.[7] According to vs. 14, the heretical teachers yearn to indulge in sinful lewdness. In the present context, this must have reference to contamination through paganism, as often in Old Testament descriptions. Into such licentious practices they are said to entice unstable souls among the Christians and are successful in this effort all too often. They are not motivated by any well-meaning idealism but only by ordinary greed, and have worked assiduously to satisfy it (cf. vs. 3a). They can count on receiving rewards from their wealthy employers (alluded to in vss. 15–16), if their agitation among the Christians meets with success. All this makes them children of a curse, as the text literally reads, that is, they are destined for damnation, just as the ancient sinners previously mentioned. The gospel must not be perverted and misused for such propaganda.

## 9. LIKE BALAAM THE SEDUCERS RECEIVE
## MONEY FROM NON-CHRISTIANS
## (ii 15–17)

II  15 Abandoning the straight path they have wandered astray. They have followed the path of Balaam, the son of Beor. He craved the reward of unrighteousness. 16 But he received a reprimand for his own transgression of the law. A dumb creature speaking with a human voice restrained the prophet from acting foolishly. 17 These are fountains without water and clouds driven by the storm, for whom the darkness of hell has been reserved.


### COMMENT

Life in the fellowship of the church is a straight path, vs. 15, but the teachers of heresy have forsaken it and are going astray. Their prototype is the false prophet Balaam who, according to Num xxxi 16, enticed the children of Israel to unfaithfulness toward the Lord (cf. Rev ii 14). In doing so, Balaam acted as the hired agent of a heathen potentate, Balak (Num xxii 7). For this reason he is said to have sought private gain through unrighteousness. In the same way the seducers of the Christians act as hired agents of foreign employers. According to vs. 16, Balaam's conduct was sheer transgression of the law. This statement is related to the fact that political agitation through such hired agents in societies and clubs was legally prohibited by Roman law (compare our remarks on vs. 13a). Furthermore it is emphasized that Balaam's transgression of the law was unveiled by a mere donkey which, through a miracle of the Lord, received the ability to speak as a man (Num xxii 28). In an analogous way, simple Christians are probably thought of as receiving the ability to correct these teachers of heresy. How irresponsible the deceivers are is finally shown in vs. 17 by the comparison with waterless fountains and clouds driven by the wind: they just depend upon others. Their punishment, however, is already determined, inasmuch as the black darkness of the underworld is prepared for them.

## 10. THE SEDUCERS PROMISE FREEDOM
### (ii 18–22)

II  18 They utter vain bombast and in fleshly lusts they entice,
by means of brutalities, men who have barely escaped from those
who live in error. 19 While promising them liberty they are
themselves slaves of corruption. For what a man obeys, to that
he is enslaved. 20 And if they have escaped the contaminations
of the world through personal knowledge of the Lord and Savior
Jesus Christ, but are again entangled and overcome by them, the
last state has become worse for them than the first. 21 Indeed, it
would have been better for them not to have known the way of
righteousness than once knowing it to turn away from the holy
commandment which was entrusted to them. 22 The point of
the true proverb applies to them: "A dog which returns to its
own vomit," and "A sow which has been washed [only] to
wallow in the mud."

COMMENT

In vs. 18, as in vs. 14, it is pointed out again that the teachers
of heresy prey upon the newly converted Christians whom they know
to be unstable in faith and easily influenced by their intrigues. A
particularly effective enticement, according to vs. 19a, is the promise of freedom given by these deceptive propagandists. That they
promised something of the sort substantiates the assumption that
these deceivers were politically aggressive. They are skilful in ex-
ploiting the social unrest prevalent in certain strata of the Roman
empire. But they cannot offer any real freedom, for they themselves

are slaves of corruption. It is a rule of life, vs. 19b, that one is a slave to that which controls him (in the Greek this clause has rhythmic form). Therefore it would have been better if these teachers of heresy had never known Christ, vs. 20, than to abandon the path of righteousness and the holy commandment, vs. 21. By forsaking them they act like a dog or a pig, vs. 22, animals that without concern revert to their natural filthiness at every opportunity. The vomit of the dog (Prov xxvi 11) is here an illustration of the aggressive propaganda of the seducers (cf. the "effusion" mentioned in I Pet iv 4, and the "froth" in Jude 13). In the figure of the sow (quotation of unknown origin), we may note that its washing is an ironical reference to the baptism of the heathen. Both dogs and swine were regarded by Jews as unclean animals, and thus suitable here to designate the false teachers.

## 11. ADHERENCE TO INSTRUCTION
### (iii 1–2)

**III** ¹ This is already, beloved, a second epistle which I write you. In [both of] them I endeavor to stimulate your sincere mind by a memorandum. ² Remember the words previously spoken by the holy prophets, and the commandment of the Lord and Savior transmitted by your apostles.

### COMMENT

In vs. 1 the author refers to First Peter and emphasizes that the purpose of both writings is the same, namely, in the form of a memorandum (cf. i 13) to urge the recipients to be watchful and awake. They must not permit themselves to be led astray by the worldly interests of the seducers, nor allow the sincere mind they have acquired to fall asleep again, but hold fast to the spirit of purity and of sonship, received through baptism. If, vs. 2, they remember or consider[8] the instruction of the prophets and apostles, they will have an authoritative rule of conduct. This shows that the apostolic traditions of the New Testament were already placed on a par with the prophecies of the Old Testament as norm-giving ideals for Christian living.

## 12. THE SKEPTICISM OF THE MOCKERS
### (iii 3–7)

III  3 You should understand this first, that in the last days ironic mockers who live according to their own lusts will appear and say: 4 "What has happened to the promise of his return? For since the fathers fell asleep all things have remained just as they were from the beginning of creation." 5 As they maintain this, they overlook the fact that long ago there were heavens and an earth sprung up from water and through water by means of God's word. 6 Because of them, the world of that time was flooded by water and perished. 7 But the present heavens and earth, through the same word, have been reserved for fire and are being kept for the day of the judgment and destruction of impious men.

### COMMENT

According to vs. 3, Peter takes it for granted that after his death, in the last days, ironic mockers[9] will arise. In their lives they will follow their own lusts without concern for the coming judgment. They arbitrarily question the promise of Christ's return, vs. 4. In support of their skepticism they refer to the fact that "the fathers" or the first generation of Christians, that is, the apostles and their contemporaries, have already passed away without any visible signs of a new order of things. Life on the earth continues as if nothing had happened. Everything operates mechanically according to the same routine. The viewpoint is similar to that of Qoheleth (Ecclesiastes); but because of the emphasis on the destruction of the world by fire, vs. 7, it is more probable that the mockers derived their attitudes from Stoicism (see below). Not least, these arrogant cynics make much of the fact that the Christians are subject to the same hardships as the rest of humanity. The hope of the return of the Son of man in glory, the reward of the faithful, and the punishment of the unrighteous, have apparently failed to materialize. The great metamorphosis did not occur as soon as the believers in the early church expected. In view of this disappointment certain groups found it convenient to reject the Christian hope and devote themselves exclusively to organizing their earthly existence as comfortably as possible. Thus they have not only abandoned all scruples themselves, but they wish to instill their philosophy in others and seduce faithful Christians to a similar skepticism and concentration on the good things of this life. For this reason the author is all the more urgent in warning his readers against the deceivers.

In answer to the skeptics it is pointed out in vss. 5–6 that prior to the present earth there was another world which was destroyed through the flood. "Because of them" probably refers to the heavens and the earth just mentioned (cf. iii 10). That catastrophe ought to serve as a warning. The author particularly emphasizes that it was God's word that brought the antediluvian world into existence, and also caused its destruction. Since it is the effective power behind everything, no one has the right to doubt God's word. This is especially absurd inasmuch as, according to vs. 7, it has also foretold the destruction of the present world, as well as the condemnation of the ungodly. A formal analogy obtains not only between the first days and the last days of the universe (i.e., between protology and eschatology), but in addition there is a common basis of operation which is absolutely fundamental: God's all-powerful word. For this word stood behind the original creation, and under the direction of God sustains the present world. If the same word now proclaims judgment and destruction upon the world, every reasonable person ought to believe it and submit to it as to the highest authority.

The contrast between the destruction of the old world through water and the present world through fire, only serves to accentuate the dreadfulness of the coming judgment (cf. also Gen viii 21 f., which states explicitly that the world will never again be destroyed by a flood).

Belief in the destruction of the present world through a universal holocaust was widely held in late Judaism and carried over into the early Christian church. For example, we read in the Hymns of Qumran (1QH iii. 29–35)[10]:

> When the rivers of Belial
> burst their high banks
> —rivers that are like fire
> devouring all that draw their waters,
> rivers whose runnels destroy
> green tree and dry tree alike,
> rivers that are like fire
> which sweeps with flaming sparks
> devouring all that drink their waters
> —a fire which consumes
> all foundations of clay,
> every solid bedrock;
>     when the foundations of the mountains
> become a raging blaze,
> when granite roots are turned
> to streams of pitch,
> when the flame devours
> down to the great abyss,
> when the floods of Belial burst forth
> unto hell itself;
>     when the depths of the abyss are in turmoil,
> cast up mire in abundance,
> when the earth cries out in anguish
> for the havoc wrought in the world,
> when all its depths are aquake,
> and all that is on it quails
> and quivers in [mighty] havoc;
>     when with His mighty roar
> God thunders forth,
> and His holy welkin trembles
> through dread of His glory,
> and the hosts of heaven give forth their voice,
> and the world's foundations rock and reel; . . .

Among the Stoics it was also natural to conceive of the destruction of the world through fire. The teachers of heresy appear to have been especially dependent on the popular Stoic philosophy, inasmuch as they, according to vs. 4, conceived of the development of the world as a mechanical, uniform process. If the author here is discussing the same troublemakers as in chapter ii, and if they represented a well-known opposition movement during the reign of Domitian, then we can reasonably count on a Stoic influence among them. For the most part the Stoics were opponents of Domitian and were resisted by that emperor. Related to this point is the statement in i 4, which seems strange in the New Testament, about Christians being partakers of the divine nature. It can best be understood as an accommodation to the philosophical concepts of Stoicism (cf. the commentary on that passage). So it appears probable that the author emphasizes the destruction of the world through fire with the idea of soliciting a response among those who were familiar with the outlook of the Stoics.

In any case the author of the epistle takes it for granted that his enemies, those skeptic teachers of heresy, are familiar with the idea of a coming world conflagration, even if at present they dismiss it. This world conflagration is spoken of in greater detail in vss. 10–12.

## 13. TWO MISTAKES ABOUT THE DELAY OF THE END
### (iii 8–9)

III  8 Let this point at least not escape your notice, beloved: that with the Lord, one day is as a thousand years, and a thousand years as one day.[a] 9 The Lord is not tardy about his promise, as some reckon tardiness. Rather he is patient toward you. He does not wish any to be lost, but that all may come to repentance.

[a] Ps xc 4

### COMMENT

Two further arguments are presented to meet the doubts of those who are impatient for Christ's return. First the author emphasizes in vs. 8 that if the readers cannot follow him in the line of reasoning previously offered, they ought at least[11] to grasp the basic difference between God's way of measuring time and that of man. A poetic image of Ps xc 4 illuminates the point. What men regard as a long time, even a thousand years, is as a single day in God's sight. The delay in Christ's second coming thus is only apparent. The observation that concepts of time are relative also permits the opposite assertion, that one day in the eyes of God is as a thousand years. On account of this, men ought constantly to be on the alert, for the end may come at any moment. It is further pointed out in vs. 9 that the relative delay is something for which men ought to be thankful, for it affords opportunity for more people to be converted. The subject is taken up again in vs. 15 (compare the discussion of God's long-suffering in I Pet iii 20).

The delay of the day of the Lord had been a problem to the Old Testament prophets (e.g., Hab ii 3). It also exercised the Qumran community during the same general period as that of the New Testament. An example may be quoted from the Habakkuk Commentary (1 QpHab vii. 6–14).[12]

*For the vision is yet for the appointed time. Though it lags toward the moment, it will not be belied.* This refers to the fact that the final moment may be protracted beyond anything which the prophets have foretold, for 'God moves in a mysterious way His wonders to perform.'

*Though it tarry, yet await it; for it will surely come, it will not delay.* This is addressed to the men of truth, the men who carry out the Law (Torah), who do not relax from serving the Truth even though the final moment be long drawn out. Assuredly, all the times appointed by God will come in due course, even as He has determined in His inscrutable wisdom.

But the twofold answer given to this question in Second Peter is original and intriguing: 1) The delay is only apparent, owing to the relativity of time; 2) It gives men additional opportunity to be saved.

## 14. THE DAY OF THE LORD
(iii 10)

III ¹⁰ However, the day of the Lord will come as a thief. On that day the heavens will pass away with a whizzing sound, the elements will burn up and be dissolved, and the earth and its works will be exposed.

### COMMENT

Both Jesus and Paul had made clear that the day of the Lord would come as unexpectedly as a thief in the night (Matt xxiv 43; Luke xii 39; I Thess v 2). On these pronouncements vs. 10 builds its argument. (Some manuscripts add the words "during the night.") The thought here expressed is also the logical conclusion of the previous exposition. No one can ever feel completely secure: The great moment may come at any time. Even the heavens will disappear with a whizzing sound like that of a storm. That is, the solar system and the great galaxies, even space-time relationships will be abolished. All elements which make up the physical world, both on the earth and in the stellar regions (cf. vs. 12; Gal iv 3, 9 f.), will be dissolved by heat and utterly melt away. It is a picture which in an astonishing degree corresponds to what might actually happen, according to modern theories of the physical universe. The writer's main interest is not in technical details, however, but in the fact that the end will come in an overwhelming fashion. And at that moment both the earth and all the works that have been done on it by man will be disclosed.[13] Thus nothing will remain hidden, and every wicked undertaking of men—like the social propaganda of the false teachers—will receive its just punishment.

## 15. PREPAREDNESS FOR THE DAY
## OF THE LORD
### (iii 11–18)

III 11 Since all these things will be destroyed, [consider] what you ought to be like, in holy living and piety. 12 You must wait and strive for the coming of the day of God, because of which the heavens will be dissolved in fire and the elements will melt from heat. 13 We are waiting for new heavens and a new earth according to his promise, in which righteousness will dwell. 14 Therefore, beloved, while waiting for these things you ought to strive to be found without spot or blemish before him in peace. 15 And recognize our Lord's patience as [a mark of] salvation, just as our beloved brother Paul has written to you in accordance with the wisdom given to him. 16 So [it is] in all of his epistles, in which he speaks about these things. In them some things are hard to understand, which those unlearned and unstable pervert, as [they do with] other Scriptures, leading to their own destruction. 17 You, beloved, since you have advance knowledge take care lest you be snatched away with the error of the lawless and give up your own stability. 18 But increase in the grace and knowledge of our Lord and Savior Jesus Christ. To him belongs the glory both now and to the day of eternity.

### COMMENT

The imminent dissolution of the whole present system, vs. 11, which will come as a catastrophic judgment upon the universe, ought to lead men to serious reflection and to holy living in godly fear. It is important, therefore, to live with the final events of history and the day of reckoning before one's eyes, as a permanently threatening possibility. The sense of danger is heightened by the awareness of the cosmic proportions and the violent character of the impending disaster, for the heavens will be dissolved in fire and the elements melt away and be consumed by the heat. Nevertheless, the Christians are advised in vs. 12 to long and strive for this decisive, final settlement. For them the critical time of judgment, according to vs. 13, will not lead to destruction and death at all, but to newness of life, which they will experience on a new earth under a new heaven. This the Lord had previously promised (Isa lxv 17 and lxvi 22). And in this fair new world righteousness will dwell; unrighteousness will not enter there. So all wickedness must be cast off here and now by everyone who desires to have part of this new life. We may compare the last chapters of the book of Revelation with its glowing description of the new earth, toward which faithful Christians may legitimately direct their hopes (Rev xxi 1–xxii 5). The conclusion, vs. 14, is that believers must strive to be found unspotted and blameless when they meet their Lord at the judgment. According to a characteristic addition at the end of the verse, this expectation and striving after perfection is to be characterized by "peace." During the time of waiting, therefore, there must be no violent exhibition of impatience, about which the author has already spoken (ii 2, 10–14), or other behavior inconsistent with Christian faith and confidence.

After this, in vs. 15a, attention logically is focused on the necessity for Christians to show patience. The long-suffering of the Lord, already mentioned in vs. 9 (compare again I Pet iii 20), is not a sign of forgetfulness or indifference, but shows that he wishes to make it possible for more people to be saved. Second Peter thus regards grace and salvation as the most important of God's actions, even though it speaks of the judgment in such a frightening way. As was particularly pointed out in vs. 9, one must not misconstrue God's long-suffering. This thought is underscored in vs. 15b with special reference to Paul, who is praised for having written with the divine wisdom granted to him. Paul did not often speak of God's long-suffering in exactly this sense (perhaps the only explicit statement is Rom ii 4). But the emphasis here is on the willingness of Christians to manifest patience, remain steadfast in faith and hope, and to avoid all schisms and inconsistent behavior. This theme is a major concern of Paul's throughout his epistles, as the author states in vs. 16. The expression "as he speaks in them about these things" shows that the author wishes to stress those epistles in which the question of the last events is discussed. In particular he may have in mind Paul's Thessalonian correspondence, in which the coming of the Lord and the judgment are principal themes (I Thess iv 13–v 11; II Thess i 7–10, ii 1–12). Part of what Paul has said, however, is easily misunderstood. Many have also twisted the statements of the apostle because of their ignorance and lack of stability in the Christian faith. Reference is probably made to those who misinterpreted Paul's teaching about Christian liberty so that they came to the conclusion that anything was permissible and refused to give heed to the congregation in matters of discipline. Paul himself had already resisted such misuse of the ideal of liberty (for example in I Cor x 23: "All things are lawful, but not all things are helpful . . . not all things contribute to edification"). Other writings as well, including Old Testament prophecies, are falsely explained by these teachers of heresy. It is significant that Paul's epistles are treated as part of the normative literature or canon of the church.

Seeing that such deceptions are to be expected, the author finally emphasizes in vs. 17 that now the believers know in advance the risks they run. Consequently they ought not to be led astray by the false teachers, but should be fully aware of the lawless activities of these men. It is vitally important that the believers not give up[14] the steadfastness which they acquired through instruction and experience in the faith and which sets them apart from the seducers in so far as these are "unlearned and unstable" (vs. 16).

A concluding admonition in vs. 18 concerns further growth in grace and knowledge of the Lord and Savior Jesus Christ. These warm personal words and the doxology attached to them make it clear that the author is not primarily concerned to preach condemnation and destruction, although he is compelled to speak very severely against the teachers of heresy, whom he recognizes as a source of the greatest danger. What constitutes the real burden of the author is God's grace and desire to save, as these have found expression in Jesus Christ.

# Textual Notes

1. To illustrate the hieratic and expressive style of Asianic prose, the following affirmations of King Antiochus in the Nemrud-Dagh inscription may be quoted: "It was as being of all good things not only a most reliable acquisition, but also—for human beings—a most pleasant enjoyment that I considered piety; and the same conviction I held to be the reason for a most successful authority as well as for a most blessed employment thereof; furthermore, during my entire lifetime I appeared to all in my monarchy as one who regarded holiness as both a most trustworthy safeguard and an inimitable satisfaction." See further E. Norden, *Die antike Kunstprosa*, I (2d ed.; 1909), pp. 126–52; J. Waldis, *Sprache und Stil der grossen Inschrift vom Nemrud-Dagh* (1920), pp. 57–59.

2. Instead of "our God and Savior Jesus Christ," Codex Sinaiticus and Syriac versions in i 1 read "our Lord and Savior Jesus Christ." This wording is more in line with vs. 2, but has obviously been influenced by the standard phrase "our Lord and Savior Jesus Christ" which occurs in i 11, ii 20, iii 18.

3. In the original, "life and godly fear," which is a hendiadys.

4. Literally "power and return," also to be understood as a hendiadys.

5. The standard Greek phrase *bebaióteron échein* means "to hold most trustworthy," "to keep to." Here *bebaióteron* is to be taken as elative.

6. Greek, *emporeúomai*, from *émporos*, "wholesaler."

7. "Deceptions" is in Greek *apátai*, and "love feasts" *agápai*. See also the comments on Jude 12a.

8. Greek, *mnēsthênai*, "to remember," used here in the sense of "to consider."

9. Greek, *en empaigmonê*, modifying *empaîktai:* "mockers appearing with irony."

10. T. Gaster, *The Dead Sea Scriptures* (1956), pp. 139–40.

11. Greek, *hén*, "only," here with the connotation "at least."

12. Gaster, *op. cit.*, pp. 252–53.

13. Greek, *heurethēsetai,* a *lectio difficilior* which should not be altered, in spite of the evidence of certain MSS, to conform with the verbs in vs. 12, or in any other way.

14. Greek, *ekpésēte,* literally "slide out of" or "slip out of," as of a garment.

# THE EPISTLE OF JUDE

# Introduction

The short epistle of Jude contains warnings against deceivers and exhortations to preserve faith, love, and hope.

Largely, this epistle is a *parallel* to chapter ii of Second Peter. Moreover, certain expressions in Jude's introductory verses are similar to Second Peter's opening verses, and the conclusion is somewhat analogous:

| JUDE | SECOND PETER |
|------|--------------|
| 2 | i 2 |
| 3 | i 5 |
| 5a | i 12 |
| 5b–19 | ii 1–iii 3 |
| 24 | iii 14 |

On the other hand, Jude contains several *independent* conceptions, and the subject matter in common with Second Peter is presented in a different context. Consequently, Jude ought to be studied as something more than a mere duplication of Second Peter.

The similarity of the two epistles naturally raises the question of literary dependence: Is Jude derived from Second Peter, or the reverse, or are they both adaptations of a common source? These possibilities have been the subject of a lively debate in exegetical literature. Most modern scholars regard Jude as the source of II Pet ii, but the opposite view has been advanced by some outstanding authorities. Arguments can be marshaled in support of either theory. In places Second Peter gives a greater impression of originality compared with Jude; in other places the reverse is the case. Jude, however, would seem to be mainly of secondary origin since it summarizes in an elegant style points which Second Peter expounds with greater effort and more detail. Such smoothness of style is

frequently characteristic of editors who condense and revise what
has been laboriously drawn up by others. If this is the proper explanation here, then Jude was an arrangement of material already in
existence. But because of certain other considerations, it is not likely
that Jude is directly dependent on Second Peter. There are numerous differences which cannot be accounted for as simply literary
variations on motifs furnished by Second Peter. The best assumption is that both epistles derive from a common tradition which may
well have been oral rather than written. Very possibly there was
a sermon pattern formulated to resist the seducers of the church:
This would explain both the similarities and the differences in a
satisfactory fashion.

The *author* of the epistle calls himself "Jude, servant of Jesus
Christ, brother of James," vs. 1. Is this Jude the same person
as one of the other Judes who appear in the New Testament? The
question is not easy to decide.

We might think first of Jude the apostle (Luke vi 16; Acts i 13).
However, the author of the epistle refers to the apostles of the Lord
as belonging to an earlier period, vs. 17. Furthermore, the father
of the apostle Jude was named James (Acts i 13), whereas this
authors refers to a brother of his known as James, vs. 1. Among
the Jews a son was not normally given his father's name, so it is
most unlikely that the apostle also had a brother named James. This
eliminates the possibility that he was the author of the epistle.

It is more reasonable to think of the Jude mentioned as a brother
of Jesus (Matt xiii 55, Mark vi 3). Even though the author calls
himself the "servant" rather than the brother of Jesus, this is fully
understandable as an expression of modesty. James the brother of
Jude would then be understood as James the brother of Jesus, and
this reference at the opening of the epistle would be important in
view of the leading position the Lord's brother James attained in
the early church. Evidence apparently confirming this supposition
is found in the *Church History* of Eusebius who reports an older
tradition concerning the grandsons of Jude. Because of their relationship to Jesus, they were revered as descendants of David, and
the emperor Domitian (A.D. 81–96), fearful of the development
of dynastic traditions inimical to the empire, summoned them before
him; when he discovered that the men were merely poor farmers
and no threat to Rome, he let them go (Eus. *Hist. eccl.* iii. 19:1–

20:6). The story indicates that Jude the brother of Jesus had some importance for later generations. Now if he wrote the epistle, it must have been before the reign of Domitian, in view of the fact that only his grandsons were involved in the emperor's inquiry. But the epistle can hardly be dated that early. Internal evidence places Jude at the end of the first century A.D. (see our discussion of the time of composition below). This speaks against the hypothesis in question. Finally, when the handling of the Greek language is considered, the authorship of the Galilean villager who was the brother of Jesus seems difficult to affirm.

We are left with two possibilities. Either the author of the epistle is a Jude nowhere else mentioned in the New Testament, in which case nothing can be said about the name, or the author has written in the name of a New Testament man known as Jude, the brother of James. This can only be the brother of Jesus, although the author is modest enough not to call him that. Jude has authority enough through his relationship to James, the well-known leader of the Jerusalem church. As is the case with the epistle of James, a personal disciple of the Lord's brother may well have written the epistle of Jude essentially in the spirit of his mentor.

The *recipients* of the epistle are described as "the called ones who are loved by God the Father, vs. 1, in short, as in Second Peter, the church in general. Jude, however, was written with more regard for Jewish Christian readers than Second Peter. Israel's exodus from Egypt and Old Testament figures such as Michael, Cain, and Korah's sons are mentioned in Jude, vss. 9, 11; none of these occur in Second Peter. Furthermore, the author cites First Enoch, a Jewish apocalypse which belonged to the Qumran library, as holy prophecy, vs. 14. It is clear that although he addressed his epistle to the church as a whole, the audience he had in mind probably consisted of Jewish Christians.

In fixing the *time* of composition of the epistle, it has been argued that the heresy referred to by Jude could not have come into existence before the end of the first century. But little is known of this heresy from other sources, and there is no historical basis on which to decide when it arose. Better evidence for dating is the information given by the epistle that the current wave of apostasy is the work of seducers in the pay of foreign masters. Two deductions can be made from this. In the first place, the Christian community must have arrived at a level of some importance to be attractive to the magnates of the Roman empire. Else why should extraordinary efforts be made to suborn Christians from their faith? Secondly, the very fact that there were numerous lukewarm members of the congregation susceptible to the influence of *agents provocateurs* shows that the Christian community had grown greatly since the time of the Pauline epistles. We conclude that Jude belongs to a later stage of church history, most likely in the last decades of the first century. Political and social factors point to the years around A.D. 90 and the situation under Domitian, as seems also probable with regard to James and Second Peter, and is certainly true of First Clement. See the commentary below on vss. 10a and 16. There is no indication of the *place* from which Jude was written (cf. note on vs. 1).

The *purpose* of Jude is the same as the main purpose of Second Peter: to warn against teachers of heresy and urge steadfastness in the faith. But the author of Jude does not feel the same need as the author of Second Peter to remonstrate against doubts concerning Christ's second coming.

As to *form,* Jude is an epistle without any specific personal emphasis. Epistolary features are evident only in the first three verses in which the writer and recipients are mentioned, a wish for God's blessing is expressed, and the present need for the writer's exhortation given. All this is said in a humble and friendly manner, but in rather indefinite phrases. The conclusion involves only a song of praise (as does Second Peter), and its simplicity is highly effective. In the sections where Second Peter and Jude run parallel, the literary styles differ to a considerable extent. Jude's language flows more evenly. He is less expressive, rhetorical, more superficial, more a literator. Emotions are restrained and not given free rein at the expense of correct form. The contrast with Second Peter's affected diction and violent moods is striking. Jude does not appear to express personal feelings and reactions but puts into effective and elegant form an exhortation already traditional. But his concern for correctness of form does not prevent the writer from speaking directly to the hearts of his audience in an intimate and soul-stirring manner.

The epistle of Jude may be divided into the following *sections:*

I. WORDS OF GREETING, THE SPECIAL OCCASION FOR WRITING THE EPISTLE, 1–3

1. *Words of Greeting, 1–3*

II. WARNING AGAINST DECEIVERS, 4–16

2. *Seducers pervert God's grace to brutality, 4*
3. *Warning lessons, 5–7*
4. *The seducers defame authorities, 8–10*
5. *Cain, Balaam, and Korah as examples of rebellion and corruption, 11–13*
6. *Enoch's prophecy, 14–16*

III. VIGILANCE, FAITH—LOVE—HOPE, MERCY, STEADFASTNESS, 17–25

7. *Vigilance toward mockers, 17–19*
8. *Faith, love, and the hope of eternal life, 20–21*
9. *Mercy toward non-Christians, 22–23*
10. *Encouragement to steadfastness; doxology, 24–25*

# Translation and Comment

## 1. WORDS OF GREETING
## (1–3)

1 Jude, servant of Jesus Christ, and brother of James, to those who are loved in God the Father and called to be preserved by Jesus Christ. 2 Mercy be with you, and may peace and love increase to a full measure.

3 Beloved, while I had every desire to write you about our common salvation, I have now got a compelling reason to write and urge you to contend for the faith which was once entrusted to the saints.

### COMMENT

Through the use of James's name in vs. 1, the author may wish to quote Jude, the brother of Jesus (as was pointed out in the Introduction). Whether this is justified or not, he presents himself in becomingly humble fashion. The recipients mentioned in this verse are the Christians in general, as no geographical location is indicated for them. Jude only remarks that they are set within the sphere of God's love and are called to be preserved for it by Jesus Christ. The same thought reappears in the concluding admonitions (vs. 21: "Keep yourselves in God's love"). It is evident that the author is deeply concerned that the Christians hold their places in the fellowship of God's love, and do not forfeit the final reunion with Jesus Christ. To this belongs also the author's heartfelt wish for his readers in vs. 2: mercy, peace, and love.

The author explains in vs. 3 that he had a general desire to write[1] to his readers and that he has now got, as a result of special circumstances, a compelling reason[2] to carry out this intention.[3] Thus he is under obligation to admonish the readers constantly to fight[4] for the Christian faith. This faith is said to have been "entrusted" to the saints. As is shown by a subsequent reference to the apostles, vs. 17, the author is thinking of the transmission[5] of the gospel from Jesus to the apostles, and from these to the church, that is, the apostolic tradition. The circumstances that have now compelled the author to write are brought out in the following verse.

## 2. SEDUCERS PERVERT GOD'S
## GRACE TO BRUTALITY
### (4)

4 Certain people have crept in among you who had of old been designated by scriptures for this judgment. Godless as they are, they pervert our God's grace into brutality and deny our only Ruler and Lord Jesus Christ.

### COMMENT

The actual reason for writing the epistle of Jude is, according to vs. 4, the behavior of certain inveiglers. As is clear from what follows, they exhibit the same destructive tendencies as the seducers excoriated in Second Peter. One possible difference is that it is not asserted about the teachers of heresy in Second Peter as of those in Jude that they have crept in among the Christians. The former, who are compared with false prophets and are called false teachers (II Pet ii 1), are treated more as authorities in the Christian church who subsequently sought connections with alien masters. The latter give the impression of being already in the service of alien masters at the time that they crept into the fellowship of the Christian church. But this difference is not important. And the Old Testament references given in the following verses of Jude rather indicate apostates.

The remark that the seducers had of old been designated by scriptures for judgment is probably based on a statement in some sacred writing. The author may have in mind the prophecy in First Enoch mentioned in vs. 14 (see below). While he speaks of "this judgment" he fails to specify which judgment or provide further details. He is apparently drawing upon a source in which the judg-

ment was described in more detail (as in II Pet ii 3). An example
of this type of material is to be found in the Qumran Manual of
Discipline (1QS iv. 9–14), where the spirits of iniquity are rebuked
in terms reminiscent of the accusations of Jude, thus suggesting the
existence of a certain tradition behind Jude's allusions. It is further
stated about the teachers of heresy that they pervert God's grace
into violence. God's grace cannot here denote his personal desire
to grant peace, but must refer to something objective which he
has given (as in Rom v 2: "the grace wherein we stand"). Evidently
it signifies the condition of grace, or the Christian life, of which it
can be said that the deceivers transform it into brutality. Likewise
in II Pet ii 2 it is noted that the teachers of heresy incite many
Christians to brutalities.

The readers undoubtedly knew to whom the author referred, as
they had had experience with these deceivers. But it is only with
the help of Second Peter that we can gain a clearer picture of them.
As in II Pet ii 1, it is brought out here that the teachers of heresy
deny Christ as their only Lord by serving other masters. That they
have sold themselves in this fashion, as Second Peter indicates with
reference to the same kind of deceivers, is not directly asserted by
Jude, but is implied in certain allusions that follow: vss. 11 (Balaam) and 12 (clouds driven by the winds); it is confirmed by
more explicit references in Second Peter. In view of this the hypothesis that Jude is earlier than Second Peter becomes more difficult to defend (see the Introduction above).

# 3. WARNING LESSONS
## (5–7)

5 I wish to remind you—you learned all about it once—that the Lord delivered the people from the land of Egypt, and the second time destroyed those who did not believe. 6 And angels who did not retain their sovereignty, but forsook their proper abode, he has kept in darkness with eternal bonds until the judgment of the great day. 7 In the same manner Sodom and Gomorrah and the surrounding cities, which like these practiced fornication and followed alien flesh, present themselves as an example by enduring the punishment of eternal fire.

### COMMENT

When in vs. 5a the author proceeds to give some illustrations from ancient history (corresponding to those given in II Pet ii 4–8), he asserts that he does this only as a reminder to his readers who are obviously acquainted with these facts. It is difficult to ascertain whether Jude assumes a general knowledge of biblical history on the part of the readers, or refers to specific instruction that they have received in these matters. On the latter alternative, the author may be thought of as alluding to a tradition that formed the basis for both Second Peter and Jude. But there seems to be no direct connection between Jude and Second Peter. Rather important differences are noticeable both with reference to the choice of examples and their application, irrespective of the obvious similarities. The deliverance from Egypt is mentioned only by Jude, while the flood and Lot are found only in Second Peter. With reference to the application an even more significant difference appears. Through the examples cited, Second Peter wishes to show how God punishes the unjust but saves the righteous. Jude, on the other hand, is interested in the people who pass or are pulled from one group to the other, namely, the apostates.

Naturally the Old Testament stories are not used to demonstrate the ultimate destruction of heathenism or unrighteousness, since this is taken for granted, but rather as an object lesson to those who slip away from the fellowship of the righteous to become co-laborers with unrighteous heathen powers. The story of the generation in the wilderness, vs. 5b, is to be understood in this way. Here the destruction of the disbelieving Israelites in the desert serves as a warning to those Christians who, like the Jews of the exodus, yearn again for "Egypt" or the land of heathenism. The author characterizes this punishment of the unbelievers as a "second" visitation of the Lord, because he has in mind the second coming of Christ, whose first coming signaled the calling of the elect. In a similar way the fallen angels in vs. 6 are an example to those who collaborate with the heathen. Their sin consisted in forsaking their proper abode and committing fornication with earthly beings. Dominated by pagan propensities, certain Christians—among them are leaders of the congregations whose function may be compared with that of angels (Rev i 20, iii 22)—have forsaken the evangelical fellowship and now conform to the heathen way of life. It is clear from the fate of the fallen angels who are in eternal bonds in horrible darkness (cf. I Enoch 10:5; Rev ix 2) until doomsday (I Enoch 10:12) that the punishment for such transgression will last until the final judgment (see also 1QS iv. 12–14). According to vs. 7 the same conclusion is to be drawn from the catastrophe which overwhelmed Sodom and Gomorrah, and the neighboring cities which committed fornication and ran after "alien flesh." Fornication may here, as often in the New Testament, refer to idolatry, while "flesh" (as in I Pet i 24) denotes human society and its violent attempts at self-exaltation. Sodom and Gomorrah represent the leaders of apostasy, and the surrounding cities correspond to their followers. As the fallen angels are punished in everlasting darkness, so the adulterous cities are visited with everlasting fire. It is imperative not to follow the example of these culprits, but to keep oneself free from the unrighteous, ungodly tendencies that prevail in the heathen world.

## 4. THE SEDUCERS DEFAME
## AUTHORITIES
## (8–10)

8 In like manner these also, hypnotized as they are, defile flesh, reject authority, and defame dignitaries. 9 The archangel Michael, when he contended with the devil in a dispute over the body of Moses, did not presume to impose a defamatory judgment on him but said: "May the Lord punish you." 10 But these defame what they do not know. On the other hand, what they understand in a primitive way like brute animals, by this they are corrupted.

### COMMENT

The examples cited from the Old Testament have shown what severe consequences ensue if fellowship with God is forsaken and one is caught by the enticements of heathenism.

It is emphasized in vs. 8 that the teachers of heresy are "full of dreams," as it reads literally; that is, they are hypnotized or blinded and do not know what they are doing (cf. Isa lvi 10–12, about the leaders of Israel who like to drink wine at great *symposia*). In the first place they contaminate and defile flesh through intimate contact with the unclean members of a godless society. On the other hand, they set aside duly constituted authority and defame dignitaries, that is, those in positions of power whether angels or men. Judging from the expressions "authority" and "dignitaries," these seducers are regarded as rebels against the existing order. Anarchistic and antinomian tendencies must be attributed to them, as is also the case with the teachers of heresy combated in Second Peter. Subsequent allusions serve to strengthen this view, for the false teachers are first compared with the devil who spoke slanderously against Israel's law teacher Moses, vs. 9; then summarizing, the author says that they murmur and grumble about their lot in life, vs. 16.

The gist of the matter is that slander or reviling spiritual or social dignitaries is contrary to God's will. For even the archangel Michael, vs. 9, who is the ruler of the angels and the protector of the elect people in the battle with the evil powers (Dan x 13; 1QM ix. 15, xvii. 6 f.; Rev xii 7), did not stoop to slander in dealing with the devil about the body of Moses. Second Peter does not mention this episode, but in ii 11 refers only to angels in general and their avoidance of defamatory statements. According to well-known authorities of the early church like Clement of Alexandria, Origen and others, the reference to Michael's contention with the devil comes from an apocryphal intertestamental book entitled "The Assumption of Moses." This apocalyptic work has been preserved and may be read in modern editions, but unfortunately the narration about Michael and the devil is missing in all extant manuscripts. Extracts from older Greek commentaries and the Slavonic legend of Moses, however, seem to have preserved the haggadic midrash for posterity. According to these fragments the devil had reviled Moses and had called him a murderer, because he had killed the Egyptian overseer. The significant detail is that the devil's slander was directed against Moses. Jude uses this as the key to his analogy: The slanders of the false teachers are parallel to those of the devil, and the dignitaries reviled by them are comparable to Moses, here as elsewhere the representative of legally constituted authority. The implied conclusion, that the teachers of heresy attacked the existing government with malicious charges, corresponds to the observation already made about these men.

A further point Jude makes is that when the devil had reviled the representative and the symbol of the law, and Michael did not revile in turn so malicious an adversary, the angel committed the judgment to God, saying only: "The Lord will punish thee." This expression is quoted from Zech iii 2, where a similar verbal encounter takes place between an angel and the devil about the high priest Joshua: The devil accuses the high priest, the angel defends

him. Jude indicates that the deceivers ought to emulate the example of this angel and of Michael but not that of the devil.

In their ignorance the teachers of heresy also revile, according to
vs. 10a, "things which they do not know." This indefinite expression
rather indicates, as does the subsequent mention of what they do
know, that the author has something else in mind besides the dignitaries of vs. 8 as the object of their accusation. Verse 9 has indirectly
revealed that the teachers of heresy defamed Moses. A following verse, 11, points to the same conclusion, inasmuch as they are
compared with Korah's sons, who rose in rebellion against Moses.
It is clear that the teachers of heresy were enemies of the law,
and of the Mosaic law in particular. As godless heathen, the deceivers are unlearned in the law, but still they challenge the holy
order of God's chosen people with scoffing and taunting. This is
analogous to the defamation of dignitaries previously mentioned, because they also represent the principles of order and authority,
though it remains uncertain whether they are thought of as angels
or men. By his allusion to the law of Moses, the author condemns
those who oppose authority in general. The parallel to Jude's
"things which they do not know" found in II Pet ii 12 is "those
whom they do not acknowledge." Here the verbs share a similar
basic meaning, but have different nuances: Second Peter refers to
the Roman authorities, Jude to the legal order generally.

The situation in Jude is similar to that described in First Clement
of Rome, a treatise written toward the end of Domitian's reign, or
about A.D. 95 (see the General Introduction). Clement also dealt
with disturbing tendencies in the social order by repeated references
to the law of Moses. The troublemakers who are opposed in First
Clement may reasonably be compared with the teachers of heresy
in Jude. This is further evidence for dating Jude during the reign
of Domitian. At the same time, the attribution of the epistle to
Jude, the brother of James, coincides perfectly with the author's
concern to defend Moses and the inviolability of the law against
slander. For as already pointed out in the Introduction, this James
was probably understood to be the Lord's brother, who was for
several decades the leader of the church in Jerusalem, and the
most honored figure in Jewish Christendom.

It is stated in vs. 10b that the teachers of heresy are corrupted
by what they, like brute animals, know "physically," that is, in a

primitive way, by instinct. The parallel text, II Pet ii 12, may offer some help in clarifying the author's reference to what these dumb animals know. It speaks of animals of prey who catch and destroy as a result of primitive instincts. Only there is the difference that Jude is concerned with animals in general. Another possibility with respect to Jude's thought is Xenophon's statement that animals know how to fight by nature (Xen. *Cyr.* 2:3:9). Jude's phraseology is strikingly similar to that of Xenophon, though it is difficult to show any dependence. In either case Jude has reference to the animal instinct for violent self-expression. The following verse supports this view by directing attention to the fratricide Cain and to the rebel leader Korah. It must be realized that in the same way the teachers of heresy will be destroyed because of their obstructive tactics. Subsequent verses also make it clear that the author regards violence and rebellion as the expression of their primitive instincts. For in vs. 15 the author speaks of eternal punishment which awaits the godless heretics on account of the iniquitous words which they speak against the Lord (cf. the vomit of the dog in II Pet ii 22); and in vs. 19 he says that they are separatists motivated by animal instincts, since they do not have the spirit. After all, the comparison with dumb animals, which do not even have ordinary human understanding, may be intended to humiliate the teachers of heresy just because they make claim to special intelligence, whether they pose as philosophers or Gnostics.

## 5. CAIN, BALAAM, AND KORAH AS EXAMPLES OF REBELLION AND CORRUPTION (11–13)

11 Woe to them! They have followed Cain's example; they have abandoned themselves to the delusion of Balaam for the sake of reward; and they have been destroyed by a rebellion like Korah's. 12 These are the hidden reefs at your love meals,<sup>a</sup> where they brazenly feast with you while looking out for themselves. Waterless clouds they are, driven about by winds; trees in the autumn, bearing no fruit, twice dead, uprooted; 13 wild waves of the sea foaming with their own abominations; straying stars for whom the darkness of hell is reserved forever.

<sup>a</sup> Another reading: "in their deceptions" (II Pet ii 13).

### COMMENT

When in vs. 11 the author compares the teachers of heresy with Cain, he presumably implies that they, like the first murderer in history, occasion the death of others. To suppose that they were actually murderers goes beyond the evidence. But there is good reason to argue that their anarchistic and antinomian propaganda compromised the believers so that they were exposed to persecution from society and even driven to martyrdom. In the First Epistle of Clement, rich in analogies (cf. comment on vs. 10, above), Cain is referred to in this way. He is emphatically presented as the archetype of those who through zeal, envy, social dissatisfaction, and hostility to society, drive their brethren in the faith to death (I Clem. 4:1–7). Among the recipients of the epistle in Corinth there were also those who by their antisocial behavior aroused the hostility of the Romans and forced the authorities to take active measures against the church. They thereby aggravated the sufferings of the Roman Christians in whose name the author writes. In this sense they and the heretical teachers in Jude are fratricides, and walk in the way of Cain. That the basis of the comparison lies in their subversive propaganda is confirmed by vs. 16, in which the teachers of heresy are flatly accused of showing and arousing dissatisfaction with society.

After being compared with Cain, these troublemakers are further charged with "pouring themselves out in Balaam's delusion" which they do "for reward." The statement corresponds to II Pet ii 15 and probably has the same meaning, namely, that Balaam's sin consisted primarily in his willingness to seduce God's people to idolatry for reward. Obviously the implication is that the seducers serve alien masters by their propaganda and receive money for their service. This *ambitus,* or gaining followers through hired agents, was common among politicians and partisans in the Roman empire, but it was severely denounced by the emperors, and was therefore fraught with the gravest risks. From a Christian point of view such a dependence on alien masters was especially objectionable as involving a denial of the only Lord Jesus Christ, vs. 4.

The heretical teachers are finally said to be like Korah, whose rebellion against Moses was notorious (Num xvi 1–35). And the general meaning of this comparison is plain. The deceivers, like Korah, are in "opposition" to, or in rebellion against the legal authorities, no distinction being made between those of society and those of the church. A related notice is found in vs. 6, where reference is made to the "angels" who forsook their proper abode and mingled with earthly beings. It was pointed out above that this alludes to leading Christians who left the fellowship of the church and joined other movements. As the instigators of such apostasy, the teachers of heresy are here compared with Korah, who gathered around him a large number of "princes of the assembly, representatives of the congregation" (Num xvi 2).

In vs. 12a it is stated that the dangerous deceivers brazenly attend the love meals[6] of the believers. This expression, which probably refers to the holy fellowship meals of the Christians, is used specifically in this sense by Ignatius, an important writer at the beginning of the second century (Ign. *Rom.* 7:3, etc.). The teachers of heresy had apparently been so successful in gaining the confidence of the Christians that they were invited to participate in their love feasts. At these they disregarded the claims of the Christian community, having regard only for themselves and seeking their own advantage, which is probably to "entice unstable souls" (II Pet ii 14). They are in fact dangerous "reefs,"[7] upon which the church may easily founder and capsize, for these inveiglers are a principal source of misfortune to the whole church because of the ill will which they stir up in society.

To complement the comparison with Cain, Balaam, and Korah, the teachers of heresy are compared in vss. 12b–13 with certain manifestations of the physical world. Jude lists clouds as symbolic of the region of the air, trees for the earth, waves for the sea, and planets for the dark outer spaces and the nether regions, too, since they rise and descend in the heavens. His presentation shows greater precision in detail and more attention to logical structure than the parallel in II Pet ii 17, which likewise follows the reference to Balaam. Second Peter only mentions waterless fountains and storm-driven clouds, the latter being counterparts to the clouds in Jude, but a comprehensive pattern is missing.

The question now arises as to the purpose of these illustrations. It may first be observed that Jude, as well as other New Testament writers, regarded nature as inferior to man redeemed by faith, since it is subject to destruction. To be compared with mere phenomena of nature is degrading, particularly for those who, like the teachers of heresy, once belonged to the believers. Furthermore the author emphasizes that these particular features of nature are futile and empty, unable to produce anything of value, like clouds without rain and trees in the autumn without fruit. The waves of the sea pound upon the rocks or against the sides of a ship, but the looming surf is froth and spray without effect. This is equally true of the insolence and "big words" (cf. vss. 15, 16) which come foaming from the mouths of the heretical teachers as they rave against society and the church. Compare the "effusion" of the heathen slanderers in I Pet iv 4, and the "vomit" of the dog in II Pet ii 22. Thirdly, it may be noticed that the dependence of the seducers on alien masters is suggested by the image of clouds driven by the winds (cf. II Pet ii 17), and partly by the parable of waves in the sea. And the erratic course of the wandering stars (i.e., the planets) points in the same direction.

These deceivers have no legitimate part in the Christian communion. In a double sense they are dead. From the very beginning they belonged to the realm of sin and death and now they have been "pulled up by the roots" and cut off from fellowship with Christ and his church. Eternal death will be their final reward, just as the planets are destined for imprisonment in outer darkness (cf. vs. 6). In sum, the illustrations based upon natural phenomena evoke complex associations of ideas in bewildering variety, but are effectively woven together about the main theme of the character and fate of the seducers.

## 6. ENOCH'S PROPHECY
## (14–16)

14 Enoch, the seventh from Adam, prophesied of these when he said*ᵃ*: "Behold, the Lord comes with his holy myriads 15 to execute judgment on all, and to punish all the ungodly for all the impious deeds which they wickedly committed, and for all the insolent [words] which they have spoken against him, these godless sinners." 16 They are grumblers and complainers who pursue their own lusts. And their mouth utters bombast while they adulate certain individuals for the sake of advantage.

*ᵃ* I Enoch 1:9

### COMMENT

In vss. 14–15 there is a citation from First Enoch, one of the so-called Old Testament pseudepigrapha. This book was originally written in either Hebrew or possibly Aramaic during the second and first centuries B.C. Until the recent discovery of several fragments of the Enoch literature in Hebrew among the Qumran scrolls, the book was known only in translation. Parts of Greek versions covering the first and last chapters of the book have come down to us. It is more completely preserved in a secondary Ethiopic translation (derived from the Greek), which forms part of the Bible of the Abyssinian church. Officially, the book of Enoch was not accepted by the Jews or the Christians as a canonical scripture. Yet it is clear that Jude regarded this writing as inspired. In fact, due to its presumed antiquity, First Enoch is placed on an even higher level than the Old Testament prophets. For it is said to contain prophecies of the patriarch Enoch dating from the antediluvian age. As "the seventh from Adam," Enoch was not only of awesome age, but summed up in himself the entire super-holy line of patriarchs, since "seven" was regarded as the number of perfection. The author of Jude therefore does not hesitate to cite I Enoch 1:9 in support of his warnings, since he regards the quotation from Enoch as an ancient prophecy of the destruction of these same teachers of heresy. We are reminded of the Qumran Commentary on Habakkuk, which consistently identifies the enemies mentioned by the prophet with the contemporary seducers of the elect, that is, with the adversaries of the Qumran community. According to this prophecy of Enoch, the Lord himself will come with his angels in order to punish the sinners who have spoken insolently against him and thus displayed their godlessness. Their cardinal failing is a haughty and rebellious spirit.

It is to be noted that the repeated and apparently exaggerated expressions "godless" and "godlessness,"[8] used in the citation, were connected by the author with a matter of immediate and grave import for Christians. Roman authorities, and Domitian in particular, eagerly prosecuted "godlessness" in the sense of disloyalty to Rome. In emphasizing again and again the godlessness of the heretical teachers, Jude alludes to their seditious tendencies. But of course he does not echo Roman charges, or champion the divine character of the state. He is rather in agreement with Paul, who asserted that rebellion against existing society was tantamount to disobeying God's disposition of matters (Rom xiii 2). Thus our author could attack the teachers of heresy for a "godlessness" which on the surface was of a socio-political nature, but which in essence was considered a religious matter.

The socio-political aspect of this "godlessness" is further elaborated in the following statement, vs. 16. Here the opponents are called "murmurers" and are said to complain about their lot in life. This dissatisfaction with society arises from their "walking after their own lusts," that is, they are driven by their passions (cf. vs. 18; a similar thought occurs in James iv 1–3). As observed in II Pet ii 18, the deceivers moreover are puffed up in their speech. Notwithstanding, they pay their respects to certain people[9] from whom they hope to derive assistance or gain profit. The phrase evidently refers to men of wealth in contemporary society from whom the seducers seek to win support for their propaganda activity. Balaam also received such payment for his false prophecies from a foreign magnate, vs. 11. In the present instance, as also in Second Peter, the wealthy men referred to may well be important Romans under Domitian who criticized the emperor (cf. the General Introduction and the commentary on II Pet ii 1c and 3a). Ancient historians describe the widespread opposition to this emperor on the part of the aristocracy who favored the republican form of government. Domitian strenuously fought the noblemen and senators whom he regarded as his adversaries. Some of the aristocrats who suffered under the heavy hand of the emperor may have been Christians, or at least associated with the church through Judaism. The most renowned of them were the consuls Acillius Glabrio and Flavius Clemens (along with his wife Flavia Domitilla); the latter were in fact close relatives of the emperor (see the General Introduction). We need not suppose that Jude had these persons in mind, especially as it has not been proved that they actually opposed the emperor. But their condemnation illustrates that fact that Domitian suspected aristocrats who had any connection with the church of revolutionary activities. For this reason Jude's warning against the rebellious complainers, and their efforts to ingratiate themselves with certain individuals, may very well refer to their negotiations with rich republican Romans, who were willing to assist the anarchistic teachers of heresy in their propaganda against the existing order of society. A similar relationship with wealthy Romans is referred to in James ii 2–9 (see the commentary on that passage). In II Pet ii 18, on the other hand, the insolent words of the seducers are not combined with any specific interest in winning Roman magnates but with a zeal for attracting proletarians by promising them liberty.

# 7. VIGILANCE TOWARD MOCKERS
## (17–19)

17 But you, beloved, ought to remember the words spoken in advance by the apostles of our Lord Jesus Christ. 18 For they said to you: At the end of time mockers will appear who will be led by their lusts to godless acts. 19 These are the separatists, sensual as they are, not having the spirit.

## COMMENT

It is clear from vs. 17 that the author writes at a time considerably later than the apostles; nor does he regard himself as an apostle. The message of the apostles, however, is not limited to the past, but is always relevant and ought to be remembered in every life-situation. Apostolic traditions and writings are becoming normative for the church, as attested also in II Pet iii 2.

What follows in vs. 18 corresponds to the statement in II Pet iii 3 that mockers are to arise in the last days, as foretold by the apostolic generation. Jude doubtless has in mind the heretical teachers already censured, though the designation "mockers" is unexpected and not entirely appropriate. Its occurrence is probably due to the fact that Jude, like Second Peter, is drawing upon traditional expressions regarding the trials of the last days (cf. Acts xx 29 ff.; I Tim iv 1 ff.; II Tim iii 1–5). Unlike that epistle, however, where the scoffers are said to focus derisive attention upon the delay in Christ's coming, Jude does not specify the nature of these people's taunts. The problem of the second coming is not prominent here; it is only alluded to later in vs. 21. Jude points rather to the source of the present troubles, the lustful appetites of the teachers of heresy (cf. vs. 16). In fact these cherish a great passion for godless acts.[10] They are the very ones, according to vs. 19, who are now causing schisms within the church. The scoffers are trapped by their lusts and consequently have only a primitive instinct and no spirit (cf. I Cor ii 14, 15; James iii 15).[11] By the use of these terms the author suggests that the teachers of heresy claim for themselves special knowledge and wisdom. They apparently pose either as philosophers or Gnostics or both. In a polemic against such intellectual arrogance, Jude declares them to be subhuman, lacking the essential quality of spirit.

## 8. FAITH, LOVE, AND THE HOPE
## OF ETERNAL LIFE
## (20–21)

20 But you, beloved, ought to build yourselves up further by your most holy faith, while you pray in holy spirit. 21 Keep yourselves in God's love, while you wait for the mercy of our Lord Jesus Christ for the purpose of life eternal.

### COMMENT

The teachers of heresy try to win followers by instigating disturbances on the one hand and enticing with sensuous pleasures on the other. Instead the believers, according to vs. 20, are to continue to build themselves up[12] or let their house be further built up (cf. I Pet ii 5) through their most holy faith.[13] Christians need only keep the faith that has been committed to them, and God will grant growth. The success of the church in the world is to come through holy prayer and not through sly tactics (cf. James iv 2 ff.). After the mention of faith and prayer there follow, in vs. 21, admonitions regarding love and the Christian hope. When the believers were called, they experienced God's love: the expression of his will to save them (cf. vs. 1). Therefore they are exhorted to remain within the sphere of God's love and thus allow its power for blessing to work effectively and continuously in their lives. They are further charged to wait patiently for the mercy of Christ which, in due time, will bring them the gift of eternal life. In short they are encouraged to be steadfast in the Christian hope. So the two verses actually sum up the most important Christian gifts of grace: faith (including prayer), love, and hope (cf. I Cor xiii 13; I Thess i 3).

## 9. MERCY TOWARD NON-CHRISTIANS
### (22–23)

22 Show mercy to some, whom you may examine. 23 Save others with fear, snatching them from the fire, abhorring the very tunic spotted by the flesh.

### COMMENT

The text of these two verses has been preserved in several different forms, and it is impossible to ascertain which is the original. Our translation is based on the Received Text,* which seems to present fewest difficulties. According to vs. 22, some people are to be shown mercy. Though it is often assumed that reference is made specifically to apostates, there is no evidence for this view. Rather, as the preceding illustration of the house being built indicates, the author's thought is of the acceptance of people in general into Christian fellowship. These individuals toward whom mercy is to be shown, however, must be critically examined.[14] On the other hand, vs. 23, some are to be rescued from death (cf. James v 20) with fear, like firebrands snatched out of the fire. The figure is borrowed from Zech iii 2 ("Is not this a brand plucked from the fire?"), but there is also an allusion to Sodom-Gomorrah and Korah, vss. 8, 11, who were punished by fire. The sinful world in which God's elect live is always exposed to the threat of annihilation by cosmic fire (cf. II Pet iii 10, 12). It is only those who are brought

* A text recension of Antioch and Constantinople, also known as the Koiné representing the mass of manuscripts in the Byzantine empire. As used in Erasmus' text edition of 1516 and hence in translations of the sixteenth, seventeenth, and eighteenth centuries, it is called textus receptus. Though generally inferior, it may in places be preferable to older manuscript traditions.

into the fellowship of the church that are saved from this danger. However, people exposed to the dangerous fire ought to be received into church fellowship only with the greatest trepidation. The author further characterizes them as those who have been so contaminated by "the flesh" that even their tunics are soiled. As the illustration of the firebrand is drawn from Zech iii 2, so the picture of the filthy garment has been borrowed from Zech iii 3–5. Since the source of contamination is external, "the flesh" must refer to the sinful worldly environment (cf. also 1QS v. 16–20). For if "the flesh" here referred to were the individual's own body, then his body should have been abhorred far more than his contaminated tunic and he would not have been received with mercy at all. Such people are not to be rejected, but the utmost caution must be exercised because of their parlous condition. They must leave every earthly possession behind, as the baptismal candidate must disrobe in order to receive a new, clean garment.

## 10. ENCOURAGEMENT TO STEADFASTNESS; DOXOLOGY
### (24-25)

24 But to him who is able to keep you from falling and to set you blameless before his glory with joy, 25 to the only God, our Savior through Jesus Christ our Lord, glory, majesty, power, and authority belong, before the whole present age, now, and in all future ages. Amen.

### COMMENT

The specific exhortation to steadfastness in II Pet iii 14 finds a counterpart in the brief but significant reference of vs. 24. While steadfastness is a primary theme of the entire epistle of Jude there is a tonal shift here. Throughout, the emphasis has been on admonition and encouragement; here it is on consolation and reassurance. The readers are reminded that God can save them from the threatening apostasy and preserve them, above reproach, at the last judgment when they will appear before him. Then there will be joy among the throngs of the redeemed.

For, as emphasized in the concluding doxology of vs. 25, over against every political authority on earth, God alone from eternity to eternity has all glory, majesty, power, and authority.

This conclusion of the epistle of Jude is grand and soul-stirring. It lifts the thoughts from earthly conflicts with which the author has been compelled to busy himself, up to the heavenly realms, where God is enthroned amidst eternal might and honor. The fight against evil forces in this narrow and dark world should always be viewed in such a luminous cosmic perspective.

# Textual Notes

1. Greek, *gráphein*, pres. inf., because the author had long wished to write; cf. note 3.

2. Greek, *anánkēn*.

3. Greek, *grápsai*, aor. inf., emphasizing the definite realization of the plan.

4. Greek, *epagōnízesthai*, pres. inf.; cf. note 1.

5. Greek, *paradídōmi*, "to entrust," "to commit."

6. Greek, *agápai*, "love meals." The parallel in II Pet ii 13 has *apátai*, "deceptions." A few manuscripts of Jude have taken over this reading of Second Peter, whereas some manuscripts of Second Peter have instead been influenced by Jude. It would seem that in the sermon tradition behind the two epistles the term was "love meals." The author of Second Peter may have altered this into the more abstract "deceptions," because it appeared inappropriate to speak openly about the love meals which had gradually become suspect. In any case a deliberate alteration in the opposite direction, i.e., from the abstract "deceptions" to the concrete "love meals," is not conceivable. Jude therefore seems to have preserved the original thought. Compare the comments on II Pet ii 13.

7. Greek, *spiládes*. This rare, literary Greek word may also be rendered "spots," as *spíloi* in II Pet ii 13. In favor of the meaning "reefs," however, there are on the one hand an overwhelming number of references in the older Greek literature, and on the other hand the extraordinary concreteness of the illustration. The author of Jude has apparently improved the literary style of the tradition; Second Peter retained both "spots" and "blemishes" simultaneously.

8. Greek, *asebés*, "godless"; *asébeia*, "godlessness."

9. Greek, *thaumázein prósōpa*, a phrase borrowed from the LXX meaning approximately, "to take an interest in a person" Lev xix 15; Deut x 17; Job xxii 8, etc.).

10. The expression *tôn asebeiôn* is best understood as an objective genitive, modifying *epithymías*. As it is in the plural, it means "godless

acts." It has the article because the author has in mind what the teachers of heresy are now doing.

11. The mockers are called in Greek *psychikoí*, inasmuch as they have a *psychê*, an "animal soul," but no *pneûma*, "spirit."

12. Greek, *ep-oikodoméō*.

13. In the Greek text, instrumental dative.

14. Greek, *diakrinómenoi*, here, "critically examining" (cf. I Cor xi 29, 31).

# BIBLIOGRAPHY

### I. HISTORICAL SURVEYS

Dill, Sir Samuel. *Roman Society from Nero to Marcus Aurelius*. London: Macmillan & Co., Ltd., 2nd ed., 1905; New York: The Macmillan Co., 2nd ed., 1905.

Hardy, Ernest George. *Christianity and the Roman Government*. London: Longmans, Green & Co., 1894; New York: The Macmillan Co., 1925.

Henderson, Bernard W. *Five Roman Emperors*. Cambridge: The University Press, 1927; New York: The Macmillan Co., 1927.

McCrum, Michael, and Woodhead, Arthur Geoffrey. *Select Documents of the Principates of the Flavian Emperors (including the Year of Revolution)*, A.D. *68–96*. Cambridge: The University Press, 1961.

Pfeiffer, Robert Henry. *History of New Testament Times*. New York: Harper & Bros., 1949; London: A. & C. Black, Ltd., 1954.

### II. BRIEF COMMENTARIES

Beare, Francis Wright. *The First Epistle of Peter*. New York: The Macmillan Co., 2nd ed. rev., 1959.

Blackman, Edwin Cyril. *The Epistle of James*. Torch Bible Commentaries. Naperville, Illinois: Alec E. Allenson, Inc., 1958.

Tasker, Randolph V. G. *The General Epistle of James*. Tyndale New Testament Commentaries. Grand Rapids, Michigan: Wm. B. Eerdmans Publishing Co., 1957.

Wand, John W. C. *The General Epistles of St. Peter and St. Jude*. Westminster Commentaries. London: Methuen & Co., Ltd., 1934.

### III. COMPREHENSIVE STUDIES

Chaine, Joseph. *L'épître de Saint Jacques*. Etudes bibliques. Paris: J. Gabalda et Cie., 2nd ed., 1927.

Dibelius, Martin. *Der Brief des Jakobus.* Kritisch-exegetischer Kommentar über das Neue Testament, 15. Göttingen: Vandenhoeck & Ruprecht, 8th ed., 1956.

Selwyn, Edward Gordon. *The First Epistle of St. Peter.* London: Macmillan & Co., Ltd., 1946. —A rich commentary, superior to all its predecessors.

Spitta, Friedrich. *Der zweite Brief des Petrus und der Brief des Judas.* Halle an der Saale: Verlag der Buchhandlung des Waisenhauses, 1885. —A broad, still indispensable study of these neglected epistles.